T0358425

The International Behavioural and Social Sciences Library

MID-CAREER DEVELOPMENT

TAVISTOCK

The International Behavioural and Social Sciences Library

INDUSTRIAL RELATIONS
In 13 Volumes

MID-CAREER DEVELOPMENT

Research Perspectives on a Developmental Community for Senior Administrators

ROBERT N RAPOPORT
WITH CONTRIBUTIONS BY
M B BRODIE AND E A LIFE

First published in 1970 by
Tavistock Publications Limited

Reprinted in 2001 by
Routledge
2 Park Square, Milton Park, Abingdon, Oxon, OX14 4RN

Transferred to Digital Printing 2007

Routledge is an imprint of the Taylor & Francis Group

The publishers have made every effort to contact authors/copyright holders
of the works reprinted in the *International Behavioural and Social Sciences
Library*. This has not been possible in every case, however, and we would
welcome correspondence from those individuals/companies we have been
unable to trace.

These reprints are taken from original copies of each book. In many cases
the condition of these originals is not perfect. The publisher has gone to
great lengths to ensure the quality of these reprints, but wishes to point
out that certain characteristics of the original copies will, of necessity, be
apparent in reprints thereof.

British Library Cataloguing in Publication Data
A CIP catalogue record for this book
is available from the British Library

Mid-Career Development
ISBN 0-415-26444-8
Industrial Relations: 13 Volumes
ISBN 0-415-26510-X
The International Behavioural and Social Sciences Library
112 Volumes
ISBN 0-415-25670-4

Mid-Career Development

RESEARCH PERSPECTIVES ON A DEVELOPMENTAL
COMMUNITY FOR SENIOR ADMINISTRATORS

ROBERT N. RAPOPORT

with contributions by
M. B. BRODIE *and* E. A. LIFE

TAVISTOCK PUBLICATIONS
London · New York · Sydney · Toronto · Wellington

First published in Great Britain in 1970
By Tavistock Publications Limited
2 Park Square, Milton Park, Abingdon, Oxon, OX14 4RN
ISBN 422 73500 0
© *The Administrative Staff College, Henley-on-Thames, 1970*

Distributed in the USA by Barnes & Noble Inc.

Contents

PART FOUR · FINDINGS AND IMPLICATIONS

APPENDICES

Foreword

Lord Fulton

The influence of education in the United Kingdom, taken as a whole, is to encourage academic virtues. This makes problems for a country whose need for managerial skill is increasing with the growing complexity of its social, economic, and industrial organization. Therefore it becomes urgently necessary to identify this kind of talent and by the right training and career development to make the most of it wherever it is to be found.

The authors of this study are modest—perhaps unduly modest—in their claims. But if we are to accept their own assessment of their work as pioneering new territory for others to cultivate more intensively in the future, we must surely whole-heartedly applaud the originality of the method chosen by which the staff of the Administrative Staff College at Henley and the Tavistock research workers enmeshed themselves in a cooperative task which gave its special character to the whole enterprise.

The result shows that not only have they contributed significantly to the re-assessment by the College at Henley of its role and scope for the future, but they have also thrown light on much that has hitherto been unknown about the principles of career development. It is to be hoped that their work will be widely read.

Acknowledgements

Many people have been involved in this research in different capacities, and the author wishes to record his thanks both to those named individually and to those whose identities may not be divulged. Eric Trist was instrumental in launching the study, and his support was greatly appreciated at various stages throughout its course. During the pilot stages, interviews were conducted by Andrew Life, Stephanie White, and Michael Foster, as well as the principal author. Karen Seashore and Rosemary Fison helped with parts of the data analysis. Barrie Irving and Linden Hilgendorf gave advice and help with the quantitative analysis. Harold Bridger helped with Chapter 12 specifically, and contributed many ideas generally. Elliott Mittler helped with some of the programming work and computer analysis, as did the staff of Survey Analysis Ltd.

At the Administrative Staff College the help of the Principal, Mr Martin-Bates, and the staff, particularly Morris Brodie, Andrew Life, Ben Aston, and Katherine Elliott, has been indispensable. The 600 or so members who participated in the research must remain anonymous, but they and their firms are gratefully acknowledged as collaborators in this work.

The task of typing the manuscript was very capably shared by the secretarial staff of the Tavistock Institute and of the Administrative Staff College, particularly Elizabeth Burrett, Angeline Agran, Pamela Rant, Susan Vlasto, Linda Francis, and Bunty Hayes.

The collaboration and assistance of the above-named people have been invaluable, and I am more than grateful. None of them should, of course, be held accountable for deficiencies in the end-product, responsibility for which remains with the principal author.

October 1969   R.N.R.

Introduction

This is the report of an exploratory study set within a deliberately broad frame of reference. Too often studies of careers and managerial development, of organizations and the use made of those who work for them, of training institutions and the role they should fill, have been undertaken with little reference to one another. In this study each has a significant place, and, to the extent that an evaluation has been attempted, it has been the sort which has brought these elements into perspective with one another, in an attempt to provide a new look at familiar problems.

Different readers will find different parts of the book of interest. Only the more social-science-orientated managers and the more 'applied' social scientists are likely to find enough in all parts of the book to hold their attention. Less research-minded managers and the less 'applied' social scientists may perhaps find certain parts tedious, if not irritating.

The core of the study is contained in Part Two. Part One – on the background of management and of training institutions and particularly Henley – is included to give the reader sufficient background to the issues being investigated, the context within which they arise and the specific institution in which the training experiences reported were taking place. It can be skimmed by those already informed on these matters and by the more academically-minded social scientists, for this part of the book is concerned with interests more specific to the men of action in the world of management and administration. Similarly, the more technical elements of conceptualization and cluster analysis in Part Two may be skimmed without too much loss by managers wanting to get to the crux of the managerial typology presented in Chapter 8. It is hoped that both administrators and social scientists will find Part Three of interest, though perhaps in different ways.

The chapters of Part Four represent an attempt to report how the study has already had an impact on the institution studied and how it might have further influence in the future.

The study itself is thus set clearly in a larger stream of events and processes, as part of a specific developmental evolution within the institution where the work took place.

A given form of career training is good or bad only in relation to the kinds of men who experience it, the use which enterprises make of those who are trained, the options open to the men and how they actually use them. This study has come out with findings which, though not entirely new, have emerged from a distinctive research approach. One hopes that the findings will enable each individual manager and each enterprise to make comparisons of sufficient interest to have justified the effort – for it took a very great deal of effort, as such explorations tend to, to arrive at the plateau represented by this book. There is a tremendous amount still to be done and said on the main topics of the study. Indeed, one of the principal aims of the study so far has been to suggest future directions that will be more purposeful and deliberate than the exploratory probes that serve as the foundations for the present report.

The very limitations of the study in time, resources, and approach may stir some to build further upon it. The perspectives of the administrators questioned ought surely to be supplemented by the perspectives of others – of their chiefs, colleagues, and subordinates and of their wives. The effects of one kind of training experience for men in middle life should surely be compared, under controlled conditions of research design, with the effects of alternatives. The exploratory interview guides and questionnaires ought to give way to more rigorous instruments, to verify and extend the patterns suggested by this first scanning of the problems of the study.

Like many of its genre, this study raises more questions than it lays to rest. For example, having established some basic types of career-development pattern, what can be learned about their 'natural histories', their interactions and transformations, as administrators encounter different career experiences? In what ways are career patterns of a given type adaptive within one setting, or in one stage in an organization's development, but not in another? Within the training institution studied changes have been taking place and more will occur, some of them attributable to the work done on this project; in which directions and on what priorities should further research be undertaken to meet its evolving needs?

This is not a last-word study, but an attempt to open up new ground by cutting across the boundaries that conventionally separate action from research. It is hoped that all readers will, in different ways, be able to make capital of it.

R. N. RAPOPORT

The Context of Management Training

Chapter 1 · General Management

A PERSPECTIVE

M. B. Brodie

Generalship is a concept that is used a great deal in practice even though it lacks its theory.

It is most familiar in the context of supreme military command, a notion which emerged in times gone by as a result of the delegation of military responsibility by the monarch. It occurs in the vocabulary of religious organization. A 'general superior' is the supreme head of a religious order in the Catholic Church, who governs in accordance with the constitution of the order and the laws of the Church and has authority over all members of the order.

The same essential idea is to be found in the notion of general management. Enterprises frequently have 'General Managers'. The attributes of generalship and the qualities of the generalist reflect the top-level nature of this role and the power and responsibility which correspond to it, for providing leadership, for looking to the broader-ranging and external issues as well as to those within the enterprise, and in particular for developing policies which integrate the activities of the enterprise and reconcile conflicting interests.

How general management is understood in practice can perhaps be illustrated by examples from the private sector of five firms invited by the British Institute of Management to present and explain their 'General Management Practice'. (The first of these presentations was in January 1966, and short papers were prepared for each.)

The Metal Box Company put the emphasis on company organization and structure, forecasting, and budgeting. F. Perkins Ltd built their presentation around the themes of planning, control, and communication. Joseph Lucas Ltd concentrated on structure and overall management, and their production and personnel policies. Sterling Winthrop Group Ltd, a subsidiary of a United

States firm, put the whole emphasis on policies for growth, on the problems of developing their business in Europe, and on personnel policies. Renold Ltd reviewed their finance, manufacturing, selling, and personnel policies, their group structure, the overseas subsidiaries, and how they saw their future.

Although there is this diversity of approach, in each instance general management is identified with the wider issues of organization and policy, with the way each main area of the business is related to the enterprise as a whole and with prospects and plans.

In the Civil Service, though pre-eminence has attached to those in positions of generalist responsibility, the concept of the generalist is now under attack, and debate has been enlivened by the appearance of the Fulton Committee Report (Fulton, 1968). The first of the half dozen main inadequacies the Committee detected in the Civil Service was 'the philosophy of the amateur (or "generalist" or "all-rounder")' (Fulton, 1968, paragraph 15), which they saw as running counter to the need for Civil Servants to be skilled managers. The Committee wrestled with the usually contrasted notions of the specialist and the administrator, to establish the proper relationship between specialists and administrators and to clarify how the career of an individual may shift him from one role to the other. An administrator in his early years had to specialize in a particular area, but 'modern administration requires men to have breadth as well as depth' (Fulton, 1968, paragraph 42), and specialisms had not to be too narrowly conceived. What was now required from all administrators was a 'fuller professionalism'. In what respects the fuller professionals differ from the generalists is not very clear from the Report, a point that illustrates the difficulty faced by the Committee in unravelling complex issues with the aid of a vocabulary lacking in precision.

As to the concept of the generalist itself, views are divided. Following the appointment of the Fulton Committee, the Institution of Professional Civil Servants commissioned an independent comparative study of the role and career expectations of the professional *vis-à-vis* the administrator. Various authors, all university teachers, were asked to look at France, Germany, Sweden, Australia, and the US, as well as Britain. Reviewing the main findings, the editor singled out one major lesson: '. . . nowhere does one find anything like a theory justifying the separation, either of persons or of functions, into generalists and specialists, administrators and advisers' (Ridley, 1968, pp. 10–11). In the comparison, Britain was the odd man out. None of the other countries had anything like the British administrative class or a recruitment policy for the higher Civil Servant on a non-vocational basis.

One critic (Hobsbawm, 1968), taking part in a series of broadcast talks following the publication of the Fulton Report, contended that it was quite wrong to equate the notion of 'the amateur' with the generalist all-round administrator. He argued that the report confused two quite separate things: specialist expertise, on the one hand, and 'a sufficient familiarity . . . with a subject to make reasonable judgements about it', on the other. Confusion on this obscures 'a crucial point that what is required today is more and better "generalists" and "all-rounders" in administration, and not more specialists' and the tendency has been in this direction in all forms of decision-making and policy-making. Another (Lord Helsby, 1968), accepting the need for a 'basic professionalism in the business of government combined with imagination and sound judgement', was not entirely convinced by the stress which the Fulton Committee placed on the specialist techniques. He was also impressed by the trouble to which large business concerns went to produce men with general administrative ability.

What are the more general areas of responsibility in running an enterprise? A leading American scholar (Cole, 1965) suggested half a dozen spheres of action which, to a greater or lesser degree, must be the concern of those responsible for the exercise of power. These are: determination of objectives and their modification as conditions require; development and maintenance of an organization; securing adequate financial resources; acquiring efficient technological equipment and keeping it up to date; establishing a market and devising new products; maintaining good relations with public authorities and with society at large.

At the Administrative Staff College, it is held to be important that those who are to occupy posts at general management level should learn

'(a) to see their role in their enterprise in relation to its main objectives and in its total environment,

(b) to understand the implications for their enterprise of government policies and of the changing domestic and international situation,

(c) to evaluate their own experience and attitudes against

those of people of similar standing and ability working in other enterprises and in other countries,

(d) to assess new knowledge, thought, techniques and methods and their application in management,

(e) to develop the skills of obtaining decisions from a group of people of diverse expertise, experience and temperament,

(f) to assess wisely and quickly what is important in unfamiliar areas and situations,

(g) to appreciate the particular responsibilities and problems of top management.'

General management is thus crucially a total-enterprise activity, a matter of making overall policy and putting it into practice, based on the view taken by those in top management of the place of the enterprise in the environment and the particular direction it should take. However, the very fact that this is a generalized activity can obscure the part of the individual more senior manager in all this.

How a manager and his enterprise interact and how they both relate to society at large are important questions. Traditional literature in this field too often treated considerations of personality in isolation, and exposés of personality requirements for management were notoriously superficial. No doubt, in part, this was due to the influence of ideas about highly individualistic, often idiosyncratic, behaviour which was supposed to characterize men of leadership and action, and, indeed, some have behaved very idiosyncratically indeed. But one unfortunate effect was to couch explanations of enterprise, success, and failure primarily in personality terms.

However, in most situations, this is now seen to be by no means the whole, or even the greater part, of the explanation, which has to be sought in a more careful analysis of the relationships between personality, behaviour, and the social context. Correctives have been gaining ground. 'Field theory' in psychology and recent developments in systems theory have helped to shift the emphasis to the study of relationships and interactions between individuals and the groups to which they belong, and between groups within enterprises and those outside it. Analysis of both individual behaviour and enterprise performance has, as a consequence, been put onto a sounder basis.

A crucial conceptual element in this has been the notion of

'role'. It links what is socially required or expected of people holding given posts with the motivations and modes of behaviour of the individuals who occupy them, and has served to clarify the nature of the problems facing those in positions of responsibility. In a complex society, an individual will hold many different roles. He has to reconcile his more personal wishes, ideas, and ways of behaving with what is expected of him in his various roles, and as a manager he must do this without sacrificing a readiness to behave in ways different from those so far socially approved or sanctioned, where he deems this appropriate. Complexity is in the very nature of policy-level situations. Tensions and conflicts characterize them, and it is the responsibility of those who fill these roles to achieve a workable and satisfactory resolution of them.

Those who occupy the higher-level positions have the particular responsibility of dealing with matters which cut across functions, departments, and sectional concerns. Much of their work is thus at the boundaries of the various 'sub-systems'. A. T. M. Wilson, referring to what he calls 'the integrative need of the executive', draws attention to the problems confronting the professional executive in his endeavours to make sense of complex situations and confusing data, and his need for a framework so that he can have an overall view of his world: 'It may on occasion force him to add up or to multiply things which cannot be added or multiplied; and it is certain to contain imperfections, inconsistencies and evasions' (Wilson, 1967). He further points to the problem which arises because this integrative task conflicts with the pluralist assumptions, concepts, and hypotheses of the wide range of people – internal specialists and outsiders – with whom he must work.

The notion of role comes in very importantly in a unique study by a professional philosopher of the moral problems which arise within large organizations. Dorothy Emmet severely criticizes the separation between sociology and ethics, and argues that moralists would do well to look at sociological studies, using the notion of role to provide the link between factual descriptions of social situations and moral pronouncements on what ought to be done in them. In a thought-provoking development of her argument, she talks about the ethics of role, the problems of a lack of clear coincidence between responsibility and actual power, and 'the morality of institutional action where the relations between personal kinds of responsibility and the impersonal kinds come to a head' (Emmet, 1966, p. 201).

It is in the creation of a new role or in changing the image of an existing one that she sees the attributes of exceptional individuals. This reflection evokes Lloyd Warner's description of managers as 'cultural mediators of the present as it moves from the past into the future, people who have to handle a structured past and yet make decisions which take them into an unstructured future, a requirement which is inevitably accompanied with conflict, tension, and ambiguity'. He asks what characteristics of personality are then necessary. Most important would be autonomy, the ability to make a decision on one's own, and to act freely, creatively, and independently. Such people must also have the ability to quickly structure what they see; they should be 'capable of putting together the changing parts of their society and the flow of events within their economic life to form them into a world of meaning and significance for action' (Warner, 1960, p. 120). As a corollary, managers must have a proper understanding of the culture within which they work and a sensitivity to the problems of cultural change. Cochran (1965) illustrates this very vividly. He puts forward a number of propositions relevant to economic growth to compare USA and Latin-American culture. He suggests, for example, that Latin-American values give more priority to family interests than to economy and profit maximization. Social and personal emotional interests are more important than business obligations. Nepotism may be favoured at the expense of continuity of able top management, and so on. He makes it clear that though these qualities may be hindrances to material progress they are not necessarily inimical to what Latin Americans would call the good life. There is a growing recognition of the importance of these basic cultural considerations and it is because they are so important that, in Cochran's judgement, a new period may be starting in which, after a generation of increased specialization, the need will be for generalists.

The growing significance of managers in society is a development which goes beyond ideological boundaries. Consider the example of Poland. Bauman, drawing on investigations carried out by the Sociological Research Bureau of the Higher School of Social Sciences in Warsaw, found that there had been

'a remarkable shift from predominantly ideological to mainly technical and managerial preoccupations; the party meetings come gradually to resemble consultative assemblies; the content of individual and collective tasks confided to people in their capacity as party members is, in much greater proportion than before, connected directly with the purely industrial life of the factory . . . Political merit and ideological virtues are no longer a sufficient qualification for the performance of party functions: one must possess vocational education and professional skill to deal with technical and administrative problems at a table with specialists of the highest rank' (Bauman, 1964, p. 214).

A study of the USSR illustrates this further. Managers have acquired a significant and recognized place in Soviet society. Their influence during the last decade or so of Stalin's rule grew. In this period, top managers gained a greater say in policy-making and enlarged the degree of autonomy of their enterprises. Indeed, one writer saw Kosygin's appointment as premier in 1964 as indicating '. . . a willingness to accord the leaders of the industrial establishment high symbolic status and a pledge of continued receptivity to managerial demands' (Azrael, 1966, p. 149).

This having been said, the question arises of the involvement of managers in politics and of how far they may constitute an independent force for political change. Azrael sees little likelihood in the USSR of the managerial elite producing political dissidents. One of the main reasons for this is the managerial recruitment and training process. By origins, selection, and education, Soviet managers, it seems, are unlikely to question the dominance of those whose primary aim is political, and he considers the argument sufficiently strong to justify a quotation from Thorstein Veblen as a preamble to his conclusion:

'By settled habit the technicians, engineers and industrial experts are a harmless and docile sort, well fed on the whole and somewhat placidly content with the "full dinner pail", which the . . . Vested Interests habitually allow them' (Azrael, 1966, p. 173).

This may leave unanswered the interesting question as to what might happen if the managerial elite actively sought to exert political power. Some interpretations of events in Eastern Europe suggest that this might be happening.

Fears of technocracy have often been voiced. Is there a danger that technical experts and managers, through their influence on organization, will form a new ruling class? Such a threat, as applied to France, is discounted by Crozier (1964), one of the most perceptive writers in this field, for an interesting reason. He contends that this fear derives from a misunderstanding of the nature of technical and scientific progress. The success of the experts and the managers is constantly self-defeating. As they rationalize processes, others are then able to take them over, and the power which comes from their expertise disappears. 'When progress accelerates, the power of the expert is diminished and managerial power becomes more and more a political and judicial power rather than a technical one' (Crozier, 1964, p. 300), which takes us back to social and political analysis.

For a fuller explanation of such findings we need to know more about the nature of the work senior managers do and the way others expect them to carry it out, though these are matters on which we must conjecture, since most studies by social scientists have taken very limited facets of managerial action and attitudes as their focus, not the complex areas of high-level policy-making.

The problem is further complicated because one facet of the work of those taking the critical decisions in enterprises has usually been related to the more elusive and individualistic qualities which in the nineteenth century were attributed to the entrepreneur. Has the era of the entrepreneur passed, or are the general managers of today what the entrepreneurs were in the nineteenth century?

One view would have it that entrepreneurship is a very different thing from management, almost antithetical to it. The entrepreneur as the bold thrusting individual with a zest for innovation, dominating the enterprise he owns, is contrasted with the career-manager, a bureaucrat concerned with stability rather than change, with little or no financial stake in the business. This view remains powerful and persistent. It helps to explain why in Britain there is an Institute of Directors with a philosophy that differentiates direction from management or why in Germany companies have a board of directors responsible for policy and a separate managerial board for operating the business (Shonfield, 1965).

The role of the individualist entrepreneur, mostly seen in retrospect, may have become exaggerated, and, with contemporary discussion of management more often journalistic than scholarly, judgement is difficult. Comparing American and British technology in the nineteenth century, Habakkuk (1962) inclined to the conclusion that men were bold and expansionist primarily because circumstances were conducive. It was favourable market conditions which brought out the capacity of businessmen, not the other way round. It was because there was a high rate of growth in the American economy that entrepreneurial talent seemed abundant. Where similarly favourable conditions obtained in Britain, there too were the men to exploit them. When an economy is expanding slowly, entrepreneurs are scarce. Habakkuk does not underestimate the social inhibitions in Britain that discouraged able men from going into business. In a society in which the ownership of land, the army, and the growing professions were all more highly esteemed than business, and where making profits was, in the eyes of many, a sordid affair, young men of ability were bound to find little attraction in business. Organizational ability as a factor in enterprise success got scant recognition or attention.

The inadequacies of too over-simplified a view of such issues are increasingly recognized. Economic theory, in particular in its preoccupation with risk-taking and profit maximization, had neglected questions of enterprise policy-making and organization and the complex relationships between them and the more definable financial and economic dimensions of an enterprise. Marris (1966) goes a long way to correct this. He puts the emphasis on the distinctive contribution of managers as organizers, and is ready to describe the capacity for large-scale organization developed by managers working together as virtually a new factor of production. As a result of this evolution, he argues, it is now more realistic to see the investor as buying a share in the organization of an enterprise than in its physical assets. Managerial teamwork has taken over from entrepreneurial individualism.

No less challenging to a common view of managers as lacking in entrepreneurial attitudes and skills is the judgement of the economic historian Postan that, in the twenty years following the end of the war in 1945, the managerial class in all Western countries 'brought to the conduct of enterprises a greater degree of rationality and professional expertise and a greater proneness to innovate than those characteristic of owner-managed enterprises also taken as a whole' (Postan, 1967).

Postan is talking here in a general way about the managerial class. In terms of social structure, are they a separate class or even, as some would have, a new ruling class? Again, only a tentative answer is possible, since as yet there are few studies which contribute towards the much-needed political science of management.

However, for analysis of present-day society it may be more useful to think in terms of elites, or high-status groups. Modern industrial society is sometimes depicted as one which has moved away from a class system in the Marxist sense to an elitist pattern, where personal ability and talent displace more hereditary and arbitrary ways of attaining power and prominence.

However, the concept of the class system provided an explanation of economic and political power, whereas the elite view leaves much more uncertain the question of whether political power goes with elite status. Bottomore puts the managers of industry along with intellectuals and high government officials as the three elites often singled out as having taken over the functions of earlier ruling classes. He is prepared to acknowledge that managers are an important functional group, but in his view neither they nor the other two groups '. . . can be seriously regarded as contenders for the place of the governing elite' (Bottomore, 1964, p. 83). Managers have not been moved by a strong sense of solidarity with one another to combine as a cohesive, independent, and powerfully organized group in society. Within society the importance of an elite with the skills of enterprise organization and leadership may be accepted, but there is no reason to attribute any special political power to its members and, as yet, the managers themselves have provided no real basis or pressure for this.

One might come to a different assessment if those who go into management were drawn from the whole of society, if promotion to the top were entirely dependent on ability, and if those who moved to the top formed a distinct and independent social group, but that is not how things seem to be. In those societies which have been studied, capitalist or socialist, it appears that managers usually come from families of men who themselves are managers, professionals, and so on. Middle-class origins predominate. That would seem to have been so in the past as well as today. A recent investigation of a sample of managers in North-West England only confirms this (Clark, 1966). Where achievement is rewarded with promotion, this may only go so far. One writer would contend that, 'The managerial ladder helps men to step up, but it rarely extends from the bottom to the Board Room' (Guttsman, 1963, p. 355). Evidently, as managers make headway in their careers, they are more likely to fit in with the prevailing social system and merge with the establishment than keep distinct from it.

Even in those countries of Western Europe where syndicalism

has had more of an impact than in Britain, and where executives have sought to combine and exert themselves as a public force (Brodie, 1965), the policies followed have tended to keep them detached from the main trade union movement and their position nationally seems not very influential.

One of the greatest concerns today is the fear of social control by the large powerful economic institutions of society. The more extreme critics would have it that 'Contemporary industrial society tends to be totalitarian' (Marcuse, 1964). C. Wright Mills (1956), in his well-known book, carried the argument further than most in contending that in the USA the means of power are now concentrated in the hands of three elite groups: the military, the politicians, and the heads of corporations. This thesis, in the way it is stated, may be more demanding than the evidence and analysis can yet sustain, but there are issues here of government–industry relationships and the public responsibilities of top managers in the Private Sector which are a long way from being resolved.

Some would contend that businessmen working in the Private Sector should be single-minded in their aims and not be diverted from seeking maximum profits by wider considerations of public responsibility. This argument rests on a theory and logic of society which are too artificial to be sound, even if the advice were not unwise on other grounds. Whether one approves of the situation or not, the facts are otherwise. Business and government interaction and interdependence have gone a long way. The relationship, in the USA, is impressively close; in the eighteen years of government from 1949 to 1967 businessmen accepted almost 180 appointments at the level of assistant secretary or higher. To take the Defense Department and the military services, the Treasury, the Commerce Department, and the Post Office, under Truman one-third of the total number of appointments went to businessmen, under Eisenhower two-thirds, under Kennedy and Johnson about one-quarter. They 'have held important policy-making posts in the four postwar administrations, regardless of the party in power' (Schechter, 1968). To suggest that businessmen at work should act as if they were not also citizens is also to ignore the fundamental point that it is society which provides the context for the exercise of their freedom and initiative.

No enterprise is an island or a law unto itself. Policies must be related to what is going on in the world at large. It is for such reasons, some would argue, that for those holding high responsibilities, and who have reached out in their careers beyond the limits of a particular specialism, an understanding of the social, cultural, political, economic, and technological environment takes priority. Hence the comments of Crozier, Cochran, Hobsbawm, and others that the importance of the generalist is growing, not diminishing.

Managers are said to be important in society; some would say of crucial importance. They are often regarded as the prime force for economic progress, or as the main hindrance to it. Internationally, it seems that there may be some movement towards a sharing of managerial values and attitudes. Yet, in a professional sense, they do not constitute a very cohesive group. The characteristics which unify them have not yet been defined with precision, and they do not seem to be much influenced by the integrating forces which shape and govern the established professions. As a group, they are neither well organized nor particularly vocal in society. We do not know much about how they see themselves; and others see them in a variety of ways. No doubt, part of the difficulty is that management itself is a loose notion. It enters frequently into popular parlance, yet it is one which social scientists and analysts would like to endow with rigour and intellectual consistency, though so far without success.

The situation may be frustrating. It is not surprising. We are dealing with something which is bound up intimately with the workings of society, with any society that is organizationally complex. Management is a social phenomenon evolving in response to human needs and initiative and not a theoretical construct, the application of which has been carefully engineered. The practice of management came before the theorizers, and the study of management raises in an acute and exciting way the interaction between practice and theory. The best early thinkers in management were themselves practising managers reflecting on their experience.

The present study of Henley managers aims to contribute something to the understanding of general managership, perhaps more to the process of becoming a general manager than the state of being one. As one wit remarked, to be a top manager is easy; getting to be one is the problem.

The findings seem to support the idea that the attitudes and requirements of generalship are shared very broadly across sectors and among managers rising from different social and specialist backgrounds. However, according to the type of person, his organizational environment, and his orientation to it, the skills of general management can develop in different ways. Three fundamentally different 'styles' of development – routes to general-ship – are described, providing insights which can add to the capacity of those in the enterprise and in training institutions to cultivate generalship in a differentiated way, rather than by a single formula.

The issues are wide and this monograph touches upon only certain aspects. It reports upon a limited study of a restricted stratum of managers in one society and of their reactions to a particular educational experience in general management. As a facet only of the contemporary managerial situation, it needs to be seen in a wider setting. It may not be possible to describe the setting in a well-delineated, unambiguous way and there are radical differences of judgement and interpretation on many important aspects, as well as severe limitations of evidence. However, the attempt to provide some perspective is a way of alerting the reader to the open-ended nature of the questions and issues which bear upon a research study such as this and to the need for sustained research in this field.

Chapter 2 · Training for Management

A HISTORICAL VIEW

E. A. Life

THE IMPACT OF THE INDUSTRIAL REVOLUTION

'She had an idea that the son of a gentleman, if he intended to maintain his rank as a gentleman, should earn his income as a clergyman, or as a barrister, or as a soldier, or as a sailor . . . There might . . . possibly be a doubt about the Civil Service and Civil Engineering; but she had no doubt whatever that when a man touched trade or commerce in any way he was doing that which was not the work of a gentleman . . .' (Trollope, 1870).

Miss Marrable's old-fashioned ideas in Trollope's nineteenth-century novel neatly summarize the attitude of the gentry towards trade and commerce at a time when the Industrial Revolution in Britain was gaining momentum. Civil engineering might have been a dubious occupation, but no doubt existed about the respectability of military engineering. Commissions in the Army, like administrative posts in the Civil Service, were reserved for acceptable gentlemen capable of purchasing them. Nevertheless, the purchase system had its limitations. Reporting on the Flanders campaign of 1794, the adjutant-general to the Duke of York wrote:

'Out of the fifteen regiments of cavalry and twenty-six of infantry which we have here, twenty-one are commanded literally by boys or idiots . . .'

While gentlemen might be able to dispense with education, those below that elite status who aspired to enter industry or commerce in the eighteenth century were assisted by a variety of new establishments created for the teaching of commercial subjects and technology. Then, as technology developed, the owners of prosperous manufacturing enterprises began to attend to the training of their successors. As Pollard has observed, the larger ironworks, for example:

16

'. . . trained not only the partners' sons as future managing partners but also others, and progressive works in general became the schools, not only of technologies, but of management techniques' (Pollard, 1965).

The same stimulus to training triggered off by technology had already made an impact upon the Army: in 1741 a school for artillery officers had opened at Woolwich. Cavalry and infantry, however, remained unaffected until the deplorable state of affairs revealed by the Flanders campaign stimulated one Colonel le Marchant in 1798 to propose the idea of a general educational establishment for officers. By the end of 1802, the Royal Military College had been founded, with a junior department in Marlow for those 'intended for the military profession', and a senior department at High Wycombe for established officers training for staff duties. The college was resited at Sandhurst in 1813, the senior department ultimately being re-established as the Army Staff College at Camberley after reforms in 1857.

This pattern of training in separate and distinct institutions was also characteristic of other professions in the nineteenth century. Candidates for the legal profession attended the inns of court; aspirants to the medical profession trained in the schools attached to hospitals; ordinands for the Anglican Church prepared for their careers in the Universities of Oxford and Cambridge, whose faculties of law and medicine had been allowed to atrophy. During the eighteenth and early nineteenth centuries Oxford and Cambridge functioned largely as extensions of the school education of Anglican upper-class youth, teaching being based on the colleges with each tutor covering for his pupils all the ground required for a degree. As Ashby has remarked:

'. . . these studies [in the faculty of arts] . . . were throughout associated with the flair for character-training which made these universities nurseries for leadership in church and state . . . the emphasis of these two universities was on the all-round education of a privileged class, not on the disinterested pursuit of learning' (Ashby, 1966).

Nonconformists and merchants alike in the eighteenth century attacked the Anglican exclusiveness and preoccupation with the classics of Oxford and Cambridge. To satisfy the demands of industrialists like Matthew Boulton and George Stephenson for an appropriate education for their sons, many clergymen opened private boarding schools which taught such subjects as accounts, shorthand, book-keeping, French, and science. During the same period, Nonconformist academies attempted to provide an education alternative to that of the Universities of Oxford and Cambridge. Although originally intended to provide preparation for careers in the ministry, law, and medicine, the academies became increasingly concerned with business pursuits. At Warrington Academy, for example, courses included commerce and political economy, chemistry, physics, and mathematics, and, of the 393 students attending between 1757 and 1783, probably 200 went into industry and commerce (Pollard, 1965).

At another level, the creation of the Andersonian Institute in Glasgow to teach science to skilled artisans created a model for the Mechanics' Institutes subsequently established in London, Birmingham, Manchester, and elsewhere early in the nineteenth century. Although the artisans were ultimately outnumbered by clerks, warehousemen, small tradesmen, and other white-collar workers, the institutes nevertheless educated J. B. Neilson, who introduced education and training for workmen at the Glasgow gasworks, James Nasmyth and many other young craftsmen whose desirable attributes of 'character, capacity, and technical knowledge' led to their appointment as managers (Gibbons, 1844).

Throughout the eighteenth and early nineteenth centuries, one observes a readiness on the part of the mercantile and manufacturing community to use its influence to encourage the development of a system of education appropriate to its needs. The Mechanics' Institutes, for example, ultimately developed into Technical Colleges, partly in response to the consternation caused by the Paris Exhibition of 1867, where manufacturers from the continent of Europe won so many of the prizes for quality products. Influential academics like Lyon Playfair drew attention to the fact that continental workshop managers were being educated in polytechnics, whereas technology was being neglected in the Universities of Oxford and Cambridge because of a greater concern with the ancient cultures and languages of Greece and Rome.

In England, the response to this situation was a compromise. Pressures developed in the provincial cities for colleges of higher education, initially to give Nonconformists and members of the lower middle classes the opportunity to pursue locally a liberal education on the Oxbridge pattern. At the same time, at the national level, there was pressure for the establishment of institutions to

teach science and technology. The outcome was the creation between 1871 and 1881 of seven new colleges, ultimately to become
universities, in which science, technology, and in most of them
economics and commerce came to be taught in the same institution
as the traditional arts subjects. Several of these colleges owed their
foundation to the energy, foresight, and munificence of provincial
businessmen.

While utilitarianism triumphed in Birmingham, Leeds, Sheffield,
and elsewhere, it made little impression upon Oxford and Cambridge. There, at that time, though science and economics were
accepted as proper subjects for university study with a substantial
content of fundamental knowledge which might be advanced by
further research, commerce and technology were rejected as being
predominantly concerned with skills and techniques.

If we turn to the social and economic pressures which shaped
higher education in the United States of America in the eighteenth
and nineteenth centuries, we find some interesting parallels to
the situation in Britain over the same period. Just as Anglicanism
had dominated the ethos of the Universities of Oxford and Cambridge in the eighteenth century, so in North America the colleges
founded before the War of Independence were intended to be
orthodox instruments of the community and its Puritan faith.
Harvard, Princeton, Yale, and Dartmouth exemplify these foundations. But whereas Oxford and Cambridge were governed by their
own members, the lay overseers at Harvard took control of the
academics in a pattern repeated elsewhere in American universities.

One consequence of lay control was democratization of the
curricula of universities, symbolized by the words of the founder
on the great seal of Cornell University: 'I would found an institution where any person can find instruction in any study.' Even in
the USA, however, the influence of Greece and Rome lingered
for a long time. At Harvard in 1867, a student reading for an arts
degree spent 57 per cent of his time in studying classical languages
and cultures; at Yale in 1875, the only full-time studies for the
first two years of the undergraduate course were Greek, Latin, and
mathematics (Ashby, 1966).

For a people who were busily building railways across the
prairies and still farming by relatively primitive methods, this
concern with the classics and the education of ministers became
less and less appropriate. Pressures for a more utilitarian education
gathered momentum, culminating in the land-grant colleges set up

by Act of Congress in 1862. This Act provided for land to be put aside in every state, the income from which was to create a fund for an institution of higher education in each state which, without excluding scientific or classical studies, had as its leading object, 'to teach such branches of learning as are related to agriculture and the mechanic arts . . . in order to promote the liberal and practical education of the industrial classes in the several pursuits and professions in life'. A century later, in 1962, there were 69 land-grant colleges, including the Universities of California and Michigan.

The education of the 'industrial classes' was not, however, neglected in the Eastern states of the USA. In 1865, the Massachusetts Institute of Technology was founded for 'those who seek administrative positions in business . . . where a systematic study of political and social relations and familiarity with scientific methods and processes are alike essential'. In 1881 the Wharton School of Commerce and Finance was established at the University of Pennsylvania to provide undergraduate courses, similar undergraduate schools of commerce being developed within the next decade in the Universities of Chicago and California. Then in 1908 came the foundation of the Harvard Graduate School of Business Administration as a department under the Faculty of Arts and Sciences of the University, with a course of study lasting two years.

EDUCATION FOR MANAGEMENT – ITS EVOLUTION IN BRITAIN AND THE USA, 1900–1940

The significant introduction of the term 'Business Administration' into the title of the Harvard Graduate School clearly indicated an intention to train young men for careers as managers or administrators. Already in Britain, in 1903, the University of Manchester had established a Faculty of Commerce and Administration, within which young men and women could be prepared for commercial careers, and local government officers could learn more about the implications of their work. The emphasis, however, was upon the economic aspects of business and social administration in local government, rather than upon management.

The major differences between the evolution of education for management in the USA and Britain readily emerge from examples. For instance, it is interesting to observe that, while

Manchester University chose to educate undergraduates with an emphasis upon the 'subjects' of commerce and social administration, the Harvard Business School was planned for graduates with a liberal education as:

> 'a separate professional school, with a separate faculty, whose object would be purely to train men for their career, as the Law and Medical Schools do' (Copeland, 1958).

Men would be taken without regard for what they had studied in college and would be taught business rather than political economy. This courageous enterprise was not without its critics:

> 'The disdain which much of the academic world felt for trade was matched in the business world by an attitude of rather amused tolerance toward the impractical theorists of collegiate halls' (Copeland, 1958).

Very quickly, however, the Business School at Harvard sought to change this image by its choice of teaching methods and of staff. In its first 'catalogue' of August 1908, it stated:

> 'In the courses on Commercial Law the case system will be used. In the other courses an analogous method, emphasizing classroom discussion in connection with lectures and frequent reports on assigned topics – what may be called the "problem method" – will be introduced as far as practicable. Visits of inspection will be made under competent guidance to various commercial establishments in Boston and in the neighbouring manufacturing centres of New England.'

Early in the history of the Business School, Business Policy was introduced as a second-year course, its purpose being to develop in students an approach to problems from the viewpoint of top management and to integrate the departmental courses of the first year. The method of teaching was to induce a businessman to present a problem from his own experience and for students to write reports which were then read and commented upon by the original lecturer. This concern with the broader view of business was thoroughly approved by the Visiting Committee in 1915, when it reported that:

> 'The Committee believes that the chief emphasis in instruction should continue to be laid on fundamentals, as exemplified in such courses as those in marketing, factory management, accounting and statistics, business policy and finance' (Copeland, 1958).

While businessmen and visiting lecturers like F. W. Taylor helped to break down prejudice on the part of industrialists against the

Business School, they were not always so successful as teachers, and for this reason were ultimately superseded by full-time staff.

During the first two decades of the twentieth century, when the Harvard Business School was struggling under Dean Gay to become financially viable, important developments were taking place in the engineering profession in Britain. In the early nineteenth century, those in the trades despised by Trollope's Miss Marrable had increased their technical competence to the extent that they felt the need for recognized status. The Institution of Civil Engineers was created to secure higher status for its members, to establish engineering as a profession, and to encourage the exchange of papers on current practice. Subsequently other institutions were formed by electrical and mechanical engineers, membership characteristically depending upon the support of a sponsor. On the Continent of Europe, however, engineers acquired their status through study and the passing of examinations, as Lyon Playfair observed in 1867. It was therefore with an eye on the status of Continental engineers that the Institution of Mechanical Engineers in Britain introduced qualifying examinations for its associate members in 1913, Part III of the examination covering 'industrial administration'.

This rather grandiloquent title for the subject carries overtones of a quest for status whereby 'industrial administration' acquired the same prestige as the work of the administrative grades of Civil Servants who helped to formulate policy, in contradistinction to members of the executives grades who carried it out. Nevertheless, 'industrial administration' as a subject tended to be narrower in its conception than the 'business administration' viewpoint adopted by the Harvard Business School, this narrowing of the subject being largely attributable in Britain to the influence of the engineering institutions.

Under the impact of World War I, the mass-production techniques advocated by F. W. Taylor and others, which were applied to the manufacture of armaments and vehicles in the USA, were rapidly extended in Britain. They had already begun to antagonize British craftsmen, and industrial unrest in engineering factories was further fostered by the growth of the shop steward movement (Jefferys, 1945). Conscious that, in future, good labour relations would depend upon the managerial skill of engineers in dealing with shop stewards, a group of engineering companies in the Manchester area in 1918 financed the establishment of a Department of Industrial Administration – the first in Britain – at the Manchester College of Technology. Since some of the departments in the college also formed the Faculty of Technology of the University of Manchester, the arrangement meant that engineering graduates there would henceforward have the opportunity to study industrial administration.

In 1919, two engineers, E. T. Elbourne and Sir Harry Brindley, further extended the concern of engineers for management by putting forward the idea of an Institute of Industrial Administration

'for the purpose of providing a medium for the interchange and development of ideas and practice pertaining to the better operation of industrial enterprises' (Rose, 1954).

They also envisaged that the Institute would aim to raise management to the status of an organized profession. The Institute subsequently came into being, in part as an examining body whose syllabus for industrial administration was ultimately modified and adopted in 1933 by the Institutions of Mechanical and Electrical Engineers.

The fillip to the study of industrial administration created in Britain by wartime experience had its counterpart in the rapidly inflated demand by returning veterans for the study of business administration at the Harvard Business School. In 1920, the new Dean of the Faculty, Wallace B. Donham, prepared a memorandum on the aims of the Harvard Graduate Business School which restated the intention to fit the student for business by 'furnishing the background of general business facts and principles necessary to a broad business point of view', by giving him practice in dealing with business problems, and by teaching him about the place of businessmen within society. As for teaching methods, Dean Donham suggested that:

'The student should be required in each course to investigate facts, to sort undigested material, to state problems, to analyze problems, to reach conclusions and to present the subject matter and his decision orally and in writing as he will be required to do in business' (Copeland, 1958).

He therefore proposed that the problem content of the courses should be enriched by getting current problems from industry as illustrations. Here, indeed, was an early recognition of the businessman as a decision-maker and of the processes involved in decision-making. Later that year, the Bureau of Business Research in the faculty undertook to collect cases and by 1924 most of the instruction was through the vehicle of cases.

By the nineteen-twenties, 'business administration' had become the popular title in American universities for what had previously been described as commerce. In 1930, there were 100 separately organized schools of business in the USA, compared with a dozen or so in 1910, and three (Pennsylvania, California, and Chicago) at the beginning of the century. In 1930, 6,958 students graduated in business, 578 of them obtaining a master's degree; at all levels, business degrees in that year constituted 5 per cent of degrees in all fields in the USA (Gordon & Howell, 1959).

We make this point about the designation of courses because the retention of the term 'commerce' as a subject title tended to obscure the extent to which British universities and other institutions provided courses suitable for young persons preparing for a career in business. Nevertheless, signs appeared that the point had been taken. In 1924, a Department of Industrial Administration had been established at the Regent Street Polytechnic in London as an offshoot of the Department of Commerce. In 1926 the courses and lectures of the Department of Industrial Administration of the Manchester College of Technology had been incorporated in the University undergraduate courses for technological students, and in the following year the college introduced a one-year postgraduate course leading to a diploma in industrial administration, with the specific object of providing instruction in the problems of industrial management.

The year 1930 saw further developments in Britain. The University College of Hull initiated a two-year diploma course in industrial administration; T. G. Rose contributed a series of lectures on management to third-year students taking the Engineering Tripos at the University of Cambridge; the South-East London Technical Institute started a two-year part-time course in industrial management using the case method of instruction in its later stages (Rose, 1954). The case method was also employed extensively in the one-year postgraduate course run by the Department of Business Administration set up in 1931 by the London School of Economics with the sponsorship of several large industrial firms. The department admitted non-graduates to the course, provided that their general level of education matched

university entrance qualifications and that they could produce
evidence of at least three years' business experience.

Generally, however, few students took the full-time postgraduate courses, the bulk of the study of industrial administration in
Britain being conducted in technical colleges, and generally
limited to those preparing for Section C of the examination of the
Institution of Mechanical Engineers, which embraced the Economics of Engineering and included Workshop Organization and
Management. This concentration within the technical colleges
derived from the introduction in the nineteen-twenties of a scheme
of National Certificates, whereby successful candidates could gain
exemption from the examinations of the engineering institutions
on the basis of either part-time or full-time study, supplemented
by practical experience in industry. As centres of instruction for
external examinations, technical and commercial colleges similarly
became associated with the Institute of Bankers, the Chartered
Institute of Secretaries, and the Institute of Cost and Works
Accountants, all of which demanded some knowledge of business
practice from examinees. It is perhaps worth noticing in this
context that with the notable exceptions of medicine and the law,
the professions in Britain in the nineteen-twenties 'remained largely
outside the university ambit', while in the USA the state universities were closely involved with them, especially in the field of
accountancy (Carr-Saunders, 1933).

The closer ties between American universities and the business
world in the late nineteen-twenties and early nineteen-thirties led
finally to courses intended for experienced practising managers in
the Harvard Business School and in the Massachusetts Institute of
Technology. In the summer of 1928 the Harvard Business School
experimented with a special session for business executives lasting
six weeks which offered courses in Finance, Marketing, Management and Economics, Public Utility, and Transportation. The
experiment was repeated in 1929 with 224 men with an average
age of 34 years, more than half of them graduates, about 25 per
cent having their expenses paid by their employers. In 1930 the
special session was reduced in length to one month and in 1931
it was discontinued, partly because of the economic depression and
partly because the teaching staff were losing their enthusiasm for
summer employment. Throughout, teaching was by the case
method. In 1936 and in 1937 the experiment was repeated, but
difficulties continued to be experienced with the range of aptitude

among the members of each session and the short period of instruction, and the experiment was discontinued.

At the Massachusetts Institute of Technology, the study of management had been introduced into undergraduate engineering courses in 1914, and in 1925 management had become a subject of study for a master's degree. Behind these developments lay the belief that an engineer could only succeed in business if his technical competence were matched by his skill in handling people and if he were a man of broad culture with a deep sense of social responsibility (MIT, 1949, p. 40).

Alfred P. Sloan, Jnr. graduated from MIT as an electrical engineer in 1895 and duly demonstrated his business acumen by becoming President of the General Motors Corporation. In 1931 Sloan and a number of other businessmen were approached by Erwin H. Schell, who invited them to support a scheme whereby a small group of promising young executives could be released from their companies to study at MIT for a year. Sufficient support was forthcoming for the scheme to be operable on a small scale, 78 men participating in one-year courses over the following eleven years, each reading for a postgraduate degree in a programme involving a formal dissertation and examinations in the traditional academic pattern. As a consequence of the quality and subsequent success of its participants, the Sloan Fellowship Program steadily gained in prestige, and after World War II was rapidly expanded to meet industrial demands.

SOME DEVELOPMENTS IN FULL-TIME COURSES FOR EXPERIENCED MANAGERS IN THE UNITED STATES AND THE UNITED KINGDOM (1940–1957)

The era from 1940 to 1957 saw promising advances on all fronts in management education and training, stimulated in part by the pressures of war. The most significant of these developments were the introduction of an Advanced Management Program at Harvard, the establishment of the Administrative Staff College at Henley, the inauguration of summer schools for managers in British universities, and the growth of staff training centres run by industries, enterprises, and consultants.

In the United Kingdom, World War II did not immediately stimulate a demand for the training of managers, although lecture courses for more than 20,000 supervisors and production planners were given in technical colleges, and 'Training within Industry for Supervisors' (TWI) with its group discussion methods was introduced from America. One interesting innovation in the university world was the mounting of courses in personnel management lasting three months at Edinburgh in an attempt to meet the shortage of trained personnel managers in the aircraft industry.

In the USA, the Harvard University Business School virtually became a military academy, apart from a special fifteen-week retraining course for men over the age of 35 who were moving across to war production work. As the war progressed, companies increasingly used this course to prepare men for more responsible positions and demanded that something similar should continue to be made available in peacetime.

In retrospect, the year 1945 stands out as a benchmark in the history of management education and training in both countries. In Britain in July 1945, plans were announced for the creation of an Administrative Staff College by its newly-formed Court of Governors who met formally for the first time in October under the chairmanship of Geoffrey Heyworth,* when the college was officially incorporated as a company limited by guarantee. The concept had been discussed since the late nineteen-thirties by a small group of men of wide experience who were familiar with the staff colleges of the fighting services and who felt that a similar kind of institution might be able to improve the administration of large-scale civilian enterprises. As elaborated in a *Times* article in November 1945 by Sir Hector Hetherington, the aims and objects of the college included the development of the manager or administrator from a person of technical competence to one capable of bearing the highest responsibility, and the extension of the practical experience of the individual rather than the enlargement of the specific fields of his knowledge in the academic sense.

Meanwhile in the USA, in September 1945, the Harvard Graduate School of Business Administration had launched its Advanced Management Program (AMP) to meet the demand exposed by its wartime retraining courses. Longer in duration than the prewar Harvard sessions for business executives, the AMP in many ways bore the stamp of the programme leading to the MBA degree, from which it was adapted. No formal entry qualifications were demanded, apart from maturity in age (averag-

* Knighted in 1948; first Baron Heyworth of Oxton, 1955.

ing between 43 and 44), substantial business experience, and good prospects for advancement. Instruction generally was by the case method.

According to Copeland (1958), men on the early programmes came from large and small companies in a variety of industries. Typically they had progressed up functional ladders as specialists and had consequently developed rather narrow viewpoints, which it was hoped would be broadened by exposing the men to the 'cross-fertilization of ideas' in the classroom and the social life of the Business School (Copeland, 1958). As described in the early nineteen-sixties (when the men in the present study were at Henley), the overall objectives of the AMP like those of the Administrative Staff College at Henley included opportunities to share experiences with, and learn from, fellow-executives from a variety of backgrounds, to view one's own career experiences in a fresh perspective, and to clarify values and attitudes affecting one's behaviour as a leader and as an individual. To this was added the characteristically American emphasis on gaining a larger understanding of one's role in 'influencing constructively the shaping of the world of tomorrow'.

To provide for the accomplishment of these overall objectives, the AMP specifically set out, amongst other aims, 'to strengthen executive competence in corporate, long range planning', 'to reinforce capacities for quantitative analysis and decision making', 'to deepen perception and refine skills in handling the human elements of organizations', and 'to examine environmental factors within the nations and the international community affecting business'. Finally, the AMP aimed to encourage a view of learning in its broadest sense as a continuous process enriching the lives of individuals. This final aim, it believed, was most likely to be achieved if the participating executive was 'a man interested in his continuing intellectual and creative growth'. Men sat no formal examinations, received no gradings from the staff, and earned no award.

The early Advanced Management Programs coincided with the return of World War II veterans and a nation-wide shortage of managers. By 1948, the Business School only admitted men sponsored by their employers, who paid their salaries and their tuition and living expenses and encouraged the men to live at the school for the duration of the programme. The school believed that sponsorship would encourage the careful selection of individuals, the assurance of high motivation and 'an atmosphere within the firm conducive to executive growth'.

In the Spring of 1948 the Administrative Staff College opened its doors to the members of its first course at Greenlands, Henley-on-Thames, the governors having appointed Noel Hall* to be its Principal. A full discussion of the policies and practices of the College and their evolution and modification over the period 1946 to 1966 appears in Chapter III, but it is appropriate to mention briefly some points of similarity and difference. Henley, like Harvard, demanded sponsorship, specified as entry qualifications only successful experience as a manager and an age between 28 and 35, and made its residential course three months in duration. And whereas Harvard encouraged cross-fertilization between AMP members by the case method, Henley chose to organize its course members into syndicates for the purpose of pursuing common tasks involving reading, group discussions under the chairmanship of a course member, lectures, visits, and other learning situations.

The success of the Advanced Management Program at Harvard encouraged emulation elsewhere in the USA in the face of a national shortage of managers and a growing concern with executive development in American enterprises. By 1955, at least 50 other American universities offered post-experience courses for executives. A similar process occurred in Britain with the innovation of residential summer schools for experienced managers in Oxford, Cambridge, and Edinburgh, following the visit to the USA in 1951 of an Anglo-American Productivity Council team to study education for management.

The first of these summer schools was organized in 1953 by the Appointments Committee at Oxford whose advisers included the then Sir Geoffrey Heyworth and Noel Hall, at that time respectively Chairman of Governors and Principal at Henley. Intended for rather younger men (average age 30), the Oxford Business Summer School was based on an intensive course in general economics lasting three weeks. The forty course members were subdivided into four groups, each supported by a tutor with a clearly defined instructional role. At Cambridge the four-week course for managers in industry inaugurated by the Board of Extra-Mural Studies in 1954 was designed to help those whose formal education ended early or whose responsibilities were widening into general manage-

* Knighted in 1957.

ment, group work being supplemented by seminars led by members of staff, and by individual tutorial sessions.

Those who had conceived the idea of the Administrative Staff College shared a strong belief that an independent institution was necessary, partly to facilitate the application of new methods, partly to allay the suspicion that the treatment of subjects would be too academic. The course of studies devised by Noel Hall eschewed traditional subject titles, being built round the study of administrative structures, the internal organization and administration of the enterprise, its external relationships, the maintenance of its dynamic, and the role of the directing authority. The summer schools at Oxford and Cambridge, on the other hand, built upon the distinctive competence of the universities to teach an intellectual discipline by the traditional methods of essay writing, lectures, and tutorials, supplemented by such innovations as group work, interviews, and panel discussions, the economic and social environment of business being a common background theme in both courses.

Shortly after these developments in British universities, the Sloan School of Management at the Massachusetts Institute of Technology in 1956 took the interesting step of introducing a 10-week programme for senior executives, aimed at an older group of men in the range of 38–50 years with substantial experience in decision-making at the policy level. This programme, reduced in length to nine weeks in 1965, took as its unifying theme the policy, planning, and control character of the executive function, with an orientation towards new knowledge and future trends based upon research and applied experience. This close link with research was forged by frequent and relatively informal contacts with members of the academic staff, including Douglas McGregor, Warren Bennis, and Jay Forrester. Apart from its emphasis upon seminars with professional researchers, the course incorporated a five-day sensitivity training programme concerned with interpersonal relations and group development, and an individual project undertaken by each executive relating his learning on the course to some of the key issues facing him upon his return to his enterprise.

The MIT programme, with its concern for research, new knowledge, change in the business environment, and the relationship of on-course learning to the 'back-home' situation of the executive, tended to be more 'executive-centred' than many other programmes in the nineteen-fifties. As we observed earlier, this in North America was a time when managerial talent was in great demand, and programmes were being designed to meet the needs of enterprises which tended to think of manager development as a process of injecting knowledge about new techniques of management and practising such communication skills as speech-making and chairmanship. Short full-time courses on these lines for middle management were also evolved in the nineteen-fifties in Britain by such institutions as the British Institute of Management and Ashridge Management College.

The courses for practising executives referred to here were generally restricted to persons sponsored by their employers, and as a consequence came to be regarded by participants as courses of some prestige within their own enterprise. In Britain from 1948 onwards, it was possible for individual managers to study for a professional qualification in management in technical colleges in their own time, the scheme involving a Common Intermediate Examination and a later Final stage administered by the British Institute of Management in conjunction with the Ministry of Education as a road to professional qualifications in general management, the standard of these qualifications being 'progressively developed so that they may become of ever increasing significance as evidence of competency for general management' (Rose, 1954).

In practice, industrialists at that time tended to reject the view that such qualifications had any significance. The authors of *Education and Training for Management* (Federation of British Industries, 1954) commented upon 'The dangerous and unproved assumption that the development of management ability lends itself to formal instruction'. It also expressed the fear that the BIM scheme 'might encourage a number of young men to press their claims to management positions on the strength of an examination qualification' notwithstanding the clear *caveat* of the Urwick Report that 'theoretical study alone cannot make a manager' (Ministry of Education, 1947).

The greater proportion of those pursuing the BIM scheme studied part-time, mostly in the evenings, although in some colleges promising individuals, usually junior managers or trainees, were released by their employers from work one day each week. Even when supported by employers, the courses leading to the BIM qualifications tended to be patronized by the less senior managers and were consequently accorded much less prestige in the nineteen-fifties than, say, the Henley course.

These limitations applied less markedly to the general management courses organized and run by management consultants. Urwick, Orr, for instance, formed their centre for the purpose of training new recruits to consultancy and then faced the problem of finding suitable courses for senior managers and directors of client firms who were reluctant to attend technical colleges. This led to the creation of general management courses lasting six weeks which aimed to give an appreciation of developments in managerial techniques, a broader understanding of managerial tasks, and the means of effecting an immediate improvement in managerial performance. Since the centres are usually staffed by experienced full-time consultants, and since the centres have to pay their way largely from fees as commercial establishments, the courses tended to be relatively expensive.

Sensitive to the feelings of senior executives between the ages of 35 and 42 who found themselves having to get up to date on new techniques, the centres of the consultants not only promised improved performance but also aimed to 'identify gaps in knowledge' and to fill them through lecture–tutorials, discussions, and case studies which encouraged the exchange and critical examination of ideas. In addition to the study of techniques and personal skills, the Urwick, Orr course tended to emphasize the theory of management and external influences on long-range planning and policy-making; Personnel Administration Ltd, at their Sundridge Park centre, similarly concentrated upon the use of standards of performance in planning and control, and problems of decision-making, coordination, and control. In both centres, the outstanding characteristic has been the emphasis upon improved personal performance and an understanding of techniques and of organization.

The same study methods have also characterized the staff colleges set up by companies and industries. After World War II, a number of large companies which had hitherto operated with many semi-autonomous subsidiaries began to modify their policies and to move towards greater rationalization and integration in order to gain the advantage of scale. In concert with this operation, many large enterprises decided to establish their own centres in which to run courses for managers and supervisors (often residential and rarely more than three weeks in length) where the emphasis was upon the nature of group operations, the creation of group loyalty, the dissemination of good managerial practice, and the improvement of personal skills. In several instances, these courses were intended to fit in with schemes for developing younger managers for greater responsibilities, men being nominated either by their own superiors or through the agency of a central personnel department.

DEVELOPMENTS IN MANAGEMENT EDUCATION IN BRITAIN POST-1957

Earlier we mentioned the introduction of residential summer schools for managers at Oxford and Cambridge universities. Industry supported these schools and released managers to attend them; industry also gave strong support to the one-week residential courses organized by the British Institute of Management during the nineteen-fifties. In 1958, the University Grants Committee in reporting on *University Development 1952–1957* commented upon the success of evening and vacation courses in management in several universities:

> 'It is clear that there is support from industry for them, including the readiness of senior and experienced industrial managers to take a substantial part both in their higher direction and also by direct participation in instruction.'

The Committee also remarked:

> 'It seems improbable, and indeed at odds with experience elsewhere, that management is so strange a skill that a systematic study of the practices that have been followed, the problems that have been met and the success that has been achieved is incapable of yielding knowledge which can be conveyed by teaching.'

It described management as a 'most difficult, multi-disciplinary field' and concluded that:

> 'The development of management as an academic discipline represents a worthwhile challenge, in facing which industry and commerce as well as the universities have an important part to play. A number of universities who are already working in this field are anxious to develop both their research and their teaching.'

Following the publication of this report with its hint that several universities were ready to develop management as an academic discipline, the Conservative and Unionist Party included in its political manifesto the statement that it would welcome the establishment of a school of Business Administration in Britain. One of its members, Sir Keith Joseph, from 1958 onwards had been discussing with a small group of enthusiasts the idea of a Foundation for Management Education to stimulate and accelerate the development of management studies in British universities. In 1959 the group invited J. W. Platt, a director of the Shell Petroleum Company, to become the first director of the Foundation, which began fund-raising in June 1960 to finance schemes at the Universities of Bristol, Cambridge, and Leeds. Although priorities for the 1962–7 quinquennium appeared to make few provisions for management studies in university budgets, the Foundation was determined to foster this development. By limiting its appeal to plans submitted by the universities which were already approved in principle by the University Grants Committee, the Foundation had, by 1961, obtained the equivalent of £30,000 per annum, largely through seven-year covenants, and a contribution of £10,000 per annum from the University Grants Committee. The Foundation believed that experiment should be encouraged and was therefore prepared to support a variety of proposals (FBI, 1961).

In the early sixties, economists began to spend considerable time in attempting to assess the economic contribution of education. This interest was stimulated by T. W. Schultz, who chose the theme of 'Investment in Human Capital' for his presidential address to the American Economic Association in December 1960. He argued that:

'Although it is obvious that people acquire useful skills and knowledge, it is not obvious that these skills and knowledge are a form of capital . . . It has been widely observed that increases in national output have been large compared with the increases of land, man-hours, and physical reproducible capital. Investment in human capital is probably the major explanation for this difference.'

This concern with investment in human capital reappeared in the April 1963 report of the National Economic Development Council, *Conditions Favourable to Faster Growth* which contained the comment,

'The dynamic economy is vitally dependent on dynamic management alert to discover new ideas, to develop new markets and to explore the possibilities of technological innovation.'

The report went on to discuss the relation between education and economic growth, emphasized the importance of management development, and urged the need for the establishment of at least one new very high-level business school.

Shortly afterwards, in October 1963, a committee under the chairmanship of Lord Robbins published its report: *Higher Education*. This commented on the lack in Britain of anything comparable to the great business schools in the United States and recommended that:

> 'at least two major postgraduate schools should be built up, in addition to other developments already probable in universities and other institutions' (p. 135).

It also observed that:

> 'there is scope in a number of centres for courses of management education for persons of mature years who wish, at late stages in their careers, to refresh their minds by instruction in recently developed techniques and by systematic discussion with academic teachers concerned with their activities. The notable success since the war of the Administrative Staff College at Henley has shown that experiments here are likely to meet with a ready response' (p. 136).

During 1963, two groups of industrialists, one associated with Lord Rootes and the other (the 'Savoy Group') with Sir Anthony Bowlby and Mr J. Parsons, had been championing different plans for at least one business school. The Savoy Group, in particular, wished to see more formal teaching of management techniques at university level. Eventually, with the help and interest of the British Institute of Management, the Federation of British Industries, and the Foundation for Management Education, Lord Franks was invited to examine the question, to take evidence, and to submit his recommendations to the two groups of industrialists and the interested institutions. In his report in November 1963, he proposed the creation of two business schools in urban surroundings to facilitate contact with industry and commerce – one in London and one in Manchester. To overcome the problem of recruiting and keeping staff of sufficient quality, the schools should be created in association with the universities but established as a partnership between university and business. Their purpose would not be to turn out specialists but to give some acquaintance with what a modern scientific approach can offer the businessman. Subsequently, in response to an appeal for £3 million for the schools which, if obtained, would be matched by an identical sum from the Government, industry subscribed £5 million, which it entrusted to the Foundation for Management Education for distribution in conjunction with the University Grants Committee.

By 1965, the two new business schools had announced their plans for courses to start in the following year. Manchester proposed as part of its plan to mount a twelve-week course for 'men and women in their thirties . . . capable of reaching senior management positions', which had as its aims to 'develop the abilities of a general manager'.

London similarly planned an Executive Development Programme as well as a six-week Senior Executive Programme. In both institutions, postgraduate courses in management subjects would be built up as quickly as possible.

Meanwhile a development in another form took place in the shape of a six-week Advanced Management Programme run by Harvard Business School professors in the summer of 1964 at Bede College in the University of Durham. This was well enough supported to justify the organization of similar programmes in subsequent years, jointly sponsored by the British Institute of Management and the Harvard Business School Club of London.

These, then, were some of the developments in management education in the period from 1957 to 1965 which were topical at Henley during the sessions of those members who answered our Survey questions.

MANAGEMENT EDUCATION AND TRAINING IN RETROSPECT

Looking back over the past two centuries at the development of training and education for management, we observe from an early stage the adaptiveness of many employers in industry and commerce. Continual changes in technology and in economic and social conditions have posed problems of education and training for successive generations of managers. Where existing educational provisions have failed to meet their needs, mercantilists and manufacturers have used their influence and support to create new institutions or to graft on offshoots to institutions already in existence. Educationalists in the newly created institutions have tended to respond by seeking to evolve learning environments and teaching methods appropriate to the process of learning how best to manage.

In the instance of Henley, its pedagogic methods, its course of study, and the roles of staff and students have reflected these processes of innovation, adaptation, and change. The College as an educational institution has been particularly responsive to the changing requirements of industry and Government, and the place of the present study in this process can be better understood by describing the College and its work in greater detail.

Chapter 3 · The Administrative Staff College

ITS CURRICULUM AND ORIENTATION

E. A. Life

As was mentioned briefly in the previous chapter, the idea of the Administrative Staff College had originated in the late nineteen-thirties although it was not until October 1945 that the college was incorporated as a company limited by guarantee, with a Court of Governors under the chairmanship of Geoffrey Heyworth (later Lord Heyworth) who was then Chairman of Unilever Limited. As a non-profit-making institution, the College was officially recognized as a charity, finance initially coming from public companies in the form of seven-year covenants or annual donations, the balance of income, about half, being covered by fees.

The general aims and objects of the college focused upon the development of the manager or administrator from a person of technical competence to someone capable of bearing the highest responsibility. This process was seen as an extension of the practical experience of each person rather than as an enlargement of specific fields of academic knowledge.

This emphasis upon 'practice' became the starting-point for thinking about the future participants, the length of the course at the College, its content and its methodology. Participants would be men or women who had already demonstrated their competence as practitioners in their chosen field, and who would be able to make a useful contribution to understanding on the basis of their experience. Staff and students alike would be described as 'members' of the College united in a common study of administration. Because of the responsibilities borne by members, a lengthy period of absence from their own enterprises was impracticable, and, after consultation with industry and the public service, the College fixed the length of its early courses at three months. It was further decided that the course syllabus would not be devised in terms of traditional subject divisions, and that the methods of work on the course would aim at the effective practice of skills relevant to management and administration. These general aims were subsequently translated into a course of studies and an appropriate methodology by Noel Hall, previously a Professor of Political Economy at University College, London, the first Director of the National Institute for Economic and Social Research, and former head of the War Trade Department in the British Embassy at Washington during World War II.

To achieve results within the limits of a three-month period, a residential College was considered desirable. This would have the advantages of freeing members from domestic or working ties and of permitting them to mix more freely among themselves, especially if the College were not in a densely-populated area. 'Greenlands', an existing riverside house near Henley-on-Thames, capable of housing 45 members, met these requirements.

THE CHOICE OF MEMBERS AND THE COMPOSITION OF SYNDICATES

Other considerations suggested the desirability of limiting the number of members. If a person were to be given the opportunity 'to cease a little from action and to think what he is doing and why he is doing it', much was to be gained from comparing the practices of different enterprises and a person's own practices with those of other managers. But a prerequisite to such exchanges would be mutual confidence and understanding based upon knowledge of each other among staff and members, and this would be hard to achieve within three months if the number of members were large.

During World War II it had been a frequent practice to establish *ad hoc* meetings between small groups of specialists to assist coordination between departments and organizations and to keep seniors informed of progress. It was observed that those attending these meetings learned much about each other and their departments in the process of discussing and pursuing a common task, this observation leading the College to believe that groups constructed in this way would be a powerful educational tool to use with mature persons. These small groups came to be called 'syndicates', a term used for many years to describe groups of senior students in the staff colleges of the fighting services. In the service staff colleges it was the custom to ensure that each syndicate included representatives from a variety of arms, services, and advisers; at Henley the syndicates were formed of members from a wide variety of enterprises and administrative bodies and from different managerial functions.

Originally the Henley syndicates consisted of nine members, representing different types of industrial company, nationalized industry, government departments, commercial enterprises, and local government or the fighting services. Later a tenth member, an overseas national, was added. At the same time, each syndicate was composed of members chosen to represent different functions of an enterprise, such as production, sales, research, accounting, and finance, or the various ancillary departments such as personnel. At a much later date, when the College had expanded to accommodate 66 members, a group of six 'unsyndicated' members was introduced, who as individuals joined each of the other syndicates in turn during the course. These unsyndicated members were used to strengthen a syndicate which might be underrepresented in a particular function or activity, to give practice in the art of introducing a new member into an established working group, and to provide a natural link between syndicates. However, it was not always easy to find the right kind of member to fulfil this role. Finally in 1965, it was decided to keep to six main 'ordinary' syndicates of eleven members, but for two areas of study to maintain the policy of forming 'modified' syndicates. These modified syndicates were constructed on the same principles as the 'ordinary' syndicates, with the same cross-section of skills and experience, but with a different selection of individuals, so that the group provided the opportunity for members to extend their knowledge of each other and of a wide range of enterprises.

Since the body of members had to be carefully constituted in order to satisfy some of the objectives of syndicate work, it was considered appropriate that the College should use the term 'session' to describe the period in residence of members attending a course, rather than to talk in terms of 'Course Number So-and-So'. Within the College, it became the practice to describe each body of members as a 'session', and to talk about 'building up a session' from the persons put forward ('nominated' in Henley parlance) by sponsoring enterprises. Understandably, among those nominated there is often an excessive number of persons with a similar characteristic, such as experience in production management in private enterprise, making it difficult to achieve the desirable balance of members for any given session. To achieve this aim, the process of building up a session has to begin well in advance of its opening, with the prospect that some nominees may have to wait eighteen months before a place becomes available.

The process just described obviously involves close collaboration with the sponsoring enterprises on the part of the Principal and of the Registrar. For this reason, the College asks each sponsoring enterprise to name a senior executive responsible for sanctioning the release of any manager put forward as a potential Henley member, together with the name of the person advising on the choice of employee, if two persons are involved. In this way the College has established an official link with a 'nominator' within each of the sponsoring enterprises who, by means of visits and sometimes by discussion with the Registrar, becomes well acquainted with the work and standards of the College.

From what has already been written, it will be evident that the choice of individual members has been a matter of great importance to the College because of the explicit attention given to planning the structure of each syndicate and its relevance to the nature of the work undertaken by members while at Henley. Since experience and successful accomplishment were prime criteria, examination qualifications alone would be an insufficient recommendation. Accordingly, from its inception, the College required each candidate for selection to attend an interview, during which the relevance of his qualifications and experience would be assessed in relation to the normal demands of a session. As far as possible, the College tried to avoid 'failing' candidates at interview by having close liaison with nominators beforehand; nevertheless, the right to reject was obviously necessary in order that consistent standards could be established and maintained in the minds of nominators. Because of the insistence upon successful experience, age, too, was an important factor; the range suggested initially was 28–35 years, later amended to 33–43 years. In practice the average age of members has remained around 39.

The College from its beginning did not lay down any demands for academic qualification for entry. Likewise it eschewed the use of any final examination by which to judge the performance of members. Many in the early sessions had had a restricted formal education, but by 1965 about half the members in any one session were likely to be university graduates.

LEARNING AIMS AND METHODS

Since, in effect, the College was trying to help successful middle managers to become successful senior managers, it aimed to give the members practice in skills which it hypothesized to be appropriate to senior levels of management. For example, it believed in 1948 that at more senior levels persuasion and consultation would tend to replace the giving of orders, so that it became important for a manager to be able to reach decisions and share responsibility with others of similar status. Also, at a more senior level, there would be a greater likelihood that a manager would have to take responsibility for the work of persons with a vocational background different from his own; this experience would introduce him to a variety of professional attitudes, to the problem of evaluating the contributions of specialists, and to the difficulties of utilizing the talents of a diverse team of individuals in pursuit of a given task. Work in syndicates at Henley was therefore designed to give practice in these skills.

Another hypothesis about the work of senior managers was that decisions at this level involved the use of a greater volume of data than at lower levels, these data also being less precise and less familiar, and that time was a factor of increasing importance. Accordingly, syndicate work was designed to involve the collective assimilation of an extensive amount of material within stringent limits of time. Furthermore, this process demanded the evaluation of the information made available, often in terms of a request for the syndicate to state its own opinions and conclusions.

It was decided that, for the accomplishment of these tasks, each syndicate would operate under the chairmanship of a specified member who would have responsibility for its work, aided by another member who would act as secretary to the group. The aim would be to put as much responsibility as possible upon the chairman and secretary, different members taking these roles in each subject. Thus, by the end of a session, each member would have had three or four spells of office in addition to his normal role within the syndicate.

This method of working was characteristic of the period 1961–6.

A College booklet of that period describes the activities of a chairman and a secretary in connection with a typical subject of the course:

> 'Having received their subject papers several days before their syndicate colleagues, the chairman and secretary go into private conference with the directing staff member in charge of their syndicate, who satisfies himself that the scope of the subject and the arrangements for its treatment are understood. This enables them to prepare their own scheme for controlling the work of the syndicate in that subject.
>
> Their next step is to examine, with the help of the librarian, the books and other printed material which will have to be shared out among the syndicate if the work is to be done effectively and within the time allotted. The chairman is now ready to conduct the opening meeting for his subject. He explains the task to the syndicate and makes his proposals for carrying it out.'

The method of working in 1969 remained basically similar to that just described. The 'subject papers' normally consist of a 'brief' for all members delineating the field of study and its relationship to other subjects and specifying the nature of the syndicate work; a note for the chairman and secretary of each syndicate referring to the procedures to be adopted and to possible sources of difficulty; details of the timetable; and an extensive reading-list.

Visits outside the College are usually arranged on three days, spread out at fortnightly intervals through the programme, providing members with an opportunity to supplement their reading with face-to-face encounters with persons involved in the practicalities of a problem. Generally members visit establishments in small groups of about six in number, having been briefed by colleagues on questions which they would like to be answered. The visits involve careful liaison with the institutions concerned to ensure that persons of authority are indeed available to answer the questions effectively. Typically the visits may involve uninhibited discussion with shop stewards and managements on such matters as industrial relations and motivation, encounters with local and central government departments and trade associations, or a flight to Brussels to examine the problems of the European Common Market. Following the visits, members report back to their syndicates on the major items of interest.

In addition to the information made available by the members on the basis of experience, visits, and reading, further material is expounded by speakers addressing the whole College or by visitors to syndicates being questioned in small group meetings. Speakers and syndicate visitors may be members of the staff or representative of a wide range of institutions – including universities, companies, trade unions, and foreign embassies.

It has always been a central feature of the work of the College that each syndicate exercise leads to the accomplishment of a definite task within a fixed time, often the completion of a report of specified maximum length on a particular aspect of the problem studied. Such reports, together with those from the other syndicates, are duplicated and circulated to all members. Each syndicate then examines critically the report of the other five for a specified purpose. This may require the selection of a number of issues thrown up by the reports which each syndicate would like to hear discussed further by the whole College at a final 'presentation' or 'conference' on the subject.

Presentations involving all the members take place in a conference room. During the period 1961–6 the Principal normally acted as the chairman of these meetings, in which members sat in their syndicate groupings with the chairman and secretary at their head. On most occasions, a presentation would open with a speech about seven minutes in length from each chairman, commenting on selected aspects of the subject from the viewpoint of the work of the syndicate, speeches being interspersed by brief comments from the Principal. Following a short break, the second half of the presentation would usually consist of a general discussion, open to all members, on an agenda of issues raised by the prior consideration of the syndicate reports. Chaired from a rostrum by the Principal or the member of staff responsible for the subject, the discussion would require members to stand on their feet and make their points in front of the body of the College. Conferences tended to be less formal, without speeches, and with chairmen putting forward points from their syndicate as the basis for a general discussion.

Over the years the College has been experimenting with a variety of plenary sessions in an endeavour to provide an extended range of learning experiences for the members. Designed to provide practice in expounding a viewpoint succinctly in front of a large gathering, presentations and conferences can inhibit the shyer members early in the course to the detriment of discussion. While retaining the requirement for chairmen to speak, the College has modified its procedures so that on occasion chairmen may speak from the rostrum or control an entire discussion. There has been also less insistence on formality in the conference room. Other developments have included the use of smaller conferences involving the interchange of views between pairs of syndicates, and the presence of expert visitors to comment on the discussion at presentations.

CONTENT OF THE COURSE OF STUDIES

The framework of the course of studies originally devised by Noel Hall fitted the view of an enterprise as an open system. The scheme envisaged four main parts to the course. The first looked at structure under the title 'Comparative Administrative Structures'; the second turned to the internal dynamics of the enterprise in the form of four subjects embraced by 'Internal Organization and Administration'; Part III incorporated four subjects concerned with 'External Relations'; and Part IV studied the problems of adaptation to change and the maintenance of vitality within an enterprise from the viewpoint of the role of those directing it. These major elements in the course were supported by other studies of the spoken word, the interpretation and analysis of financial statements, sources of current information, and biographies of famous men and women.

This pattern evolved for the managerial world of 1948 was modified from time to time over the intervening years. 'The role of the directing authority' soon demanded attention as a fifth major part of the course of studies, but other modifications were contained by adjustments to the nature of the subjects within the other four parts. By 1961, for example, the problems of technical innovation received separate attention within Part IV, and a special study was being made of the economic position of the United Kingdom.

Having in essence adopted a systems view of the enterprise, the College chose its 'subjects' in terms of the processes involved in administering an enterprise, rather than in terms of the limits imposed by conventional academic disciplines. As the managerial world changed, so adaptations continued. By the end of 1966, for example, the advent of computers and the possibilities of using an increasing range of quantitative techniques influenced the course of studies in the direction of more specific attention to Statistical Aids to Planning and Control, the Interpretation of Accounting Data, and the Use of Figures in the Management of Operations. Similarly, as the role of Britain in world affairs changed, more time was given to an extensive study of Britain and the International Community.

Some subjects perform a dual function not always apparent to the outsider. The study of Comparative Administrative Structures, for example, required each member to describe the organization of his enterprise in his own terms. Being the first subject of study, it enabled each individual to speak with relative authority in syndicate from the moment of assembly, besides helping to establish the nature of the normal working environment of each member for the benefit of colleagues who might wish to explore it further in discussion. Human Behaviour and Management Practice, another early subject, similarly invited discussion of behaviour in the working environment and at the same time prepared members for later discussions of their own behaviour as a syndicate.

Other developments in the content of the course of studies had a closer relationship to the findings of the research described in these pages. Accordingly, they receive separate attention in Chapter 12.

THE ROLE OF THE STAFF

The staff are called Directing Staff or DS. It was decided at the outset not to give them academic titles such as 'lecturer' because of the wish to emphasize a practical rather than an academic approach. A member of the Directing Staff is assigned to each syndicate. He briefs the chairman and secretary for each subject and attends most of the ensuing syndicate discussions and all plenary sessions. Throughout the discussions he is expected to be available to give guidance on College methods and resources, including reading matter.

Individual DS contribute to discussions according to their own 'style' and experience. Their contributions are often felt to be wanted when the syndicate is evaluating its handling of the subject or its performance in a plenary session. To fulfil his role well, a DS must be constantly in touch with the work of the syndicate in each subject, to ensure that the main issues are not neglected, and that the resources available are utilized fully. In addition, the skilful DS can help the members of his syndicate to gain insights into the dynamics and decision-making processes of the group by drawing upon their own immediate experience. Consequently individuals on the Directing Staff must be thoroughly conversant with the individual experience, capacities, and needs of the members of their syndicate, and well informed over the whole field of the course of studies.

In aiming to help members to maximize the value to be obtained from the course, a DS may intervene in syndicate discussions through the chairman if he has factual information to offer, or appropriate knowledge and experience not otherwise available to the group. If he has specialized experience, such as skill in leading case study discussions, he may be required to exercise this for the benefit of the syndicate. He also makes himself available to individual members for private discussions outside syndicate time.

Each member of the Directing Staff has a responsibility for one or more sub-divisions of the course, for which he prepares the documentation. This responsibility requires him to keep up-to-date on subjects by means of personal study and contacts outside the College, and to discuss significant developments and proposals for change with his colleagues. He may write a paper to support the subject in the course of studies or be responsible for commissioning one from an outside authority. In addition, he may have to make arrangements for talks from visiting speakers, and for visits by members of the College to other institutions.

The activities of the six syndicate Directing Staff are coordinated by a colleague who holds the post of Director of Studies, usually for a period of one year, the post being rotated. He chairs regular meetings of the syndicate Directing Staff, prepares the course timetable, allocates members to syndicates and to the offices of chairman and secretary for each subject, coordinates arrangements for presentations and conferences, and, through the Course of Studies Secretary, provides clerical services to the course. The Director of Studies also takes personal responsibility for a number of subjects.

Over the period 1961–6, the role of the Directing Staff was gradually extended to permit more active participation in the course of studies and to offer more scope for initiative. Other changes in the role, such as the greater incidence of formal lecture presentations by members of the staff and involvement in the review by syndicates of their own behaviour, are discussed in Chapter 12.

The experience and qualifications of the Directing Staff concerned with sessions between 1961 and 1966 varied very widely. Their previous occupations included high-level administration in central government and the armed forces at home and overseas, industrial management and direction, university teaching and administration. Several persons also joined the College on secondment as temporary members of the Directing Staff for one or two sessions, bringing with them direct industrial experience.

For staff and members alike, the work required is exacting. Syndicate periods normally last one and a half hours, with two meetings each morning and one after tea, while presentations and talks take place after dinner on three evenings each week, leaving time during afternoons for reading, drafting reports, and informal discussion. Meetings also take place on Saturday mornings and Sunday evenings, excepting the three weekends arranged during each course to allow members to return home briefly.

THE COLLEGE IN RELATION TO ITS MEMBERS

One thus sees the Administrative Staff College as aiming to influence men and women who are moving upwards in their enterprise. In so doing, it creates a temporary community of similarly placed men and women in their late thirties and early forties chosen from a range of major institutions in British society. These individuals interact extensively within an environment which is orientated towards their eventual social roles in many ways: for example, they study the lives of eminent men and women; they meet and talk with visitors who are currently leaders in their own fields; they meet representatives of political parties and foreign countries. This is done 'without political, social, or economic bias', with a deliberate attempt to search for elements of the administrative process that are common to all types of complex enterprise.

Institutionally, the College reflects the social changes following World War II, in which managers found themselves 'achieving' status rather than having status 'ascribed' to them by virtue of their social position. Indeed, the willingness of senior administrators to assist in the creation of Henley and to sponsor managers attending its courses was an open acknowledgement of the importance of the manager to an enterprise, and once again illustrated the institution-building skills of businessmen and public servants in Britain. At the same time, the importance attached to successful managerial experience as a qualification for entry to Henley, as opposed to formal examination qualifications, was reminiscent of the conditions of entry to the engineering institutions in the nine- teenth-century when high practical qualifications had been de- manded. Indeed, the Institution of Civil Engineers had also been born out of a dining club, in which civil engineers 'mingled social activities with informal but serious discussions of their common problems'. This is a description which also reasonably fits the activities of the Greenlands Association, a self-administering body with more than 3,000 members drawn from Henley 'alumni' who meet from time to time on a regional basis and publish a Journal twice yearly. For its members, one useful function of the Green- lands Association is to act as an informal source of support when there are difficulties at work or when the enterprise is going through an unsettling period of reorganization.

Reinforcement to this role is given by the review courses held by the College eighteen months after each session, when members of a particular session return for a short period to confer on speci- fied issues of topical importance and to compare experiences since leaving the College. From 1958 onwards, the College has organ- ized conferences for members in attendance ten years previously, and, more recently, for those whose original session ended five years before, both types of conferences providing formal tasks as well as time for informal discussions between individuals. Besides meeting an educational need, the conferences also provide the College with a further means of remaining in direct contact with practising managers over a considerable portion of their careers.

THE INTERNATIONAL INVOLVEMENT OF THE COLLEGE

This account would not be complete without a reference to the interest of other countries in the Henley approach and experience.

As early as 1949, the success of the College attracted attention in India, and in 1957 the Administrative Staff College of India was established at Hyderabad with the support of the Central Government and of businessmen. In the same year, the Australian Administrative Staff College opened its first session, having been established in 1955, both colleges having been helped in the formative stages by members of the Henley Directing Staff on secondment. This active help also extended to the Pakistan Administrative Staff College, which was inaugurated in 1960, and to the Philippine Executive Academy, which is attached to the University of the Philippines; in these instances, additional advice and assistance was made available from American sources.

This direct involvement by Henley Directing Staff in institutions overseas similarly occurred with the East African Staff College, the University of Tehran, and the University College of the West Indies.

In addition to seconding its staff to overseas institutions, the College has for many years permitted the attachment to its staff of Staff Observers, usually for periods of three months, observers having come from many countries, including Egypt, Ghana, India, Iran, Iraq, Israel, Jamaica, Kenya, Mexico, Pakistan, Somalia, Yugoslavia, and Zambia.

At the same time, the College has maintained by various means a practical interest in problems and developments in other management education and training centres throughout the world. Members of the College staff have undertaken missions for the United Nations Development Programme Special Fund in Ceylon, Colombia, Ghana, Poland, and Hungary and have independently studied the provisions for management education in extended visits to Belgium, Czechoslovakia, the Netherlands, Spain, and West Germany, besides undertaking visits to institutions in North and South America.

This international traffic in ideas has enabled the College to examine the extent to which its organization and methods are appropriate to different cultures and to countries in different stages of economic development. Its methods seem to be appropriate to the other Administrative Staff Colleges, all of which cater for experienced administrators and managers in their late thirties and forties, although some run shorter courses for other age-groups. Comparative research may later show that organization by syndicates, opportunities for group discussion, and residential study all contribute to a learning experience of particular value to managers in mid-career in a wide variety of cultures.

RESEARCH AT HENLEY

At an early stage in the history of the College, it was recognized that DS could benefit from the support of other colleagues whose main interests were in improving material used within the course and in improving course design. In 1950 a person with these functions was first appointed, primarily concerned with College documentation in the form of course-of-studies papers written anonymously which aimed to be factual and non-contentious.

This concern with the development of the course of studies remained paramount until the early nineteen-sixties, when it was decided to prosecute research more vigorously. While the three members of the small research unit continued to devote some time to the development of material for the course of studies, they were also committed to make an original contribution to knowledge relevant to the work of the College. An important issue was the relationship between the experience of attending Henley and a member's subsequent career pattern. With this concern in mind, the College began to explore the prospects of making a collaborative study of the problem with the Human Resources Centre of the Tavistock Institute of Human Relations, believing that a larger and more uninhibited response would be forthcoming if members knew that an impartial body would be analysing the data and maintaining the confidentiality of individual responses.

The study undertaken with the Tavistock Institute of Human Relations provides an example of the way in which involvement in research and development has become diffused between all members of the Directing Staff. The Registrar was closely involved in the early stages of a pilot study and in questionnaire design; members of the research unit carried out interviews in the pilot study and with members of the Directing Staff contributed ideas for the questionnaire. As soon as provisional research findings became available, they were considered by the Directing Staff in terms of their implications for course content, learning situations, and staff roles.

Once research had become an integral part of the activities of the College, the terms of reference of each DS were modified to include long-term responsibility for the development of a subject, with planned periods of time away from syndicate responsibilities to do longer-term thinking and work. Much of this work has in practice stemmed from periodic reviews of the course and its component parts undertaken in connection with long-term development meetings held under the chairmanship of the Principal. Staff were also encouraged to write papers and books under their own names rather than anonymously.

Overall, the College has aimed at working in fields of interest to both the Private and the Public Sectors of the economy and to take problems as starting-points for research without regard to disciplinary boundaries. This policy has led the College to become involved in a working collaboration with several other institutions: the University of Aston; the Industrial Training Research Unit of University College London; the London Graduate School of Business Studies; Reading University; the European Association of Management Training Centres. In the project described in the following pages, the basic disciplines of those involved in the research included social anthropology, mathematics, physics, psychology, geography, and economics, but all had come together because of a shared professional interest in the study of managerial development.

Experiences of Henley

Chapter 4 · The Concept of a Developmental Community

THE RESEARCH CHALLENGE

When the idea of conducting research investigations collaboratively between the Tavistock Institute and the College was first mooted, it was clear that there might be a number of possible ways of approach. One could concentrate on the College, on managerial roles in the client firms, on members' careers and personal development patterns, and so on. One could attempt an experimental comparison between the effects of the College and the effects of some other training experience or of no training experience; or one could simply describe what happened as it appeared to all of the parties concerned without exact control groups. One could concentrate on a critical 'audit' of the College's work in relation to its goals, or one could focus on growth points in an era in which many changes are under way. Our decisions were based partly on what we would have considered desirable from a research point of view – both methodologically and substantively – and partly on necessity. Control groups are an attractive research idea, but methodologically have serious limitations for a study such as this. Desirable though we would have considered it, for example, to have a controlled comparison between the effects of Henley and of other training experiences of comparable groups of managers, this was simply not feasible at the time. Many of the firms sending men to Henley did not have comparable men whom they did not send. Furthermore, desirable as it might have been to compare men sent to Henley with similar men who underwent different kinds of training programmes, this was simply not on the cards at the time the research was initiated, because the basis for such comparisons did not then exist. Perhaps in the next stage of research such controlled comparisons could be achieved.

The work was defined at the outset as a collaborative project, in which the research staff of the College and the Tavistock staff researchers worked together to define issues and strategies for the investigation so that it would evolve in a way that was interesting and useful to both groups. We recognized at the start that the question of focus was as much a diplomatic as a scientific one. The College was, of course, interested in reassessing its work, and made continuous efforts in this direction independently of the research. This was in a sense the crux of any venture associated with the College. On the other hand, it was thought that an indirect rather than a direct approach to this task was more likely to be effective, particularly if it were then accompanied by a follow-through of implications of the research for the actual College programmes. Given the fact that we considered the different foci of research to be highly interrelated – the focus on the College, the focus on the members' careers, the focus on the managerial role in different environments – this seemed a reasonable strategy. We therefore began by exploring managerial role-requirements. In the first year, we conducted exploratory interviews, following them up in the second year (1967) with a survey of members' careers. Beginning in the second year of the work, a parallel effort was undertaken to relate the research perspectives to the work of the College. Group discussions were held involving the Henley staff with the research worker directly concerned with the careers study (RNR), and with another member of the Tavistock staff who was experienced in the implementation of research results (H. Bridger). We have thus developed the work in stages, with the emphasis of the first stage on the environment of managers in their firms (1966); of the second, on their careers following Henley (1967); and of the last, on the implications of these observations for the College itself (1968–9).

THE COLLEGE AS A DEVELOPMENTAL COMMUNITY

In order to put the Survey results on members' careers into perspective, we must add to the description of the College that has been presented in the earlier chapters a sociological conception of the nature of the College's work. From an analysis of elements in the College's own conception of the nature of its work, it is clear that the idea of development is absolutely central. The Principal reasserted this emphasis in the College's most recent announcement of its aims.

'Our main object is to encourage personal development, and by this we mean a man or woman's capacity to manage, not only in his present job but also in the kinds of tasks he may be faced with in the future.'

A sampling of staff remarks made about the impact of the course on members indicates that the concept of development that they hold is fairly complex:

'Despite his position (pretty high in marketing) he had been sheltered from the cut and thrust of life. Here he was brought face to face with a lot of elements normally outside his own job which shocked his system a bit, mostly I think because of the general directness with which they were discussed.'

'. . . really had his eyes opened.'

'. . . he started out badly. He was belligerent and somewhat disdainful of the possible value of the course, but he became the focal point of his syndicate and then its natural leader . . .'

'. . . held himself back at first, then when he got a chairmanship never looked back once he realized his own ability . . .'

'. . . showed a noticeable growth in self confidence . . .'

'. . . increased in judgement and grasp of the situation . . .'

'. . . he didn't look like much on paper or at first when he came here, but at some point he "got the message" and began to contribute and to relate the new conceptions that he was getting to the problems of concern to him in his job.'

'. . . he blossomed toward the end of the course – an accountant who came away from the narrow straightlaced approach.'

'He had an emotional experience . . .'

'Came from an industry where he wasn't given much scope . . . we certainly broadened his horizons . . .'

The development process is thought of as being facilitated by several elements in the situation. *Role-disengagement* is one. It is seen as important to give managers a break at a critical point from their ongoing pressures of career when they are ready to pause and integrate the personal and professional significance of their life-experiences so far. From accounts of the early work of the College it would seem that some of the clients and members took this point of view to mean something more recreational and less purposeful than subsequent interpretations have stressed. Sir

Noel Hall, the first Principal of the College, stressed the importance of the experience as providing a transition from the more specialist requirements of middle managerial roles to the more generalist requirements of more senior roles. In this view, recreation was an important but secondary element.

Role-disengagement, then, is not enough. The *cultivation of positive role-conceptions* is also important. This includes elements of leadership, self-confidence, breadth of perspective, balanced judgement, and emotional maturity. In discussing their members after they have completed the course, the staff consider that about 25 per cent 'grow' a great deal, another 50 per cent grow to some extent, and the remaining quarter do not grow appreciably. They have in mind this complex of criteria. The transition that is implicit in this conception, then, is one that is *away from* a more subservient or uncertain orientation, a narrower perspective, or a less balanced and less mature capacity for judgement and decision-making. These are all, of course, matters of degree and the College's standards for admission are such as to make descriptions of their candidates in deficiency terms somewhat ludicrous in most cases.

Indeed, the overriding conception as first set forward by Noel Hall and later elaborated and refined, is probably closer to that conceptualized by A. T. M. Wilson, who indicates that there is a role-discontinuity in managerial careers, so that development entails *traversing a role-discontinuity*. A person rising from specialist to general managership has to make a *qualitative* leap (Wilson, 1966). A man rising to the top of his special function – e.g. accountancy within a large firm – does so more or less regardless of his capacity for policy-making. It is technical excellence and the execution of policy that make for his success up to the top of his special ladder. The policy-maker, in contrast, must be a man of breadth and wisdom, capable of understanding and employing men of specialized competence in various functional fields, though he himself has only limited competence in the fields themselves. In the past, when recruitment for the top may have been done independently of recruitment for middle management – e.g. through elite or family connections – one could use different standards. In an era of meritocracy the channel to the top lies, on the whole, through the obstacle courses of functional specialisms. It has therefore been considered necessary to provide a transitional experience in which minimally the perspectives of the aspiring senior were 'stretched' and 'broadened' and, in some instances, even 'unlearned' so that they could be relearned in a way more adapted to work at the top. This particular role transition is a critical one for managers moving from specialist to general managerial status.

This picture is made complex as the range of different managerial skills and types becomes more complex. Be this as it may, the paramount element in the College's conception of development is the reorientation of managers from a narrower set of perspectives to a broader one prerequisite for effective functioning at senior levels. Proponents of this view hold that increased technical expertise in middle management makes the need for a transitional experience of this kind *even more* relevant than in the past. How, then, is this done?

As indicated earlier, the work of the College is centred on the syndicates. This approach consists of group discussions and presentations organized around management tasks which resemble those confronting directing bodies of large organizations. In the terms of the College's Guide:

> 'The College deliberately throws the responsibility of learning on the members themselves, considering that they will learn more effectively if they take an active part in the process of discovery and participate in the direction of the work.'

The staff help the members to define the syndicate task and give advice and consultation on the use of resources available at the College, but they consider that 'in the end it is the individual himself who must use the opportunity and the facilities to learn by his own efforts'.

Ideally the move outward and through the College articulates with the individual manager's move upward within his organization.

The performance of the individual in the environment of the Administrative Staff College reflects his accumulated competence and tendencies after passing through previous social environments of home, school, and employer organizations. The College has elements of each of these environments. Like the work environment, it is concerned substantively with problems of administration. However for the members it is not 'for real', in the sense that the survival of the College itself does not depend directly on the conclusions reached or decisions made by the member-trainees during their studies. It is like a school, in that there is the goal of learning which is paramount. However, it differs from many schools in that the members are already comparatively well established in careers. It is their personal values and perspectives that are being revised rather than their technical competences. In this regard, and in the residential aspects of the experience, there are overtones of a familial quality to the experience, though here the differences from 'real' family life are very plain.

The Administrative Staff College resembles more than anything else a residential 'progressive' school. It functions according to principles which were popular earlier among progressive educationists – permissiveness, student-centredness in the learning experience, etc. – which for a time became *passé* with the introduction of highly technical syllabuses, but which are now again becoming popular with 'discovery' methods of teaching. Ackoff gives an account of how higher education is moving toward an emphasis on the 'learning' as distinct from the 'teaching' elements in the university system (Ackoff, 1968).

The staff considers that its role is to guide and advise the members in the organization of their work and in the use of available resources. They do not attempt to provide a formal course of instruction, but if necessary give assistance to the individual who has deficiencies. As with schools of this type, the technical part of the education is communicated along with the human relational part (which in this case is inextricably connected with the technical part). The College Guide for new members emphasizes the way in which syndicates are constructed and conduct their work as being a microcosm of the actual world of managerial activity: '[the syndicates represent] a live situation of a management team in action'.

Conceptualizing this situation in sociological terms, we would suggest that the Administrative Staff College is an example of what we term a *Developmental Community*. By this, we mean the sort of organization that has as its primary goal the development of its members, and that has as its primary method for achieving this goal the operation of a community. Obviously, there are many kinds of community, and in a sense it is stretching the term community very hard to use it in relation to an institutional community (as do physicians in using the term in relation to 'therapeutic communities', or training-group devotees in relation to T-group 'learning communities'). This is a special type of community in which there is a group of transient members and a permanent staff group who continually reassemble new members for a community learning experience. The essential point about its community character stems from its sense of *interdependence* which is created by the removal of the members from their usual set of role-relationships (both occupational and familial) and placing them for a considerable period of time in a residential situation which becomes salient for them personally and in which they become intensely involved. It is a 'temporary community', which provides a grounding for work with future groups having the character of a 'temporary community' (Miles, 1964; Bennis and Slater, 1968).

The two cardinal elements of the developmental community as we see it are:

(a) *role-disengagement*: i.e. the separation of the individual from the demands of his prior role-relationships; and
(b) *role-rehearsal*: i.e. the provision of a new set of role-conceptions based on an analysis of those that the managers are likely to have to take on at work following the College experience, together with an opportunity to rehearse these roles in a constructive environment.

Seen as a type of developmental community, the College has, as indicated above, greater resemblance to some other kinds of institution that it does to many other management training institutions. There are two dimensions that differentiate institutions aiming to 'develop' people. These are the amount of *formal input* that the institution aims to inject into its developing members, and the degree of emphasis placed on *influencing personal values and motives* (as distinct from purely technical or formal role-behaviour) in the course of the experience.

In some institutions there is low emphasis on both variables – e.g. the sabbatical-year experience. Individuals are expected to define their own interests and not be constrained to take in anything formally from their sabbatical institutions other than what they themselves wish to adopt. Centres for advanced study, select fellowships, and so on exemplify this sort of situation. At the other extreme, some institutions place a very high emphasis on formal inputs from the institution and also on influencing personal values and motives. The extreme example of this would seem to be 'brainwashing' as practised by the Chinese communists (Schein,

1961; Lifton, 1961). Schein conceptualized the process associated with what we call role-disengagement and role-rehearsal as 'unfreezing' and 'refreezing'. One general conception of all studies of social learning is that once-adopted attitudes tend to become somewhat crystallized and that the loosening of established attitudes and restructuring of new ones occur only under the impact of pressures. These pressures may be internal (Jaques, 1965) or external through life crises (Caplan, 1964), role changes (Rapoport, 1963), or coercive persuasion (Schein, 1961). The persuasive power of intellectual or logical inputs alone has been stressed by some educators, particularly in technical fields, but this is now being reassessed.

An example of the traditional technical educational emphasis which gives high attention to the formal inputs but low attention to the issues of personal value and motivation of its trainees is the typical engineering course. There is nothing in technological training that makes this intrinsic or necessary as a didactic method, and some technological training institutions are experimenting with new methods; but young engineers-to-be tend to be given a series of lectures packed with technical details imparted by experts in the relevant fields and are expected to absorb the information and demonstrate their competence in it at the end of the course. The faculty are, characteristically, not highly involved in the students' motivations or personal values. If the student is in difficulty, he may be referred to a physician or psychologist for assistance when his tutor cannot deal with the problems arising. The obverse example – where motivation and personal values are in focus and the inculcation of formal didactic materials is minimal – would be seen in therapeutic communities or in T-groups (Rapoport, 1961; Bradford et al., 1964). In the recent anthology of T-group writings by Bradford et al., the way in which T-groups function to help individuals to develop is summarized as follows:

'The value of the T-Group lies in the fact that the process by which individuals develop a group in which they participate effectively is the process of learning. The conditions include exposure to the problem areas, collection of data, analysis, experimentation, generalization, and application to other situations. Its genius lies in the deep involvement and expenditure of energy called forth by its unstructured nature coupled with a process of inquiry, action and evaluation.'

The four types of institution assessed above may be seen in *Figure 1*.

Figure 1 Types of Developmental Institution

		Degree of Formal Didactic Input	
		Low	High
Degree of Emphasis on Changing Personal Values and Motives	LOW	Sabbatical	Technology Course
	HIGH	T-Group	Brainwashing

All types of developmental institution have elements in common, and some members passing through any one of them may perceive it to be like others. For an academic taking a sabbatical year, for example, the element of personal value and motivational reappraisal and overhaul may be the paramount aspect of the experience. He may liken his experience to a therapeutic one. For some members of a therapeutic community, the implicit theory of motivation which they learn may be for them a more prominent part of their experience than it is in the intentions of the staff, who may emphasize the permissive and individual-centred nature of the programme. For such members, the therapeutic experience may be likened to a course in psychopathology and psychodynamics. These differences of perception need not be elaborated, but it is important to recognize that they exist and that there is a problem of articulating the intentions of the practitioners in a developmental institution and the impressions made on the trainees themselves. We shall discuss this at greater length in subsequent chapters. The issue at the moment is where the Administrative Staff College at Henley fits into this schema and what the relevance is of placing it in such a conceptual framework.

It would seem that the College is intermediate in the framework presented above. It differs from some management training institutions in being closer to the T-group quadrant, whereas some of the newer training institutions – particularly those based on what we might call the technological management science model – are closer to the technological course quadrant.

The pragmatic inclinations of managers have led to an emphasis on the wish to learn techniques, as contrasted to the desire to acquire insight or grasp of motivation. This is explained by John

Davies, formerly Director General of the Confederation of British Industry:*

> 'Managers, on the whole, are not much given to visiting psychoanalysts. The nearer they are to top management the nearer the bottom they are likely to relegate such visits in their order of priorities. Perhaps it is a pity. The psychoanalyst's role is to uncover and explain the motives that actuate men in the way they live their lives. Managers, more than most, brush aside their motives as secondary to their own performance.'

The growth in size and complexity of organizations, however, has led to an increase in the need to develop on both fronts – the technical and the human.

The T-group writers emphasize the other side of the coin: managers are seen as needing learning experiences 'for change'. Members of the group learn this by constantly reorientating themselves in a situation with minimal formal structural guidelines. Contradicting the more formal educational systems, the emphasis is on the 'here-and-now' observable data of the needs, goals, and inhibitions of the group's members – rather than on learning what was learned and demonstrated 'there and then'. Learning to learn through helping to evolve a supportive group structure within which the work of learning can take place is the goal of the T-group. Some institutions, like the Coast Guard Academy described by Dornbusch (1955), present themselves on the formal didactic model of the technical course, but on sociological investigation are revealed as having an informal dimension – e.g. in the 'hazing' practices of the students' peer group – which function at the motivational and personal value level, complementing the technical inputs of the didactic programme. The overall effect is that of a *rite de passage*, with the emotional aspects of passage from one role to another dealt with informally while the technical-competence aspects are dealt with in the formal system. In a sense, the Henley course turns this approach on its head. The formal system deals with the development of the person, while it is only informally that he picks up specific technical competencies.

In management training, the explosive growth of technical knowledge associated with management science and practice raises challenging issues as to how these two dimensions are best

* The Federation of British Industries became the Confederation of British Industry in 1965.

integrated. While the more 'heuristic' or 'participative' approaches are clearly important, they can no longer be considered to be sufficient on their own. Increasing a man's 'grasp' (Gold, 1965), his 'understanding' (IMEDE, 1965), his 'self-expression' (Bakke, 1959), etc. through a 'psychological moratorium' (Chowdhry, 1964) are valid goals of the type of training programme orientated to human development, but in what relationship to technical competence? Given that such development tends to occur adaptively only when informed by technical knowledge and competence, increased knowledge inputs are also called for. The managerial role is rapidly increasing in its professional content and calibre (Evan, 1961; Burnham, 1962). An initial reaction in such a situation was to swing toward the opposite pole and to emphasize the formal didactic approach almost exclusively. However, there is increasing realization that there is a danger of throwing out the baby with the bathwater. Though trained to a high level of technical competence, some graduates of highly didactic science-based management courses feel that much of their training is irrelevant or difficult to apply in subsequent management work because it is too theoretical or technical, and their colleagues and bosses feel more than ever that formal technical qualifications alone are no charter for effective management. A purely didactic programme does not cultivate the capacity to apply the knowledge creatively.

It is becoming generally accepted that the key problem for the field of senior management training as a whole is how best to combine the two types of input, the critical re-evaluation of personal values, motives, and role-playing capacities, on the one hand, and the increase in technical information, on the other. Each emphasis – the human-development emphasis and the technical-didactic emphasis – has a certain internal consistency that makes it possible to develop a programme around that dominant orientation and value system. We are in an era where there is a general recognition that the two approaches must be married to make the most effective sort of developmental community for those in top positions in a technological society. It would seem that the emerging mixtures of technical and human-relational programmes for senior managers will benefit maximally by having strong components of both approaches. The real issues are how much, with what organizational approach, and for what kinds of manager.

In a sense, this is part of the larger issue facing education, particularly the form of education to which Henley belongs, the 'progressive' education of recent times (Curle, 1968). With the challenge of advanced technologies and many technical specialisms flourishing, there seems to have been a trend toward mirroring them in education. That is to say, where technical competence in man-machine relations has been the rule in making the world of work operate most efficiently, it has been assumed that a style of similar values and interactions is appropriate in educational programmes. This has led to setting up training programmes which are geared to the man-nature or man-machine models – mastery of techniques rather than of insights, judgements, and relationships. In fact, education programmes are in the sphere of man-man relationships where different models and values prevail – and different problems present themselves for solution. The one, without a good underpinning in the other, however, may prove ineffective, and the challenge for contemporary training institutions is how to synthesize the two.

The statement of 1963 by the Federation of British Industries about managers rising into senior positions is probably as true now as it was then. It said:

'They can benefit from close contact with first-class minds from their own and other industries and the academic world. The broader aspects of administration, organization and inter-relation of government, society and industry will now begin to assume a real practical significance. The handling of resources, the assessment of progress and achievement, and the effective handling of complex human organizations are all aspects of higher management which can be better understood after comparing ideas and experiences with able contemporaries from other walks of life' (FBI, 1963).

However, what it assumed and what is becoming increasingly apparent is that there are different levels of communication and therefore different degrees of effectiveness of such contacts and interchanges. The interchanges are the more effective to the extent that they occur on a platform of a fairly high common denominator of knowledge of technical problems and processes. When group discussions are reduced to the lowest common factor of purely human and personal interaction process – as is deliberately fostered in T-groups – the developmental process becomes a part-process of the overall work that a College like Henley is trying to do. The College seeks to prepare the whole person for senior management roles. T-group work could be an ancillary form of discussion here as it would be for a more formal lecture programme. It could not do the whole job.

Let us now turn our attention to what the job is, and how much of it seems to be getting accomplished. We can then discuss more intelligently the issues of adapting the developmental community.

THE RESEARCH CHALLENGE

We have argued that the challenge for a developmental community – specifically from the point of view of the College – is how continuously to readapt its methods of training to suit a managerial environment in which technical considerations are mounting explosively. While its assumption that human considerations are more important than ever in such a technological society is taken to be valid, the development of managers as human beings is seen to be most effectively accomplished in the context of their technical role-requirements.

The research challenge in this context is how to formulate a problem for investigation which is both meaningful in scientific terms and relevant in policy terms to the training challenge faced by the College. Viewing the College in the context of other institutions designed to change people's perspectives is one sort of contribution. The College is also of general interest to social science as a specimen of a 'developmental community', ultimately to be compared with other types of developmental community. Closer to the focus of the current research, however, is the issue of the individuals who are developing, partly by having passed through the experiences provided by the developmental community. In social-science terms this is a problem of adult socialization, or, more specifically, of adult socialization at mid-life. This is of particular interest because most theories of development have concentrated on earlier phases of the life-cycle, with such studies of later adulthood as have been done indicating a continuous decline in faculties after the age of about 30 (Neugarten, 1964; Soddy, 1967).

The task of the research was to formulate problems that are scientifically interesting and to investigate them in a methodologically sound manner. The task of consultation with the College, with its own quite distinctive purpose, was that of translating the implications of the research into terms amenable to being useful for College policy. This is a separate though linked task – in this case accomplished through a division of labour between the author (RNR) who defined his role primarily in research terms and his colleague (Harold Bridger) whose role was defined primarily in consultation terms. The ventures, though necessarily distinct, are linked in that the choice of research topics, from among the nearly limitless range of possibilities, was made partly on the basis of some expectation of relevance to College policy.

Chapter 5 · Client Orientations to the College

NOMINATORS AND PROSPECTIVE MEMBERS

In a narrow sense, Henley's clients are the nominating firms. As indicated earlier, at the time the College was founded the most sensible use of training resources nationally was taken to be for men who had proved their mettle in actual management jobs and in whom their firms felt a further investment of costly and time-consuming courses to be worthwhile. This perspective fitted well with the prevailing perspectives on the nature of a man's relationship to his employer. The ideal situation, as expressed in contracts, pension plans, etc. was for a manager to expect to spend his working-life within an organization, and for the organization to assume responsibility for developing the manager as a human resource.

It is beyond the scope of the present work to mark out in any detail the degree to which the context of management has changed. The professionalization of managers which has accompanied the development of more systematic management knowledge and methods has increased the autonomy of the individual manager (Evan, 1961). The credentials of formal training programmes – e.g. at universities – have gained growing acceptance on the management job market. With growth in complexity of organizations and with the dynamic shifts entailed by mergers and other forms of reorganization, individuals have had increasingly to look after themselves in the managerial career market. All these trends, and others, in the more diffuse cultural environment of the 'managerial revolution', have made the individual manager more active as the architect of his own career, reducing somewhat the classical gap between entrepreneurs and managers.

We shall have more to say about this in the analysis of career patterns of Henley members, but for the moment it is important to note that we are inclined to deal with the question of who are the clients in terms of a double rather than a single relationship.

69

The formal clients are, to be sure, the nominating organizations. However, there are at least two reasons why the members, past and prospective, should be considered clients as well. The first is, as implied above, that the member-managers are increasingly important as opinion-setters. Not only do they rise in their own organizations into nominating roles and express their attitudes to the College directly in this way, but they form a part of an increasingly articulate and intercommunicating professional community whose evaluations of their training experiences have a diffuse effect far beyond their own organizations. With increasing circulation of managers from one employer to another this is even more marked.

The issue of 'clienthood' has important implications, both for the College and for the research methods used here. Because the employing organization is technically the client, releasing its managers for this specific training and paying the bills, the College accordingly recognized the necessity of satisfying the organizations. This is further reinforced by the awareness that the satisfaction of the client is the best available evaluation of management training at this level. Pragmatically it makes sense to assume that if the 'output' of the College meshes with the requirements of the organization for its managers moving into more senior posts, the College's programme is in part achieving its objectives.

On the other hand, the College recognizes its obligations to the members – and in this sense the fact that they represent a part of the client picture – in several ways. The College recognizes the importance of free communications for the developmental process, and treats them as privileged in a sense not dissimilar to the communications of clients to doctors, lawyers, or priests. Communications by members while at the College are respected as confidential. The College does not 'report' formally on its members' performance, and disclaims an evaluative function on behalf of the employers. It is assumed that the evaluation of the man by the employer has already been done and that the College's function is to work within a positive evaluation framework. Finally, the Principal expresses the College's sense of obligation to the individual members by providing a final personal session in which he attempts to encapsulate the College's impression of the member in relation to his career. This constructive feedback is felt to be of special value to the member, giving him something to take along with him in making the transitions back to his firm and into whatever new roles his subsequent career may hold in store for him.

From the research point of view the issue of clienthood is important because any evaluation of training is sensible only in the context of objectives (Hesseling, 1968). Training for the performance of a relatively delimited and definable set of tasks can be evaluated against the defined criterion. Training for a wide range of tasks, difficult to define and changing continuously, is another matter. Though there has been a good deal of work in recent years toward defining the tasks of senior managers (Schein, 1961; Stewart, 1967) there is also evidence that there is a very great range of variation (Barna, 1962; Horne & Lupton, 1965).

The College seems to strike a middle ground between the conception of senior managers' roles that is entirely open – seeking to develop the individual's personal capacities only (as with T-group work; cf. Bradford, 1964) – and the approach which seeks to equip the managers with a definitive armamentarium of skills that are assumed to pertain to managerial roles (Simon, 1960). Its assumption is that for senior managers the two are interrelated and that they should therefore be approached integrally. To ignore that a senior manager, to be effective, must be competent in a number of technical areas such as the interpretation of economic and statistical information would be foolish; and yet, to treat these technical competences as sufficient would be similarly short-sighted. The cultivation of breadth, judgement, intuitive and creative capacities is closer to the heart of the College's programme, but linked to a process of 'filling in' where gaps in managerial competence are apparent.

How do the clients themselves feel about what they want from the College? Combining the insights we are able to achieve through our exploratory interviews in 1966* with survey data on initial expectations of Henley as recalled by a series of past members,† we are able to put together some kind of picture, though its tentative nature must be stressed.

---

* In 1966–7, when exploratory discussions were under way about how a research investigation would contribute to the work of the College, eight nominators were interviewed representing three Civil Service Departments, a large clearing bank, a nationalized industry, and a large market-oriented private-sector organization. Also 27 ex-members, prospective members, and non-Henley men of comparable standing in the organizations were interviewed to get some idea of attitudes to the course.

† The survey, to be described in greater detail in subsequent chapters, was a lengthy and detailed postal survey of all Henley members who attended the College in the period 1960–6. Among the areas of information sought was the topic of their initial expectations and how these aligned with what they actually experienced at Henley and afterwards.

THE NOMINATORS

The basic organizational scheme used by the College in composing the membership of courses is a fourfold one. The four major categories are Public Sector (including the Civil Service and Local Government agencies); Nationalized Industries; Banks; and large Private Sector firms. Members also come from a miscellaneous group of organizations and include military representatives, trade union executives, small businessmen, and representatives of foreign governments and organizations, including other training institutions. This was the framework within which our exploratory interviews were conducted.

Once having interviewed a range of representatives of the client organizations, the overriding impression was one of enormous complexity. Within the Civil Service, for example, there are great differences in the types of work done by the different ministries, the degree of centralization or decentralization in the structure of a given ministry, and in the attitude of the particular establishment officers incumbent at the time. Compare the situation of an establishment officer from the Ministry of Technology sending a scientist from a field research station in the North with that of an establishment officer in the Post Office sending someone from his own personnel office; or even within a single ministry, e.g. in the then Ministry of Labour, the difference between a factory inspector from the Midlands and a headquarters research economist. In the electricity industry, there are great differences between area boards in orientation and requirements, and great differences between the type of men sent by area boards generally and those sent by the generating side of the industry. The latter tend to be technologists, while the former tend to be business managers in the Public Sector, often former sales managers. Within the Private Sector there seem to have been very great differences not only in the function from which the man was rising toward general managership, but in the kinds of experiences and attitudes he might have developed because of his particular career experiences. For example, a man who had been a manager for a British company in an African or Far-Eastern country had probably had a great deal more experience and knowledge about politics and public relations with governmental agencies than did a man who had come up mainly through a headquarters specialism like finance in the London headquarters. On the other hand, he might be out of touch with the most recent developments in central administrative services. It was only among the Bankers that there seemed to be a fairly standard kind of experience, with men following a very similar career-timetable and developmental pattern, rotating upward in a series of moves into and out of headquarters posts through larger and more important branch managerships. Their differences were mainly in the speed at which they spiralled upward in the banking hierarchy and the degree of momentum they enjoyed in their ascent to general managership.

Again, the organizations differed in the process by which they made nominations, the location in the organization of the initiator of nominations, and the general attitude of the nominator toward Henley.

The literature that attempts to systematize dimensions of organizational analysis so that meaningful cross-comparisons may be made is so vast that it does not make sense to try to summarize it here. Much of the work is classificatory and rather static (Hall, 1962–3), though some of the analyses fix on a particular dimension of the functioning of an organization – its technical system in relation to its social organization (Woodward, 1965; Emery, 1960; Trist *et al.*, 1963); its authority structure and decision-making processes (Jaques, 1956); its organization relative to response to innovation (Burns and Stalker, 1963) – and follow through the implications for an organization of its position on the particular dimension (Lupton, 1970).

The importance of the economic base of the organization for its goals in management development has been stressed in a number of publications. The College's own publication on *Accountability* (Ennis, 1965), spells out in detail the implications for policy of the different forms of accountability under which organizations in the private and public sectors operate. Numerous writings by other organizational analysts elaborate this point still further (Sisson, 1959; Shonfield, 1966).

There are differences other than accountability in the client organizations that contrast them in their orientation to management training programmes in general and to Henley in particular. Differences in dominant goals and values in size, structure, and cybernation (mechanization, automation), in the organization's history and philosophy of management, in special problems relating to the content of the work, all make for a diversity of attitudes in regard to management training.

To make an exhaustive analysis of the differences in orientation to training would itself have been a major task. We have not been able to do more than form impressions about what might distinguish the Henley nominators from other potential nominators, and within the group of Henley nominators the critical differences affecting the success of the member in getting anything by way of development out of the Henley experience. Obviously, we have more on the latter than the former, as our survey analysis will show. However, on the former our impressions are very unsystematic indeed, being based on general information about the field and tangential interview data.

It would seem that there are at least four types of attitude prevalent among non-nominators – those who do not use Henley (and were not interviewed directly in relation to this study). The four major non-client orientations would seem to be:

(i) The *technocratic* – where the emphasis on the human element in the development of managers is so low that no need is seen for courses in relation to these factors. Training investments in such a situation tend to concentrate on technical courses, with the development of the manager as a person seen as either automatically accompanying his growth on the job, or as enhanced by short sessions such as T-group courses.

(ii) The *charismatic* – where training programmes are seen as a waste of time and money, particularly for senior men, because of the belief that management is an 'art' and that top men cannot be trained. The good manager is one because of a 'gift' for management.

(iii) The *overloaded* – where it is felt that no one in the firm can afford to take the time off for a training programme. This is particularly found in smaller firms, but may also apply in large organizations where senior men are under pressure. Training in this context is seen as a luxury.

(iv) The *uninvolved* – where there is little recognition of the development of managers as part of the human assets of the enterprise and where there is little knowledge of or interest in training courses and their relative merits. Indifference rather than a positive counter-rationale seems to be the prevailing attitude – and a high-level 'I'm all right, Jack' atmosphere.

Looking at the nominators who *were* interviewed, it is useful to note two major dimensions that differentiate them. This is all within the framework of recognizing that we are observing a positively biased sample, in that whatever the attitudes of specific managers or nominators may be toward Henley, their organizations are in fact Henley clients. The two dimensions that we shall mention are:

(a) Position of the nominator in relation to his organization. By nominator in this context, we mean the actual initiator of a nomination, regardless of the machinery for approving it. Approval in all organizations tended to be at a very high level relative to the administrative structure of the organization – but initiation might be either central or in an operating unit – a department, branch, factory, or station of some kind. Thus a highly centralized organization, like the Administrative Class of the Civil Service, can and does use decentralized techniques for naming and screening nominees.

(b) The attitude of the nominator (i.e. the person initiating a nomination as distinct from the 'official' organization's attitude) toward the course at Henley.

We have found it useful to distinguish three major attitudes:

(i) the committed
(ii) the experimental-minded
(iii) the sceptical.

An example of the *committed* attitude, slightly paraphrased, is as follows:

'When I wrote my report on Henley, outlining how much the organization needed training of this kind for its top men, they said to me, "you want it, you do it", and I've been running the training programme ever since. We send our best men to Henley when it becomes clear that they are likely to be on their way to the top.'

An example of the *experimental-minded* attitude:

'We believe that Henley has a special place in the training of senior managers, but it is difficult to weigh up the relative merits of the

Henley programme and the business schools programmes for specific types of people. We have begun an experiment in sending men in roughly comparable situations, one to each of the new business schools and one to Henley simultaneously. Then as they return we intend to hold a series of discussions among them on their experiences.'

Another example:

'Henley served a very useful function as a model in building up our own training facilities, and all of our early Henley graduates put in a spell as instructors in our own school. Now, we are increasingly combining the Henley syndicate approach with other approaches, mixing in lectures on specialized subjects, case studies, and so on. The Henley approach is best for learning about the general environment in which business operates, the business school approaches are probably better at teaching the "tools of management".'

An example of the *sceptical* approach:

'I've reviewed all the management training programmes, and have come to the conclusion that at the present time there is no rhyme or reason to them. People have put together various programmes in one way or another, and it is very difficult to evaluate them. After the war this got to be quite a business, and they became rather commercialized, each trying to sell its own programme, but there being very little evidence that any of them was better than just giving a man a chance to get away from his work for a bit. In some cases, it might be just as well to let him go back to refresh his knowledge of Latin grammar, and then return with a fresh mind to his job.'

Or another example:

'When the call comes around to put up a man for Henley, we certainly want to take advantage of it, but the tendency is to say, "who is available", and "who can be spared", rather than "who is our best man". The best men are too much needed and, given the uncertainty about the value of such courses, they certainly need the experience less than men in more limited jobs.'

All the large organizations that we visited had centralized approval processes in the form of review boards for the consideration of potential Henley members. They varied, however, in the extent to which the review board exercised authority in relation to the selection procedure. Towards one extreme is the Bank, where there is a systematic programme for the development of managers and every man in the entire system is known centrally and his career in the organization is under the control of the central authority. Selection and review are both headquarters functions. In the case of the large market-oriented firm in the private sector, there is centralization of management development functions and a well-developed philosophy and programme, but considerable local autonomy of operating units as well. Thus while selection ordinarily is left to the authority of senior managers at the operating unit level, to be then screened by the review of a central personnel committee, the personnel committee may itself initiate suggestions, as well as approve or decline them. The local operating unit must then consider the proposal to release the individual from work commitments in order to attend the course. This is a mixed pattern representing active interplay between centre and units.

The Nationalized Industry represents another form of interplay. Owing to the relative autonomy of local area organizations, these organizations have authority to propose members to a central body which reviews them, screening out inappropriate candidates, to put up a short list for the consideration of the Principal of the College. Because the training requirements of the industry are very great relative to the numbers of places available, there is no problem about producing sufficient numbers to provide a regular flow to Henley. However, the fact of decentralization of selection gives rise to an issue of the variations in standards and values attached to the training experience. Areas vary considerably in the number of candidates they produce and their criteria for selecting them, according to their differing attitudes to management training and career development. Part of the central office's mission is to work in the direction of coordination, but its structural position makes this a matter of persuasion rather than authoritative rationalization. The allocation of places to Henley is one instrument in this process.

In the Civil Service the tendency toward heterogeneity is carried still further, with the influence of the central review body on the component selection agencies still less. The Treasury training director has no comparable mission to that of the Nationalized Industry in relation to the various ministries, departments, and so on of the Civil Service. Self cites the Civil Servants' conception of Treasury control as 'to satisfy themselves that we are properly satisfying ourselves about the economics of particular schemes' (Self, 1965, p. 33). Policy is set in the Treasury to invest a certain amount of money in this type of training. Notifications are distributed, and reviews are performed of selections submitted. However, there is neither active initiation of nominations, as in the personnel office of the Private Sector firm, nor a programme of persuasion as in the Nationalized Industry, aimed at the co-ordination of standards and selection practices. There is simply a surveillance of the process with a view to avoiding inappropriate allocations of places. Of course, informally and in the Civil Service's own training programmes, there is a good deal of exchange of views and opinions on all this which plays a part in influencing the nominating process, but structurally the process is as described.

We thus see emerging a pattern which may be represented as follows:

TABLE 1 *Nominators' Attitudes in Relation to Authority Structure*

Attitudes	Authority Structure		
	Centralized	Shared with Operating Units	Decentralized
Committed	Bank		
Experimental		Nationalized Industry Private Sector Firm	
Sceptical		Some Civil Service Ministries	Some Civil Service Ministries

The tendency, where there is relative local autonomy coupled with strong scepticism, is to send along men who 'can be spared' or who are being sent for reasons other than those congruent with the College's aims and self-image (e.g. as a sabbatical, a reward, or a consolation). Some Civil Service units showed this pattern, where local scepticism goes along with a strong degree of decentralization of the nominator's role. Where decentralization exists and yet the central nominator is more committed to the values of the Henley programme, as in the Nationalized Industry, a pattern emerges where some of the component units function appropriately in relation to the selection of candidates and others do not, though efforts may be continuously under way to standardize procedures. The particular Private Sector firm looked at had a policy of shared authority between central and operating units, but in certain respects had more leverage to promulgate central personnel policy in the operating units, particularly in relation to the issues of movement into more senior posts in the company. In both instances the orientation to the Henley course tends to be experimental, to an extent because of the fact that it is part of a complex process of interplay between headquarters and the operating units. What headquarters might like to be committed to might be negatively valued in some of the operating units, for reasons indicated earlier in the description of non-client attitudes. Experimental-mindedness may be adaptive in such situations where no overall policy can be easily imposed. As the central authority increases, we speak of a centralized rather than a mixed situation in relation to the organizational role of the nominator. The fact that the most centralized structure, in the Bank, is coupled with the most committed attitude is not surprising. In centralized structures with more sceptical or negative attitudes, one would presumably not find the flow of candidates that would have brought a firm for consideration into our study. A centralized sceptical system would tend not to be found among the nominators. There seems to be some evidence to support the idea that decentralization, as well as allowing for an experimental or sceptical form of usage, increases the chances of inappropriate nominations, while firms showing great centralization also either show a high degree of commitment to the Henley programme or do not use the College at all.

Aside from issues of coordination of policy among diverse segments of their own firms, dilemmas confronting nominators, once assuming commitment to training and learning, involve on the one hand the optimal choice of men for Henley and on the other the optimal choice of programmes for the firm. While there are some firms in which virtually all the top men have been to Henley as part of the overall organizational development programme, in many situations there is a tendency *not* to send the best men because they are too vitally needed on the job – and, anyway, they may be felt not to need training – and not to send the poorest men at the relevant levels because they are not considered worth the investment and may, it is feared, not make a good showing for the organization in the world of Henley men.

It is the men 'in between', who are 'quite good', but who 'need working with', who are often selected: aggressive ones who need taking down a peg or two; shy ones who need building up; men who need added confidence in terms of becoming more able to talk and mix with a variety of other men of rising status in a higher-class type of life-situation at the College, where they need not fear making 'cultural errors' and are not in direct vital competition with one another. Henley is seen by most of the nominators interviewed not primarily as a place to test the mettle of a man, for he is selected as having come through the firm's ordeals in this regard, but to prepare him for effective and serious continuing engagement at another level with the demands of senior management. Within this 'social training' orientation, the whole range of attitudes about the actual technical content of the Henley course may be found.

One nominator in the Nationalized Industry, for example, indicated that he nominated men of promise for senior posts for two kinds of reasons: to knock rough edges off the more arrogant ones, and to build up confidence in the more diffident ones. He said that he personally did not go for some of the actual management philosophy of a place like Henley because he felt that decisions had to be made by decisive individual action and not by committees.

In contrast, one of the Civil Service nominators, a sceptical one, said that he tended to name people who were 'average'. The problem he faced was 'what can we do for the average people, because the best ones do it for themselves?' His scepticism about Henley did not relate to the committee method of helping to arrive at decisions, but the inconclusiveness of the putative benefits of training programmes. He personally felt that a sabbatical year was as useful as anything for the more self-directed and talented administrators.

Some of the remarks of the Bank's nominators are at the other end of the continuum, in relation to the relative part to be played by an individual as against that of the environment, whether employer or training college, in the developmental process:

'Henley claims to give breadth. Bankers are thought to suffer from inbreeding. This is true to some extent, though we are probably too sensitive about it. In some of our West End branches we deal with everyone from archbishops to kings . . . but it is true that most bank managers need a different kind of experience. We reckon that we can train a bank manager up to a certain level – but then more than a bigger branch is needed to widen his experience . . . Most men are better than they think, but they need a special challenge to bring it out.'

Contrasting a manager he would not send to Henley with one at the same level he would, he had this to say:

'This chap [the non-Henley type] never thrust himself as a powerful personality. He is solid, reliable, trustworthy in a clerky way . . . He got up to being a manager on one set of qualities, but would need other qualities and the support of other types to go further. You can only go so far with this dotting of "i's" and crossing of "t's" . . .'

Contrasted with another whom he did nominate:

'This man grows all the time. He has a gentle wisdom. When I first knew him he was a clerk, and as we've met from time to time since I'm more and more happy to deal with him as an equal and he is finding it more and more possible to deal with me . . . Getting on for this chap is doing what comes naturally – he is terribly thoughtful about staff matters and would be a good staff controller, may bring in some new ideas – this is a complex area . . .'

Not all nominations have led to the same degree of success in relation to expectations. One man whom this nominator would not have sent himself, though he acquiesced to pressure from a general manager to send him as part of a policy of distributing the benefit among different categories of managers, was characterized as 'a bit thick'. He only managed to use Henley for 'making contacts' and would probably not go beyond his next branch managership. Another man was disappointing because he got stuck in a provincial town which his wife liked and then for domestic reasons turned down a never-to-be repeated opportunity for promotion. Another man will be successful in his career, but didn't get mellowed in the way his nominator had hoped:

'He has a keen, sharp mind – draws blood. His only weakness is that he doesn't suffer fools gladly . . . This has led to not delegating enough . . . choking off good subordinates . . . he will be a full-blooded general manager, but whatever he does he still is likely to leave a few aching skulls . . .'

Polish up the rough ones, take the arrogant ones down a peg or two, get the in-bred ones to mix with others, take the blinkers off the narrow ones, stretch the ones who have become preoccupied with detail, broaden the ones who have been only concerned with machinery. These are prevalent expressions encountered among the nominators interviewed, together with an endorsement of the notion of a qualitative gap to be traversed between middle and senior management roles – a discontinuity requiring new kinds of learning not easily acquired on the job or in the context of the employing firm.

Table 2 shows the patterning of retrospective perceptions of ex-members in the Survey as to why they were sent to Henley.

TABLE 2 *Members' Perceptions of the Main Reasons why they were sent to Henley**

(Percentages are listed only for reasons given by 10 per cent or more)

Reason	Private Industry (PI)†	Bank (B)	Nationalized Industry (NI)	Public Sector (PS)
Pure chance	—	10	—	17
Asked for it	—	—	—	—
Sabbatical	—	—	—	—
Reward, good job	—	—	—	—
Assess potential	—	—	13	—
Fill in areas of weakness	15	15	17	—
General broadening	56	55	47	44
Indication of being 'earmarked' for senior post	—	—	10	11
Compensation	—	—	—	—
Other	—	—	—	—
N‡ =	(300)	(82)	(87)	(103)

* This table, and all others having these *N*s, are drawn from the 1967 survey of all members who attended Henley 1960–6. This figure represents the returns of a postal questionnaire sent to all members who went through the College in this period (excluding observers, foreign participants, and other 'irregulars'). A response of over 70 per cent was achieved, which was unbiased for sector, specialism, time of training, or the College's rating as to the men's success as developers in the course of their training.

† In subsequent tables the abbreviations only (PI, B, NI, PS) will be used to denote the main categories of members.

‡ Total *N* = 576. Four Trade Unionists in the sample are included only where overall figures are cited, since they are too few in number to be reported as representing their sector. Percentages in *this* table will not add up to 100 % because items chosen by under 10% of respondents are not recorded. The policy used in all subsequent tables is to round off each figure to the nearest per cent, so that totals will not always add up to exactly 100%.

'General broadening' is the main reason given by the greatest proportion of members from all organizations. However, the Civil Servants follow this up with 'pure chance' as the second most frequently mentioned reason, while the others indicate 'fill in areas of weakness in managerial skills or knowledge', as the second most frequent reason.

Bankers are the only other group having 10 per cent of their numbers who give 'pure chance' as the main reason for having been sent. Substantial proportions of the Nationalized Industry members and Civil Servants also feel that they were sent because they had been 'earmarked' for more senior posts.

PROSPECTIVE MEMBERS AS CLIENTS

The significance of having been invited to go to Henley varies with the type of organization and its career structure, and with it the sort of thing a prospective member is likely to want from the Henley experience at the outset.

Of the few types of enterprise examined in the exploratory phase of the study, it was clear that the Bank was at one extreme, with its centralized system of appraisal and selection, its streaming according to performance, and its relative 'closedness' (i.e. few men enter in senior posts and few leave to go to other organizations, once established within the system). Men are involved in a highly rational system of management development, but it is controlled from the top. They are offered appointments when openings occur, according to a central appraisal system at headquarters, and participate relatively little in decisions about stages in their own career development. In such a system, men watch for cues to infer whether they are on the 'fast track' or the 'slow track' in their ascent towards the top. Two major indicators of approval in high places are whether or not they are selected, earlier in their careers, for a period at headquarters in the general managers' department, and, somewhat later, whether or not they are nominated for Henley. Being chosen for the general managers' department, like being chosen for Henley, is a sign of being marked out as one of the 'bright boys' who is likely to go far. Turning down a bid to go to Henley is simply 'not done', however much other preferences of a personal or familial kind might be present.

At the other extreme, as in some of the Civil Service departments, the situation is very 'open'. Many career lines are available within the Civil Service, even though there is a tendency for men to be tied in by the pension scheme in the mid-career years, and advancement is based to a larger degree on seniority. There is continuous assessment of performance and relatively little un-certainty about where one stands. Receiving 'the nod' to go to Henley is not as eagerly sought as a sign of status within the system. There are indications, both in what the nominators say and from the men who have been selected, that there is a greater tendency to turn down the invitation to Henley for a variety of reasons – not wishing to be away from one's family for so long, not feeling the need or desire for this kind of course, etc. At the same time, be-cause of the very great diversity of Public Sector posts and the discontinuities involved in making many of the transitions, a man who is 'earmarked' for a more senior post may welcome the train-ing experience as an opportunity to receive help with the transition, but the choice to go or not to go is more his own.

In between these two extremes is the Private Sector company, which is more like the Bank, in that men on the 'fast stream' are chosen to go, and, when given the chance, a man ordinarily *goes* unless there are exceptional reasons not to. Here the compulsion to accept is less than in the Bank, but a man accepts if he is given the chance, as a matter of course. Unlike the Civil Service, men from the Private Sector company feel that Henley is the sort of place where men like them automatically go to, on their way up. The Nationalized Industry is like the Civil Service in its range of variation, but more in the direction of the Private Sector situa-tion, in that once a man is selected he is likely to go, particularly if he is ambitious and seeking a headquarters-type of position.

Thus, eagerness to go to Henley would seem to relate to at least two kinds of factor: the extent to which it relates to the individual's 'career timetable'* within his firm, and the image he has of what he is likely to get from the experience. It will be noted from *Table 3*, in which three of the four organizations are represented, that the career timetables in all organizations 'slow up' with age, but that there are differences among the organizations studied.

This career-timetable analysis suggests that young men move about a great deal in their earlier and middle-management years,

---

* The concept of career-timetable has been applied by sociologists in a number of institutional contexts. F. Davis has applied it to the course of a physical illness, E. Goffman to the hospital 'career' of mental patients, J. Roth to treat-ment experiences in general hospitals, and M. Scott Myers to industrial work careers.

just over a job a year for the Henley-calibre men, and this seems to be a general pattern across organizations. Men move less as they move upwards into the more senior age and rank groups, but here differences among the organizations emerge. The Civil Servants become more stable compared with the businessmen, who in turn stabilize more than do Bankers, who continue to move from one post to another fairly frequently, even in the senior ranks.

Though we do not have quantitative demonstrations of this point, our interview material suggests that contrasts in promotion pattern as between Henley men and non-Henley managers of

TABLE 3 *Career-Timetable of Ex-Henley Members in Three Organizations**

	Average Number of Years per Job (Post-Henley)		
	B	PI	PS
Younger men (at Henley ca. 1960)	1·1	1·2	1·1
Older men (at Henley ca. 1955)	2·1	3·1	4·1

* The figures in this table were arrived at by an examination of career histories of samples of ex-Henley members at the two age levels in each organization. Because numbers were small these figures must be dealt with as suggestive only.

comparable age and seniority vary among the organizations. For the Bankers, Henley probably is more associated with continuous advancement than for the Private Sector men, and for the latter more than for the Civil Servants.

These are tendencies, and cannot be said to hold for all individuals or for all firms in the sectors indicated. In each of the organizations there are highly stable men who have remained for many years in a senior job in which their services were found valuable. Each organization also has men who have continued to move about rather rapidly throughout their careers, and for various reasons some of these movements are in the direction of increased responsibility and remuneration, particularly in the Private Sector (see Chapter 7), while some of the movement simply reflects the organization's needs and policies.

When one examines the members' own expectations of Henley,

we have some initial impressions from the exploratory interviews with the small sample, which are partly supported by the cross-sectional data from the main survey. In the Bank, where there is a relatively closed, highly mobile system of careers, the expectations of the men interviewed centred on learning a new kind of role. They emphasized broadening in the direction of the cultivation of human relations skills, particularly 'public speaking', 'report writing', 'how to deal with staff', and how to 'mix with senior men in other organizations'. One man illustrated a greater attention to the 'calculative' elements in the situation, expecting that the experience would 'stir up his thinking' on a number of topics which he would follow through to mastery later, and that he would learn more about the jobs of senior managers in other organizations and how their organizational structures worked. This is seen as useful in assessing clients and the reliability of their organizations (Etzioni, 1961).

The Civil Servants when they spoke of 'broadening' meant learning more about the economic and administrative skills that men in other organizations apply. Factory inspectors, for example, are already 'broadened' in the sense of having an acquaintance with a wide range of organizational settings, and men in the Administrative Class are already broadened from the point of view of having a national overview of various environmental issues bearing on the conduct of any specific organization's work. In learning to take over more senior roles for which they may have been earmarked, the Administrative Class members felt that they knew enough about some of the 'broadening' skills such as how to conduct committee meetings, how to delegate, and how to write reports, but that they might lack the more technical knowledge of modern business organization. The more technical men, scientists and technologists, felt somewhat more in awe of the whole administrative process, and 'broadening' for them was a more elementary conception concentrating on the management of human relations.

In the Nationalized Industry and the Private Sector firm, we interviewed only one pre-Henley man each during the exploratory study, so our impressions from this stage of the work are particularly fragmentary and tentative, though the men were interviewed as 'informants' about prevailing attitudes in their organizations as well as being individual 'respondents' about their own personal views. The Nationalized Industry man represented the 'Civil

Service' type within his organization, being involved in a broad range of administrative functions. He considered himself well equipped in the formulation and implementation of policy in complex organizational settings, but saw that he had something to learn from new developments in private industry. He wanted to be 'put in touch with new ideas, techniques, and terminology', e.g. cost–benefit analysis and the use of computers. His conception of broadening involved 'a look at the wider world, seeing something of the big wicked world of private industry'. He felt this as necessary because 'people in the Public Sector tend to move around in their sector, rather than from a Public to a Private Sector industry'. His requirements were different from the men in the technological side of the industry (who resemble the technologists in other sectors) or the local area men, who resemble in many ways the small businessmen.

The Private Sector man felt that having been selected to go to Henley was an overt acknowledgement of a 'stage having been reached' in one's career. The 'platform' notion was quite pronounced in his thinking, and, as with other men in his firm, there was emphasis on the sabbatical aspect of the nomination. The idea of having a spell at Henley was thought of as desirable, as normal and expected for those in the 'fast stream'. The emphasis is on consolidation and comes perhaps closer than any of the others to the initial description of Henley's mission by Sir Hector Hetherington. The man in our sample saw it as a 'sabbatical experience', tinged with the expectation of having 'a good time'. He saw it as providing an opportunity to meet people outside the company for the purpose of discussing how they tackled common problems. More important, perhaps, was the expectation that he would have a chance 'to think about the job while away from it and see it in perspective' – in relation to the larger theory of management and organization. The 'feedback' he had received on Henley had made him feel that he would not learn much in a practical way, and that the Henley attempt to build up a sense of pressure in the work was only to be regarded as rather amusing in the light of normal pressures in the company. He did, however, expect to be 'stretched' intellectually – reading, discussing, considering authoritative theoretical writings and research on the topics of his practical involvement. He also thought that meeting people in government and nationalized industry would be useful to him in terms of contacts; not for gaining business, but for facilitating the functioning of his business in so far as government constraints operate in its environment.

While the members' conceptions of their firms' reasons for sending them to Henley conform on the whole to the 'public' reasons agreed by the College and the firms, i.e. general 'broadening' and 'filling in' of managerial information and skills, the individuals themselves show a greater range of specific expectations. In the larger survey conducted in 1967, the members were asked what their *initial* expectations from Henley were. They were allowed to indicate as many as they felt applied, and the patterning of response was as follows:

TABLE 4 *Members' Initial Expectations from Henley*
(Percentages)

	PI	B	NI	PS
Complete break	26	28	24	35
Chance to compare experiences with others	66	74	78	68
Better understanding of senior role	66	30	63	55
Better understanding of organization in relation to environment	26	37	42	41
Improved ability to work with others of different experience	20	18	26	22
Improved ability to handle a new situation	38	27	30	31
Increased understanding of self	23	18	16	14
New knowledge and skills	31	33	30	15
Useful contacts	14	18	15	9
Nothing specific	4	9	1	4
N =	(300)	(82)	(87)	(103)

The initial impressions gained from the exploratory interviews are thus modified in the light of more adequate cross-sectional data that the survey makes available. The individuals interviewed unquestionably represent certain types of manager in their organizations. However, it is clear that these may be types which are not the most characteristic of their organizations. Thus, while there are many Private Sector men like the one interviewed who see the Henley experience as a 'break' in their work (a sabbatical or 'psycho-social moratorium'), this particular orientation is *more* prevalent among the Public Sector men than among men from other organizations.

Perhaps the most striking thing is the *resemblance* among the sectors. The wish to compare experiences, for example, was the reason most highly chosen by men of *all* sectors. More of the Bankers and Nationalized Industry people felt this way than did the others (and was consistent with our exploratory information), but it was the *top* aim for most of the men from all the organizations. Consistent with the explicitly stated goals of Henley was the comparative rareness of references to the acquisition of new skills and of personal insights.

We shall return to these expectations in the next chapter when describing how Henley was actually experienced. There are some interesting contrasts between what members 'initially wanted' and what they 'actually got'.

Men in all organizations except the Bank mentioned the reluctance of their wives to have them go for such a long time, and in some cases there was added to this their own sense of reluctance at being away. All sorts of family issues seemed involved – working wives, ill relatives, new households to establish, and so on. However, in the Bank and in the Private Sector, Henley was seen as a normal and expected stage in a systematic management development programme for fast-stream men, following specialized courses and in-firm courses and sometimes itself to be followed by attending a management programme in the USA. Both types of men mention 'contacts' as an important by-product, but for the Bankers this may relate more to the quest for business in a competitive market, while for the Private Sector men this may be more related to the continuous testing of legal and political boundary conditions in relation to their companies' policies.

For those from Nationalized Industry, as for the Civil Servants, the Henley situation offers an opportunity to break out of their usual network of Public Sector contacts and to learn more of the actualities of the business world. Measuring oneself against the businessmen, who have high prestige as innovators and practitioners of the new skills of the 'managerial revolution', seems to be a part of their wish to learn more about this world. The sustained personal contact is therefore seen as an important part of the experience, not adequately dealt with by reading and attendance at lectures in which the information is disembodied from those who put it to use in the performance of their roles.

Chapter 6 · The Henley Experience

RETROSPECTIVE ACCOUNTS BY MEMBERS, 1960–1966

Given the variegated picture of how each member happened to come to Henley – the interplay of his own wishes and ambitions, his firm's pressures and expectations, and his overall life situation, it is not surprising that, for whatever combination of motives, most of the members were keen to attend.

Table 5 shows the pattern:

TABLE 5 *Recalled Initial Reaction to being Nominated to go to Henley*

(Percentages)

	PI	B	NI	PS
'Enthusiastic'	58	45	64	44
'Keen but diffident'	34	43	29	40
'Not very keen' or 'resentful' or other	8	12	7	12
N =	(300)	(82)	(87)	(103)

Fewer Bankers and Civil Servants proportionately were 'enthusiastic' about going than were members from the other two groups, but their reasons may have differed. Our exploratory interviews suggest that *diffidence* indicated in the second response had different connotations for both groups. The Bankers may have had greater doubts about the relevance of their experience for a course in managerial training than did the others, hence some diffidence about how they would perform 'in public'. The Public Sector people's lower level of enthusiasm may have stemmed from their relatively greater reluctance to leave their personal and private situations and their feeling of scepticism about the relevance of the course to them.

This line of interpretation is supported not only by what has already been said about the expectations of the course by members before they come, but by the patterning of responses to other questions. For example, members were asked how hard they worked on the course – 'very hard', 'moderately hard', 'not very hard', or 'not hard at all'. Sixty-six per cent of the Henley ex-members considered that they worked 'moderately hard' with 27 per cent considering that they worked 'very hard'. Among the Bankers, however, 37 per cent considered that they worked 'very hard' – a significantly greater proportion, indicating their feeling of the need to apply themselves more to the work of the course.*

The other element in the situation – the reluctance to disengage oneself at the early family stage of the life-cycle for a lengthy residential course – seems to be stronger among Public Sector men. When asked whether the residential character of the course was disturbing to them, the ex-members answered as shown in *Table 6*.

TABLE 6 *Perceived Degree of Disturbance by the Residential Character of the Course*

(Percentage indicating that they felt disturbed)

	PI	B	NI	PS
N =	9 (300)	11 (82)	17 (87)	15 (103)

The ex-members were also asked if their wives found it disturbing, and the responses follow the same pattern by sector, with the

* It is interesting to note that the staff did not feel that Bankers applied themselves more than others to the work of the course. Indeed, when asked to rate a sample of men from the four sectors for 'application', Bankers and Nationalized Industry people showed the lowest proportion of 'high application', and Bankers the highest proportion of 'no special effort'. The Private Sector people were considered to be the highest; this contrast with their own declared reaction is interesting. It seems to represent a 'throw-away' attitude. As 'top dogs' in the management line, they seem to want to convey the impression that it is all a lark for them, yet at the same time there is an underlying recognition on their part that the Henley experience has a reality in a sense that may be more poignant than in the more public sectors. This duality of orientation is interesting in the light of other research (e.g. Gruenfeld, 1966) which indicates that the greatest learning is likely to take place where there is an attitude of humility and personal deficiency rather than the 'cocky' or 'top-dog' attitude.

percentages of disturbance for the wives higher than for the men themselves.*

The work of the College has been described in formal terms. What we are concerned with here is attempting to assess what members draw from their participation in such a programme. The programme has been evolved by the staff interactively with successive classes of members, to be sure, but in an intuitive way. The programme 'feels' right, and the 'feedback' from members is sufficiently positive to be reassuring. How can this type of continuing assessment be refined? The first step is to have the evaluative queries made by a detached person or organization – such as the research team in this instance.

In the pilot study, the twenty-seven ex-Henley men interviewed were asked to rate the different aspects of the Henley experience in terms of relative influence on them, and the following rough pattern of responses emerged:

TABLE 7 *Aspects of Greatest Influence at Henley*

(Percentages, $N = 27$)

Informal Interaction with Peers	Syndicate Method	Longish Residence	All Other Influences
60	30	10	—

The numbers are very low, and these results must be taken as very tentative. Though no equivalent question was asked in the larger survey, there is supportive evidence that it is the informal interaction, both among the members and between members and staff, that is felt to be the key element in the learning experience, rather than the more structured aspects of the course. Ex-members were

---

* A probable contributory factor here is the tendency for the wives of Public Sector men to have had a higher level of education than the others and to be in some form of employment. The problems of family management where both partners are employed are described in Rapoport and Rapoport (1969). In such family structures, it is more disturbing to the equilibrium for one of the partners to be away, since the domestic division of labour tends to be more equally distributed between them than in the one-career family.

asked if, in their opinion, 'there should have been more or less of the following in the organization of the Henley course' – and to indicate for each of nine aspects of the course whether they felt there should have been 'more', whether it was 'about right', or whether there should have been 'less'. *Table 8* shows the pattern of responses:

TABLE 8 *Attitudes towards Aspects of the Course*

(Percentages, $N = 576$)

	'About right'	'Should have been *more*'	'Should have been *less*'	Net 'Popularity' Score
Report-writing	73	9	18	64
Informal member contacts	72	22	6	88
Informal staff contacts	70	26	4	92
Reading and private study	57	21	22	56
Outside visits	56	36	8	84
Syndicate method	55	3	42	16
Talks by outside visitors	40	54	6	88
Public speaking	30	10	60	−20

Obviously it is hazardous to treat the net score – calculated as the percentage considering an element 'about right' plus the percentage wanting 'more' minus those wanting 'less' – as an accurate 'popularity' or 'influence' score. Equally, it would be erroneous to attribute the same significance to a minor aspect of the course (e.g. outside visits) as to a major aspect (e.g. syndicate work), simply because they received similar proportions of 'about right' votes. Likewise, to indicate that there should be 'more' of something could be either a sign of high praise and attribution of value or an implied criticism. The 26 per cent who indicate that there should be more informal contact with staff probably contain some with each of these orientations. Nevertheless, it remains of some significance that it is the informal interpersonal elements (members and staff contacts, talks by outside visitors, and visits to outside enterprise) that rate highest in the series, and the more formal performance elements, especially public speaking and to a lesser degree syndicate work, that rate lowest in this series.

THE HIGH VALUATION OF INFORMAL INTERACTION

What is it that the ex-members get out of the informal interaction? There seem to be at least three kinds of gain – which are inter-related and will be discussed again in Chapter 7. They are:

(a)   de-stereotyping of other organizations
(b)   objectification of one's own organization
(c)   increase in self-esteem.

Examples of each of these will be given. The interviews indicate that comments of the type used illustratively here are very wide-spread among those that are positively orientated to the experience as a whole.

De-stereotyping of other organizations is very frequently encountered. Many businessmen tend to have negative stereotypes about Civil Servants and vice versa; Bankers tend to have similar stereotypes about the incompetence of men from other organizations in financial matters, and so on. The de-stereotyping aspects of the Henley experience are as follows:

'nothing but good can come from a situation like that at Henley, where all sorts of people mix together and force one another to see the other side of all sorts of issues.'

'a mutual opening of doors and increase of understanding of how things work in other kinds of organisations . . .'

'All these different types of organizations operate in one world, but they play a different role in it. We are all trying to adjust to the same environment but coping with it in different ways.'

'The fresh perspectives made us think. This was a shock to the system and involved a lot of re-thinking.'

Associated with this is the '*objectification*' of one's own organizational environment. As one man put it: 'When you get away and work with other kinds of people, you see your own people with fresh eyes when you return – you make a mental reappraisal of your job and your colleagues.' Other expressions of this objectification process are:

'Stimulating to have your attention focused on matters that you may have been vaguely aware of but could easily skip over in your usual round of work. When you go back you see them differently . . .'

(A Private Sector man) 'You develop a new sense of civic responsibility for your firm.'

(A Civil Servant) 'You know, the Civil Service gets such bad press in terms of red-tape, inefficiency, resistance to change, and so on that one gets to believe with part of oneself that these things are true and that we are an inferior lot. When I went through the course at Henley I realized that many of the problems we face are the same as those of any big organization, and that smallness means inefficiency rather than efficiency. I came back with an increased respect for how some of our chaps are handling these problems when I saw how others handle them. I realized that we are doing jolly well with some difficult issues.'

Though objectification need not necessarily be accompanied by an increase in self-esteem, it seems very often to be. As one Private Industry member put it: 'I don't know what it is about it, something about the general atmosphere, but it makes you grow up.'

'Growing-up' may involve a superficial drop in overt displays of self-assertiveness. One of the Private Sector men representing a very large and successful company said: 'We have a very high opinion of ourselves at——.' As will be indicated below, these men did not show as high a development score as others. However, to the extent that self-assertiveness represents inner uncertainties, a growth of 'real' self-esteem may actually be accompanied by a decrease in overt egotism. And, there are some members whose egotism makes them maladapted to their managerial roles. They may, in the course of being 'taken down a peg or two', increase in their own self-esteem as well as in the esteem of others. By and large, however, the indications are that most managers have doubts and uncertainties about their capacities in senior roles and they benefit by increasing their confidence to perform adequately. Confidence in public situations, ease in dealing with different kinds of people, and reassessment of one's own areas of competence seem to nurture general self-esteem at this stage. The Banker can contribute a facility with dealing with financial issues that makes him valued in group discussions even though he has never produced anything tangible for the market and may not have a higher degree; the Civil Servant can display his facility with report-writing and presentation; the scientist or technologist can develop a logically reasoned analysis; the industrialist can offer plenty of case materials of effective operations in manufacturing.

This putting oneself in perspective is described by a senior manager in the Private Sector as follows:

'I believe that I benefited from . . . Henley in that I gathered additional information, recognized more clearly my weaknesses and their extent, made a number of friends, had an opportunity of seeing how other disciplines approached management (or . . . administration) and returned considerably stimulated . . .'

SYNDICATES AND PUBLIC PRESENTATIONS

The same man illustrates some of the reasons underlying the widespread wish for less emphasis on formal elements of the course, including the syndicate method. His remarks are very widely representative:

'My disappointment centres more or less on the fact that little of the realistic management situation was introduced and insufficient practical management problems were presented for members of the session to study and solve . . . far too much academic influence within the College . . . I valued tremendously the syndicate method, but I am sure that it could stand a lot more interfering influence from the permanent staff members without losing significantly, if at all, anything of its value: Henley tends to treat the syndicate method as a bit too sacred . . .'

Though 42 per cent felt that there should have been less emphasis on the syndicate method, only about 10 per cent of the respondents in the questionnaire made adverse comments about the syndicates. The 'lessening' attitude is one of emphasis rather than of fundamental disagreement. Representative comments are:

'Too much time spent in syndicates exchanging relatively trivial experiences . . .'

'. . . discussions . . . based on theory and incomplete facts gleaned from books in a short space of time were useless and frustrating.'

'. . . the size and static composition of the syndicate [meant that] the potential for learning from others quickly dried up in the later stages. One could amuse oneself by forecasting the "line" various members would invariably take . . .'

'Too much time-waste . . .'

'. . . lack of rigorous or stimulating scientific approach to management problems. Most members lacked rigorous techniques when they started and were allowed to continue with "mere debate" in syndicate . . .'

'. . . time wasted in abortive work; the blind leading the blind . . .'

'. . . hours of wrong discussion on subjects or pseudo-subjects which were not adequately defined at the outset . . .'

'. . . unreal formal presentations . . . bogus and time-wasting . . .'

'. . . do not think College conferences . . . reflect a situation paralleled in industry . . .'

'. . . the system of presentations which dominates the course is laborious and finally archaic . . .'

'. . . course work on too high a place . . . should have devoted more time to everyday problems that confront us . . .'

'. . . failure to encourage a professional approach to management; indecisive conclusions to many exercises . . .'

'. . . academic approach to solving and discussing problems was not tempered by the harsh realities of a practical situation . . .'

'. . . idealistic . . .'

'. . . overindulgence in "moral issues" . . .'

'. . . insufficient time available to pursue subjects of interest in greater depth . . .'

'. . . only came into contact with 50 per cent of the members through syndicate work: would have preferred more . . .'

'Study of management *in vacuo* . . . needs more "practical work" . . .'

Certain of the views expressed by these managers, who went through Henley in the early 1960s, were in fact shared by members of the staff, and subsequent developments have taken account of them. This will be described in Chapter 12. The important thing to remember is that a majority of the members felt that the syndicate method was about right, but a substantial minority felt that it needed modification. The modification suggested was almost uniformly in the direction of increased structure. This also bears on members' views about the role of the staff.

STAFF ROLE

As we have indicated above, the staff role is by design a facilitating one and not a formal leadership or authoritative role, despite the misnomer of 'Directing Staff'. In the exploratory interviews, there was a good deal of criticism expressed towards the DS role. It was the single thing about the programme most mentioned in critical terms:

> 'There is always a DS in the background of the syndicates, like an *éminence grise*, whatever is being done. Some of the projects could be done better without them. It would give more freedom to the groups as men are often behaving in such a way as to get "good marks" in the eyes of the DS.'

The ambiguities in the definition of the DS role would seem inevitably to lead to the arousal of fantasies based on prior images of the 'silent observer'. Such men are thought of as wielding secret power, scrutinizing, inspecting, judging, examining. All of these are roles from which men at the threshold of top management positions may be struggling to free themselves. These images retain overtones of childhood, schooldays, or lower-echelon experiences which were perhaps fraught with a certain amount of anxiety, and towards which residues of negative feeling persist. The DS, in their passivity and relative anonymity, become suitable objects onto which to 'project' these feelings, whether or not they are valid in purely objective terms. Most criticisms of the DS were for not exercising more leadership:

> 'DS are often intelligent and charming men, but their qualifications for running a course on top management are questionable.'

> 'The DS are out of touch'; or 'not up to date'; 'not in contact with recent developments in the external world' or 'the blind leading the blind'.

In some cases, as with one Civil Servant, the model of the relatively passive group leader was accepted, being rather a familiar one in committee work in the Public Sector, but he was very critical of the way in which the DS performed *within* this model:

> 'A group can develop quite a lot when left to its own devices, but at the same time informed tutorage can accelerate the process of crystallization.'

While these critical comments on the DS were fairly frequent, there were also positive comments in relation to their role. There is a strong thread of acceptance of the College's definition of the role, particularly among more senior men and among those in the nominator's position. This is perhaps best put by one of the more senior men from the Private Sector who was interviewed in the pilot phase:

> 'The DS are often criticized for not contributing too much. But I see this as their job. Their job is to sit there and be relatively unobtrusive and only to jump in when things go off the rails.'

It is difficult to quantify the extent and intensity of the criticism felt about the DS role as distinct from the syndicate method of working. Added to this, it is even more difficult to separate the 'rational' and objective bases for this criticism from the 'projective' bases formed under the impact of a growth experience. The latter experience, with its need for objects onto which to 'hang' feelings of rejection as one moves to a more advanced stage of career development, will be discussed in Chapter 12. In the present chapter we shall attempt only to assess how widespread the criticisms are and what their substance is. There were several questions in the questionnaire that approached these issues indirectly. Members were asked in which of the following ways the staff contribution was 'most valuable' to them and in which ways 'could the staff contribution have been of more value'. This phrasing emphasized the positive, and indicated a number of ways mentioned in the exploratory discussions with both members and staff in which the staff were considered helpful:

> private advice and encouragement
> help in social mixing
> help in self-appraisal
> joining in discussion
> career advice
> direct teaching,
> other – specify if chosen
> none of the above

In their responses, a roughly similar percentage of members chose all of these as important. Private advice was chosen by 17 per cent, social mixing by 14 per cent, self-appraisal by 14 per cent, joining in discussion by 22 per cent, direct teaching by 7 per cent, and 'none of the above' by 26 per cent. No one indicated 'other ways' in which the staff helped. It may be said, therefore, that there is no 'typical' Henley member reaction to the staff role in terms of its most positive aspect. 'Joining in discussion' comes closest, but it is exceeded by the ambiguous and ambivalent category of 'none of the above'. One inference from this is that many members felt that the staff had not been particularly helpful. In addition, as is consistent with the teaching philosophy, the smallest number felt that 'direct teaching' had been the main contribution of the staff role.

Looking at the second part of the question, however, where it was asked how the staff could have been more helpful, 'direct teaching' becomes the most important category, with 30 per cent choosing it. A high proportion of the members want the staff to perform as experts and to teach their expertise whatever it may be.

We get some indication as to the favoured kind of expertise wanted from at least a sizeable proportion of the members when we see that 23 per cent of the members indicate that 'help in self-appraisal' is an area where the staff contribution could have been more valuable. Examples of what they meant by this are the following comments written into the questionnaire forms by those indicating this wish, under 'suggestions for the future':

'. . . I feel that there should have been more personal guidance by the staff to assist the efficiency of individuals, for example, in speeches and organizing meetings.'

'More direct appraisal of one's work by the staff and thereby not such an oblique approach to work of students.'

'Staff . . . should be encouraged to reach better social rapport with their syndicate members so that they can give, if asked, knowledgeable and disinterested appraisal of the syndicate member (e.g. the impression he makes, annoying habits, etc.).'

'There could be a few private – i.e. individual – seminars at, say, monthly intervals in which personal progress through the course is discussed.'

'There should be more direct knowledge. We all always need self-knowledge and knowledge of people.'

'. . . greater help from the DS in personal counselling on one's own ideas and performance. Without this latter one's assessments are too subjective about what ideas have been absorbed or are worth following up.'

These 23 per cent are, remember, not the 30 per cent who indicated the wish for more direct teaching, though their expressed value is consistent with this in a specific area, that of personal appraisal. The members who pushed for more direct teaching had in mind information about new management techniques, use of computers, economics and statistics, and so on. The majority of the members indicating this wish implied that they wanted it not instead of syndicates, but as a supplement to the syndicate work, making the syndicate work more meaningful and laying a basis for greater depth of syndicate discussion. Examples of these views, written in under the request for suggestions about future organization of the course at Henley, are as follows:

'Unless Henley specifies previous management training as a requisite, there should be more personal teaching to supplement syndicate discussion, which is often rambling and indecisive.'

'I think that the early part of the course dealing with internal organization and administration is first rate. Too much time was, however, diverted to syndicate discussion on external relations, particularly central and local government. This would have been better and more quickly handled by direct teaching; it being more factual, one cannot formulate syndicate views as one did in the organization and administrative phase.'

'Somewhat more *teaching* of new technologies – e.g. OR, O and M, use of EDP.'

'I think that there should be more teaching and expert guidance in the technical subjects. Starting from scratch in some subjects meant that little depth was penetrated.'

'Keep the excellent "syndicate alchemy". Introduce a massive transfusion of direct teaching of business skills by first-rate teachers with business experience.'

'I feel that there should be some formal teaching of basic subjects initially i.e. simple cost accounting, personnel principles, together with supervisory and general management principles.'

'More teaching of fundamental management principles – less "abstract discussion." '

'I would not change the basic character of the Henley course. However, it might be useful to some members to attend *voluntary* lectures on [some subjects] to obtain at least a nodding acquaintance with the subjects.'

'More positive teaching, possibly on a tutorial basis, to meet particular individual needs. This should not be at the expense of the obvious benefits of the syndicate.'

'More clear instruction after *some* syndicate discussion. Less reliance on experience within the syndicate which isn't there.'

'One or two projects with a strong element of expert teaching.'

'Henley must realize that some subjects are better taught than arrived at by the syndicate method. Members of syndicates, however well chosen, do lack some experiences, so the rate of input is slower than necessary.'

'The opportunity should be more available to obtain more direct instruction – probably no more than an acquaintance with the currently developing management techniques.'

'More expert staff personnel teaching.'

'Slightly more emphasis on direct teaching – there was often much uninformed discussion in syndicate.'

'There is a distinct need to teach or have a planned logical sequence of lectures on some subjects, e.g. management sciences, OR, statistical methods, since the syndicate method is not always an effective one.'

It can be seen from these comments that the primary motivation behind the desire for more direct teaching for most of the respondents is *not* an out-and-out rejection of the syndicate learning method. Members do not feel that lectures should replace syndicates, but see them more as providing the technical inputs that would make the syndicates more meaningful. In addition to information on new management methods, lectures are widely desired on economics, financial aspects of administration, and so on, in association with the syndicate work.

In addition to the emphasis on active teaching, which more directly affects the staff role, there was a great deal of mention of the value of the case-study method and of business games.

The fact that the two highest proportions of members' responses to the question of how the staff could have helped more were 'direct teaching' and 'self-appraisal' is significant and will be returned to in Chapter 12.

Twenty per cent of the members expressed the wish for *more* joining in by the staff. Examples of what they wrote are as follows:

'I also liked the "do-it-yourself" approach, but at the same time I would have welcomed a little more direct summing up by the staff at the end of projects.'

'I think, without sacrificing the overall policy and character of the course, something could be done – by a little more frequent and a little more forceful intervention by the DS – to tighten up and point syndicate discussion.'

'More direct participation by DS . . .'

'DS should challenge members more – possibly on the line of a "professional irritant".'

'Although [I] appreciate that finding your own way out of problems is part of the object of the exercise, I advocate . . . a *slightly* greater participation in discussion by DS when foundering – mainly to save time.'

'A more positive contribution on the part of the staff at Henley, for example, by summarizing at the conclusion of projects the considered opinion (or opinions) of the relevant authorities, especially when research has been carried out by specialist groups.'

The fourth reason – indicated by 11 per cent of the ex-members – was that the staff should give more 'private advice'.

These four opinions on how the staff role could be more helpful together account for nearly 90 per cent of the opinions. This indicates the wish, on the one hand, to have more structure and demonstration of staff expertise and, on the other, to increase *self*-understanding and awareness of how to handle personal problems and issues. It would seem that many members do not want either an increase in personal insight *or* more technical input but *both*. And they want them to be interrelated.

This impression is reinforced by the members' assessments of what they got out of the course. The members' initial expectations of what they wanted to get from the Henley course gave the greatest emphasis to the 'officially declared' objectives of the course. They considered that they were sent to be 'broadened generally' and to be 'filled in' with management knowledge and skills. They themselves wanted to compare their own experiences with those of men from other organizations, and to learn more about the senior managerial role. They did not expect much by way of the acquisition of new skills, nor did they expect much by way of benefit from the fact that they were having a complete break from their usual routines and that they would interact personally with others and through this process learn more about themselves as persons. *Table 9* shows the differences between initial expectations and actually derived benefits as members retrospectively perceive their experience. This is the picture, with minor variations, for members from all sectors.*

* The Civil Servants showed a somewhat greater rise than the others in relation to the acquisition of new skills and in relation to the handling of new situations. The Private Sector people showed the greatest rise in learning about the relationship between their own organizations and the wider environment. The members from Nationalized Industries showed, more than the others, gains of

TABLE 9 *Initial Expectations and Perceived Benefits of the Henley Experience*

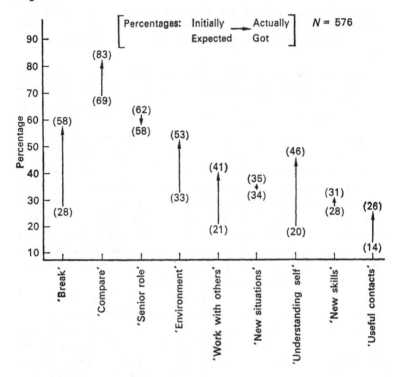

It is clear from this table that the greatest overall gains of actually realized benefits over initial expectations come in the related areas of 'complete break from work loads and associates' (gain of 30 per cent), and 'increased understanding of yourself as a person' (26 per cent gain overall). The fact that there were relatively lower gains in 'comparing one's own experiences with others' and gaining a 'better understanding of the senior role' are not, of course, to be taken as indications that these areas are

---

actual benefits over expectations in the two areas of 'complete break' and 'understanding of self as a person'. Except in the two areas of 'senior role' understanding, and 'new skills' – both of which showed little difference between expectations and gains – the movements were all in the same direction, with all members by and large indicating many more gains than expectations. Four per cent indicated that they expected 'nothing very specific' and three per cent indicated that they actually got 'nothing very specific'.

unimportant. They were high expectations and remained high as realizations. The two areas of greatest gain were so, partly because they were low as expectations. The 'complete break' aspect of the experience has, of course, been recognized as important from the beginning of the College's life, and relates to the emphases earlier mentioned by Hetherington and Noel Hall. However, given the temper of the times, this way of putting a potential benefit is not highly esteemed. In an era of careful cost-benefit analysis, the vacuum implied in the expression 'complete break' must be filled with definable content of some kind. The importance of 'self-understanding' as a kind of content will be discussed in Chapters 12 and 13. However, it is worth noting at this point that this is an unrecognized kind of benefit, not because it is not known to exist by the Henley staff and members, but because it is an element of the programme that is left implicit rather than made explicit. Psychological insights, self-analysis, the analysis of interpersonal relations, and so on are elements that are known to be important, but that tend by performance-conscious managers to be left implicit. Managers are not psychologically-minded, on the whole, and the Henley staff do not see themselves as psychological counsellors. Be this as it may, the men themselves have indicated that for many this was an unexpectedly great gain from the course, and the staff have been credited with having brought it about to a large extent. Many members wanted even more staff effort in this direction.

DEVELOPMENT AT HENLEY

A more thorough discussion of the process of development is reserved for Chapter 12. However, it would seem useful at this point to indicate in very broad terms what the overall pattern of 'growth' was felt to be by the members in relation to their experience at Henley.

First, a cautionary reminder that we are working with retrospective data. We know that people tend not to recall their reactions in situations very accurately. Also, the intervening time between members' attendance at Henley and their being asked to evaluate the experience has introduced all sorts of new and complicating elements into the situation. All of these things make for a potential unreliability of such estimates. In addition, self-ratings for an experience like this are suspect because of the possible tendency for members to wish to express a positive attitude toward the course, particularly those who responded to the questionnaire. One researcher describes this hazard as follows:

> 'The generosity of the participating executive's comments is doubtless reinforced by his feeling that he is expected to respond in this way, by his recognition of the favourable implications of his selection and by his satisfaction in associating under pleasant circumstances with other men of intelligence, ability and varied experience' (Andrews, 1959).

This tendency to aggrandize the benefits of any experience which is advocated as being helpful and which is considered at least implicitly as relevant to career success is very real and widespread.

Countering this are several other factors worth mentioning in the situation. The Henley experience, because it was such a major event in the lives of the managers who attended it – even for those who were not so favourably disposed towards it – cannot easily be confused with other events. Furthermore, the group studied were all recent members – not members who attended 10 or 15 years back, though some of these were interviewed in the exploratory phases. While there might have been a tendency to aggrandize the positive gains of the experience within their own firms where promotions were at stake, the fact that the research organization was associated neither with the College nor with the employing firm diminished the probability that the ex-member would want to aggrandize the effect either as an expression of gratitude or as a way of currying favour. In addition, we had some reliability checks.

In the pilot-study stage it was possible to draw upon an analysis of staff ratings, without jeopardizing confidentiality, for the men in the four organizations included and for members in the two years 1955 and 1965. This seemed to indicate two things: first, that the earlier men showed less 'growth' in the staff's view than did the later members; second, that there was quite a range of variation according to organization. Overall, the staff considered that only about 55 per cent of the members in the two groups (1955 and 1965) showed any growth worth noting, with Civil Servants and Bankers showing the greatest degree of growth (about 65 per cent, compared with only about 40 per cent for those from the Private Sector firm and from the Nationalized Industry). These overall totals were lowered by the lower 'growth' ratings for the earlier group (1955). In addition, the particular Private Sector firm whose members were interviewed and scored was one in which managers generally had a 'very high opinion' of themselves they felt that they were 'tops' in their field and, while they felt they might benefit from being at Henley, would not have expected to 'grow' in the same sense as members from less advantaged backgrounds in terms of managerial training and experience.*

At the same time, the interviews held with the ex-members during the pilot study were coded for their own conceptions of whether or not they had developed at Henley. About 35 per cent indicated unambiguously positive attitudes, about 55 per cent indicated some benefit along with quite complex reactions, and only about 10 per cent had predominantly negative things to say.

There was partial validation for this in the reports made to their own organizations, some aspects of which were made known to us. In one Civil Service ministry, for example, where it was made clear to the men that there was nothing to be gained by aggrandizing the experience and a frank and critical appraisal was called for, 40 per cent of the people on returning from Henley indicated that they would rate the course as 'high' in terms of value to their work and 60 per cent gave it 'some value'. No one found it useless.

In the larger survey – 1960–6 – ex-members were asked whether and how much they felt that they had developed as a consequence of Henley. Here the issue was broken down into 'developed as a *manager*' and 'developed as a *person*' to test out members' conceptions of the relationship between the two – one of the fundamental postulates of the College.

For both aspects of development we used four ratings and *Table 10* shows how the overall percentages distributed themselves.

This table shows that very few of the ex-members indicate that they did not develop *at all* as a consequence of Henley, and at the same time very few felt that they developed a *great deal*. Most were in between. Furthermore, the two aspects of development, 'as a manager' and 'as a person', are very significantly inter-correlated. This finding supports the fundamental position of the College on the importance of personal development in the transition to general managership.

* A somewhat comparable phenomenon was found in a study of the growth pattern of Henley members conducted by K. M. Elliott, the College Registrar, which showed that greater growth scores were in fact achieved by members with somewhat lower formal educational qualifications or by those from technical colleges rather than from universities.

TABLE 10 *Members' Conceptions of their Development as a Consequence of Henley*

(Percentages, $N = 576$)

	Developed as a Manager	Developed as a Person
A great deal	7	5
A fair amount	50	48
Not very much	41	38
Not at all	2	7

A comparison of staff assessments with the self-assessments of the members, made well after they were out of Henley, makes it clear that these staff and member assessments are also very significantly intercorrelated. *Table 11* shows this:

TABLE 11 *Staff Assessments of Members' Development Compared with Members' Subsequent Self-assessments*

(Percentages)

Members' Self-assessments of their own Development	Staff Assessments		
	A Great Deal of Growth	Little Growth	No Growth
A great deal	12	6	4
A fair amount	58	50	43
Not very much	28	43	50
Not at all	2	1	4
TOTALS % =	100	100	101
N =	(138)	(307)	(131)

Looking at organizational differences, a somewhat different pattern emerges from the survey as compared with the indications of the pilot study, but not of such magnitude as to be considered highly significant. Taking all of the firms together in the early sixties period, the greatest expression of benefit is from Private Sector members, 62 per cent of whom indicated that they developed 'a great deal' or a 'fair amount' as a result of Henley.

Nationalized Industry members, too, had 60 per cent in these categories. Bankers and Civil Servants were discernibly lower, both showing just under 50 per cent in these two categories of response. The members themselves in all organizations showed only negligible numbers, under 2 per cent overall, in the 'not at all' category of perceived benefits.

Chapter 7 · The Post-Henley Career, 1960–1967

To the extent that Henley succeeded in providing a complete break for its members, the 're-entry' following Henley must be seen as carrying special hazards of its own. Ideally, of course, the member is welcomed back, refreshed, broadened, full of new enthusiasms, which the firm is eager and waiting to harness. In actuality, this is true in the most ideal circumstances only. Sometimes the man himself is apprehensive about returning; sometimes the firm is indifferent or even unfriendly toward his new ideas and enthusiasms; sometimes he is keen and his firm receptive but the task of making the transfer and application of lessons learned at Henley more complex than anyone envisaged.

In this chapter we shall trace the overall picture of the post-Henley period and discuss some of the types of problem confronted. In the next chapter we shall analyse different career patterns and their relationships to perceived development in the course.

THE AFTERMATH OF HENLEY

When asked about the relevance of the Henley experience for the subsequent demands of their jobs, members were given an opportunity to indicate whether they found it *directly* relevant, of

TABLE 12 *Members' Perceptions of the Relevance of the Henley Experience for Subsequent Work*

(Percentages)

	PI	B	NI	PS
General relevance	76	68	73	73
Little or no relevance	12	24	14	17
Direct relevance	11	8	12	10
N =	(300)	(82)	(87)	(103)

general relevance not easy to specify, or of little or no relevance to subsequent work. *Table 12* shows their response, by organization.

The 'typical' Henley member saw the experience as having *general relevance, not easy to specify*. The differences between organizations are not great, except that among Bankers a higher proportion saw the course as having little or no relevance to their work than was true for members from other organizations.

JOB MOBILITY

Members were asked about their movements. The 'typical' Henley member *stayed with the same employer* (14 per cent had one or more change of employer in this period; the figures ranged from 17 per cent of the Private Sector people to 6 per cent of the

TABLE 13 *Promotions Since Henley**

(Percentages)

No. of Promotions	Overall	PI	B	NI	PS
0	26	24	16	26	34
1	50	48	44	50	54
2	21	21	32	20	10
3 or more	4	7	7	4	2
N =	(576)†	(300)	(82)	(87)	(103)

*These percentages represent promotions, uncorrected for period of time out. However, as the different sectors have roughly the same proportions of members in each of the courses over the period of study, and roughly proportionate response rates to the questionnaire, proportions in each sector who have been out of Henley 7, 6, 5, 4, 3, 2, and 1 years are constant.
†Overall totals include 4 Trade Unionists.

Bankers). Typically a member received a promotion within a year or two of having attended the course.

In relation to job changes, as distinct from promotions (there are more of the former than the latter), there is, as one would expect, a time factor involved. Those members who had been away from Henley longest had had more job changes. Still, nearly 15 per cent of the first nine sessions represented in this Survey (i.e. those at the beginning of the 1960s) had not yet had a job change by the time of the Survey.

This figure compares with about 33 per cent of the men in the six more recent sessions who had not yet been promoted. Over time, the trend appears to be a job change within a year of leaving Henley, and then a second change two years later. Job changes and promotions are intercorrelated for Private Sector and Nationalized Industry people. The Public Sector men indicate more job changes than promotion, and Bankers the reverse.

The four sectors seem to share comparable increases in responsibilities and in the management content of members' jobs. However, this is not equally represented in terms of promotions and remuneration. Bankers have more promotions than the others but Private Sector men the highest salary increments. Civil Servants are lowest on both criteria. *Table 14* shows the changes in salary patterns from 1961 to 1967:

TABLE 14 *Members' Salary Patterns, 1961–7, Pre- and Post-Henley*

(Percentages for 1967. In parenthesis, the percentages in each salary range in 1961.)*

Salary level (£s)	Overall	PI	B	NI	PS
Less than 2,000	2 (16)	2 (14)	0 (23)	0 (15)	0 (15)
2–3,000	14 (53)	12 (44)	18 (61)	17 (61)	17 (72)
3–4,000	42 (21)	33 (26)	37 (12)	56 (22)	64 (14)
4–5,000	24 (7)	26 (12)	26 (1)	22 (1)	17 (1)
Over 5,000	17 (2)	28 (4)	19 (2)	4 (1)	2 (0)

*This is uncorrected for the drop in value of the £ in the period 1960–7 – of the order of 20 per cent.

Salaries are a rough but unreliable guideline to increased responsibilities; the type of organization within which the member is developing his career determines what potential there is for salary increases. How does this relate to the pattern of increase in managerial responsibilities as the members saw it? We expected that increase in managerial responsibility would be indicated by rises in the following:

'Number of decisions taken without referring to higher authority.'

'Magnitude of decisions taken without referring to higher authority.'

'Amount of involvement with others of different specialities.'

'Amount of dealings with people outside the firm.'

'Amount of your work that can be done by machine aids.'

'Amount of your work that you can delegate to other people.'

'Participation in long-term planning.'

and a decline in

'Constraints on freedom of action.'

We accordingly asked members to compare their current jobs with their pre-Henley jobs in relation to these factors.

The 'typical' Henley member showed a pattern in accordance with these expectations, with one exception (i.e. the amount of work that could be done by machine aids – this remained the same or decreased for most, particularly Bankers and Civil Servants).* The number and magnitude of decisions taken without referring to higher authority increased most, with about 70 per cent indicating increases. Participation in long-term planning also increased markedly, with nearly 70 per cent of the ex-members indicating this change. The amount of involvement with others of different specialities increased for about 60 per cent of the members, and the amount of work that can be delegated increased in nearly 55 per cent of the cases. The amount of dealing with people outside the firm increased in about 47 per cent of the cases and constraints on members' own freedom of action decreased in over 50 per cent of the cases.

Variations in the pattern by organization were not enormous, but they did show some interesting contrasts. The 'typical' Private Industry member was more likely than the rest to have increased

* In fact, this indicates the lack of utility of this item as a general indicator of increase in managerial responsibility. Machine aids was too inclusive a term – suggesting desk calculators, etc., as well as sophisticated management resources like computers.

in the *magnitude* though not the number of decisions taken and was slightly more likely than managers in other sectors to have increased his involvement with others of different specialities.

The 'typical' Banker was quite a lot more likely to have increased the magnitude and number of decisions taken without reference to higher authority, and his feeling of constraint is more likely to have decreased. However, he is quite a bit less likely to have increased his participation in long-term planning or involvement with others of different specialities. These patterns reflect the relatively 'total' working environments of Bankers and the centralization of their long-range planning at the very top. In Banks the use of machine-aids decreases markedly as one rises, probably because the smaller machine-aids are so prevalent at lower levels.

The 'typical' Public Sector member, aside from the tendency, as mentioned above, to have a greater decrease in the use of machine-aids than others, tended to have more of an increase in the degree to which he has felt constraints on his own freedom of action following Henley. Unlike managers from other sectors, the typical Civil Servant feels more rather than less constraint on his actions as he rises.

PROBLEMS AND PROBLEM-SOLVING

Some further insight into the post-Henley experience of the members is contributed through a consideration of the types of problem they face. *Tables 15* and *16* produce an interesting pattern. In *Table 15* the ex-members' responses are summarized in terms of the types of problem most frequently encountered in their work.

TABLE 15 *Most Frequent Problems Encountered*

(Percentages listed in order of overall frequency)

	Overall	*PI*	*B*	*NI*	*PS*
Economic/Financial	31	30	38	27	23
Human relations	31	30	25	29	30
Technical	24	23	22	27	21
Intellectual	9	9	12	9	12
Political	5	6	3	8	14
N =	(576)	(300)	(82)	(87)	(103)

The list is in order of overall frequency of choice of each item. It is remarkable that the order of frequency is very nearly *the same for all organizations*, though the relative emphases vary somewhat. As might be expected, the Private Sector people are more concerned with problems of finance, the Bankers, naturally, most of all; more of the Public Sector people are concerned with political problems than are other managers, though for them as for the others these problems are lowest in frequency of choice from the list provided. Both the Public Sector and Nationalized Industry members are a bit more concerned with human-relational problems than with technical problems, unlike the other members, and the higher proportion of the Nationalized Industry members concerned with technical problems reflect their specialized work content.

Thus, the 'typical Henley member' most frequently encountered a trio of problems – economic/financial, human relational, and technical (the first being highest for Bankers; the second relatively high for the Private Industry members and Civil Servants; and the last being relatively higher for the Nationalized Industry members). However, these are the problems presented to them for solution in their managerial roles. They do not necessarily reflect the relative challenge or difficulty of the different areas. Members were thus asked which of the problem areas were most 'irksome' to them.

When one examines the reports on the 'most irksome' problems encountered, the picture changes dramatically.

TABLE 16 *Most Irksome Problems Encountered*

(Percentages listed in order of overall frequency)

	Overall	PI	B	NI	PS
Political	39	35	34	43	44
Human relations	26	29	25	21	25
Technical	16	14	31	21	14
Economic/Financial	15	16	1	11	13
Intellectual	5	5	9	4	3
N =	(576)	(300)	(82)	(87)	(103)

While the 'typical' member does not find political problems the ones he most frequently encounters – indeed, they are the least frequent (except for Civil Servants, for whom the meaning of the term has a special duality) – he finds them the most irksome. The political problems displace economic/financial ones as his main source of irritation, and it is really only the human-relational problems that maintain a comparable level of salience in terms of *both* frequency and irksomeness of occurrence. Here, as with frequency, it is remarkable how uniform the pattern is found to be *across* organizations. The Public Sector people are more irked than the others over 'political' problems, but for all this is the paramount area of irksomeness. Technical problems are more irksome to Bankers than to others, but financial problems less so, presumably because this is their area of expertise, the management of which is fairly well routinized. Examples of what the ex-members mean by problems in these different areas are as follows:

Political problems overlap to some extent with human relations problems, and seem to relate to circumstances where the ex-member is subjected to awkward situations in relation to higher authority. The sorts of problem mentioned are:

'. . . dealing with pressure groups . . .'
'. . . sorting out inter-functional rivalries . . .'
'. . . recognizing the effects of other people's ambitions . . .'
'. . . interference from the top; bosses more trouble than juniors . . .'

Human relations problems

'Dealing with people's problems and trying to release their talents . . .'
'. . . trying to keep the staff happy . . .'
'. . . dealing with contractors over unfulfilled promises . . .'
'. . . protracted fruitless discussions with the union . . .'
'. . . making judgements of people . . . whom to trust . . .'
'. . . have to argue for a point of view and put a case across, sometimes with an awkward individual involved . . .'
'. . . would be easier if one could get rid of certain people one wanted to get rid of who prevent certain developments from taking place . . .'
'. . . helping people to adapt to change . . .'

Technical problems

'. . . making forecasts . . . manpower calculations . . .'
'Keeping the plant running . . .'

'. . . learning about the new areas of work I'm responsible for on a new job . . .'

Economic/financial problems

'have to watch overdraft being run up and take action to avoid difficulties . . .'

'problems of setting up rates, collecting tariffs . . .'

'. . . making analyses of commercial potentials in new situations'

'planning for company responses to anticipated profit situation . . .

'. . . the company has been undergoing financial reorganization, and I do not understand it sufficiently well – don't like leaving it too much to financial types.'

Intellectual problems are difficult to differentiate from technical problems and this may account for the low frequency of this category being chosen. However, it would seem that, aside from such borderline problems as those of economics or finance, the sort of thing meant by members who chose this item seems to have included not knowing enough about the specialisms of people working under them, having to give advice on matters while knowing one's deficiency of information, lack of time for thinking through problems, and difficulties in finding solutions to problems.

Ex-members were asked how these problems are typically handled in their work environment. The 'typical' Henley member handles them by complex negotiation rather than by drawing on clear-cut technical solutions or by decisive action from the man on the top. There are, however, differences, according to the member's organization, in the ways the problems are dealt with, as is seen from *Table 17*.

TABLE 17 *Ways of Dealing with Most Problems*

(Percentages)

	PI	B	NI	PS
Complex negotiation	51	24	60	60
Technical experts	20	24	26	18
Strong action from top	19	30	10	14
Other	10	22	4	8
N =	(300)	(82)	(87)	(103)

The typical Nationalized Industry member is somewhat more likely than the others to use technical expertise; the typical Banker is somewhat more likely than the others to use or experience strong action from the top; the typical Public Sector men, and those from Nationalized Industry, are more likely than the others to work things through by complex negotiations. However, as with the prevalent problems at work and reactions to them, the resemblance between members from different sectors is very striking.

Ex-members were asked to describe how they dealt with the changes they encountered and what their main strengths and weaknesses were in coping with the challenges they met. The strengths and weaknesses they described were then coded into six pairs of categories, one-half of the pair being used where the type of trait was found and used as a strength and the other half where it was a weakness, either because of the member not having it or because it was present in the wrong form or amount for the job. The six areas overlap a good deal (salesmanship, for example, can be considered a management skill, a human relations skill, or a technical skill, depending on the sort of emphasis the person gives it), yet are informative as major groupings.

1   *Management skills*

    (a) *as a strength* – these were the greatest source of strength, reported as helpful in over 40 per cent of the responses:

'My main strengths are in being good at production control and delegation of authority.'

'ability to organize and administer'

'producing new ideas which are acceptable'

    (b) *as a weakness* – only 10 per cent of the ex-members reported weaknesses in this area, e.g.

'[I have] problems in rating priorities'

'Not happy . . . accounting to Board regarding Branch performance'

2   *Technical knowledge or skills*

    (a) *as a strength* – 41 per cent of the members mentioned strengths in this area, e.g.

'My strength is commercial acumen.'

'Flair for invention' (resulting in patents).

'Salesmanship.'

'Interest and enthusiasm for technical problems' (in an engineering firm).

    (b) *as a weakness* – 13 per cent mentioned weaknesses in this area, e.g.

'Difficulties in making decisions affecting men junior to me but who nevertheless know more than I about specific aspects about the problem . . .'

'. . . in tasks requiring numeracy.'

'. . . in understanding the financial structure and basis for management action . . .'

'Lack of technical expertise. I was trained in a different field of engineering from the ones on which I have to make decisions . . .'

3 *Bureaucracy and political aspects of the job*

    (a) *as a strength* – only 2 per cent indicated that they liked or were good at this sort of thing –

. . . my views now carry more weight in the interpretation of [the organization's] policy . . .'

    (b) *as a weakness or dislike* – 38 per cent indicated that they disliked or were poor at this, e.g.

'I dislike the politics . . . procrastination.'

'I resent time spent in futile negotiations . . .'

'Interminable and wasteful committee meetings . . .'

'. . . views of seniors clash with mine on management philosophy.'

4 *Human relations*

    (a) *as a strength* – 37 per cent of the members – e.g.

'I am good at obtaining support of juniors . . .'

'I have made a contribution by establishing harmonious relations with new colleagues.'

'My main strength is in getting on well with people.'

    (b) *as a weakness* – 10 per cent – e.g.

'I am not a quick thinker, and often lose force through not having a *bon mot*.'

5 *Moral traits* (e.g. of individual character)

   (a) *as a strength* – 27 per cent mentioned items classifiable in
        this way – e.g.

'Hard work.'

'Enthusiasm.'

'I enjoy the power when responsibility is delegated to me.'

'I had to use all of my discretion and tact . . .'

'My adaptation in the face of challenge has been developing in me
an increased sense of vocation . . .'

   (b) *as a weakness* – e.g.

'I dislike expedients and procrastination, hence I sometimes seem
indecisive. I also have a tendency to idleness.'

'Stubbornness.'

'Intolerance.'

'I feel that I can do a job better than anyone else, so have difficulty
delegating.'

Some 'moral' traits were difficult to classify because of the
'double-edged' character of the usage – e.g. 'I am not ruthless
enough', to which an implicit 'thank goodness' was often sensed
in the overall tenor of the ex-members' remarks.

6 *Self-expression*

   (a) *as a strength* – 18 per cent answered using traits classi-
        fiable into this category, e.g.

'. . . persuading the Board to develop R & D . . .'

'[I am] good at putting across my ideas . . .'

'I like to lecture – show off – be a big fish in a little pond . . .'

   (b) *as a weakness* – 10 per cent, e.g.

'My weak points include a dislike of dominating people or achieving
objectives by being aggressive.'

Overall, there was marked similarity in response patterns across
the different types of employing organization. Dislike for bureaucratic problems is stronger among the Public Sector people, including those from Nationalized Industry; technical skill as a
source of strength is high in those from Nationalized Industry;
self-expression as a strength is high in those from the Private

Sector. These variations are small, however, and are in expected directions.

ORIENTATION TO THE JOB: THE WORK ENVIRONMENT

A number of questions were asked to characterize the work environment of the members, in terms of the feeling of *security* it engendered as opposed to *insecurity*; the degree to which it was felt to be *exciting* as opposed to *boring*; *warm* opposed to *cold*; *permissive* vs. *strict*; *conventional* vs. *unconventional*; and *united* vs. *divided*.

The 'typical' ex-member characterizes his work environment as 'secure' in a positive sense (51 per cent), except for Private Industry members, of whom 52 per cent characterize their work environment typically as only 'average' in security. Ten per cent of the Private Sector and 9 per cent of the Nationalized Industry men indicate 'insecure', as against only 1 per cent of Bankers and 2 per cent of Public Sector members.

The 'typical' Henley ex-member characterizes his work situation as 'exciting' (53 per cent). Private Industry and Nationalized Industry members find it most exciting (58 per cent), and Bankers find it least exciting (38 per cent). Only 5 per cent or less of all types of managers find their jobs 'boring'.

The 'typical' Henley ex-member characterizes his work environment as neither terribly warm nor cool (57 per cent say 'average'), though Bankers and Private Industry members typically characterize it as somewhat warmer than the others. These are small differences (31 per cent and 32 per cent vs. 23 per cent and 26 per cent). The 'typical' Henley member (48 per cent) also characterizes his work environment as 'average' in the permissive-ness-strictness spectrum; the greatest proportion saying per-missive – 37 per cent – are the Private Industry members; the greatest proportion saying strict – 11 per cent – are the Bankers.

On conventionality, the 'typical' Henley ex-member also regards his work environment as 'average' (54 per cent). The Bankers have more saying 'conventional' (35 per cent) than do other members (this is the modal pattern for Bankers), and the Private Industry members have the highest proportion describing their work environment as 'unconventional' (23 per cent), this being their modal category.

The 'typical' ex-member's work environment is also seen by

him as 'average' (47 per cent) or united or divided continuum, though the Banker typically sees it as united (55 per cent). Most frequently mentioned as 'divided' were Private Industry and Nationalized Industry.

To sum up, as compared with the most general picture, the Private Industry member will typically feel his work environment to be more *insecure,* but more *exciting, warm,* and *permissive;* the typical Banker will be likely to feel that his work environment is more *secure, united,* and *conventional;* the typical Nationalized Industry man will feel that his work environment is more *exciting;* Public Sector members are likely to feel that their work environment is more *secure* but less *permissive* than the others.

JOB SATISFACTION

How does this relate to job satisfaction? We asked members how satisfied they were with their jobs prior to going to Henley, and how satisfied they were at the time of being surveyed. The typical member was and still is *moderately satisfied* with his job. Bankers and Public Sector members showed the greatest before/after increase in 'very satisfied' responses. Private Sector members diminished their 'very satisfied' proportions and increased their 'dissatisfied' proportions, while for all the rest the proportions indicating 'dissatisfied' decreased. *Table 18* shows the pattern:

TABLE 18 *Job Satisfaction: Pre- and Post-Henley*
(Percentages)

	PI		B		NI		PS	
	Pre-Henley	Post-Henley	Pre-Henley	Post-Henley	Pre-Henley	Post-Henley	Pre-Henley	Post-Henley
Very satisfied	33	29	34	41	29	31	38	41
Moderately satisfied	45	46	54	49	55	57	45	49
Moderately dissatisfied	16	19	11	7	13	10	11	5
Very dissatisfied	4	3	0	1	0	2	2	1
N =	(300)		(82)		(87)		(103)	

Weighting these responses 2 for very satisfied, 1 for moderately satisfied, −1 for moderately dissatisfied, and −2 for very dissatisfied, the net gain was greatest for Public Sector people (18)

with Bankers second (11), Nationalized Industry (6), and Private
Industry people showing a net loss in overall satisfaction (−11).

The 'typical' Henley ex-member following the course tends to
spend more time on his work and less time with his family than
previously. There is a slight overall tendency for leisure to decrease and for participation in organized community or public
service activities to increase. These changes are accompaniments
of advancement to more demanding posts, and in some instances
to posts that engage the manager in the firm's relationships with
the community.

Ex-members were asked to characterize their feelings about their
work. The two extremes were 'pride and fulfilment' and 'rage and
despair'. For each, the ex-member was asked how often he felt that
way. Typically, the Henley ex-member feels more 'pride and
fulfilment' than 'rage and despair' in his work, with the typical
Banker showing more 'pride and fulfilment' and less 'rage and
despair' than the others. The Public Sector member tends to feel,
like the Banker, low 'rage and despair' but he does not tend as
much to feel 'pride and fulfilment' at work. The Private Sector
member tends to feel least 'pride and fulfilment' and most 'rage
and despair' relative to the others.

MANAGEMENT PHILOSOPHY

Eighteen propositions were presented to members, and they were
asked to indicate their views by circling 'strongly agree', 'mildly
agree', 'mildly disagree', or 'strongly disagree'.* When the responses are broken down into the basic dichotomy of agreement/
disagreement, it is clear that there are three sorts of response
patterns (see *Table 19*): one grouping of seven items with which
there is overwhelming agreement – and thus we may say that the
'typical' Henley man agrees with these; a second grouping of three
with which there is overwhelming disagreement – and thus the
'typical' Henley men disagrees; and a third grouping of eight
where nearly half agree and nearly half disagree i.e. within 5 per
cent of 50/50, so that there is *no 'typical' Henley member philosophy*
but two contrasting viewpoints.

Several things are interesting in the overall pattern of response
to these items of management philosophy. First, there is a very

* A number of these items are adapted from a study by E. Schein (1967) of
changes in philosophy under the impact of a training programme in America.
Comparisons, where possible, will be drawn below.

TABLE 19 *Management Philosophy and the Ex-Henley Member*
(Figures in parentheses are overall percentages agreeing)

'Typical' ex-Henley member agrees	*'Typical' ex-Henley member disagrees*	*Views are split*
'The most important skill for managers in future is planning and controlling change.' (93)	'Most managerial jobs require a person to compromise with his moral standards.' (27)	'The man who gets ahead is the man who knows the right people.' (46)
'Most workers are capable of taking more responsibility.' (86)	'Most people who rise to the top find that they are less happy than when they were in more junior posts.' (31)	'The quality of individual decisions is generally higher than the quality of group decisions.' (54)
'Top managers are willing to take decisions that hurt others.' (86)	'The most important objective of an organization is to facilitate the development of its employees as individuals.' (32)	'The burdens of senior posts outbalance the rewards.' (47)
'A clearcut hierarchy of authority and responsibility is the cornerstone of a well-functioning organization.' (84)		'A young man who is aiming for a top post should be careful in selecting a wife to make sure she will fit into his career plans.' (54)
'In management decisions the human factor is at least as important as the economic factor.' (85)		'The average worker prefers to avoid responsibility, has little ambition, and above all wants security.' (55)
'The same personal qualities are required of the man at the top whether he is running an industrial organization, a bank or a ministry.' (85)		'There are many sound principles of management that should not be changed, even if economic and technological conditions require that they be modified.' (51)
'Too much of most senior managers' energy goes into work, to the detriment of other aspects of living.' (81)		'It is the tough, driving impersonal man who gets to the top.' (48)
		'It is more important than ever today that the man on the top should be a bold leader more than a skilled administrator.' (47)

high degree of uniformity of attitudes among the members from different sectors. Where there are differences, they tend to be within a range of 10 per cent. The differences existing make good sense in terms of the differences between the sectors as generally understood and as expressed in the patterns of response of the members to other questions about the characteristics of their work. For example, the Public Sector members (who, as indicated above, see themselves as 'idealistic') feel less than others that managers have to compromise their moral standards in their work. The Public Sector men typically agree more than the Private Sector members with the proposition that 'the human factor' is as important as 'the economic factor' in management decisions and so on. For one of the 'tradition-mindedness' items – there are many sound principles of management that should not be changed – Private Sector members showed less inclination to agree (48 per cent) than did Public Sector members (56 per cent).

For most elements of management philosophy the Public Sector and the Private Sector were most in contrast with one another, with the others in between, but there are some items in which they resemble one another. This is not necessarily by virtue of having the same viewpoint; rather it is by virtue of the fact that they both disagree with a proposition. Perhaps the best example of this is the proposition that the same qualities are required of top managers regardless of organization. Bankers agree most with this (90 per cent) while both Public and Private Sector members show somewhat less agreement (83 per cent and 82 per cent).*

* Comparing relevant selected items on management philosophy with Schein's findings on American managers (Schein, 1967), fragmentary observations of a tentative kind may be made. The item on 'compromise of moral standards' is like one that is a part of Schein's 'general cynicism scale'. Eighteen per cent of his control group of ordinary business managers agreed with this, and about a quarter of his academic types (Sloan Fellows and MIT graduates and faculty). There is a rough correspondence with the Henley members' response to their slightly differently worded statement. Overall, about a quarter of the Henley men agreed, but in this instance the business managers agree *more,* and the Public Sector people less. The British Public Sector people were talking about their own jobs, whereas in the American sample the academics were talking about the jobs of managers outside in business reflecting a possible negative stereotyping effect.

From among his 'general management theory' items, we adapted two – the one on 'clearcut hierarchy' and the one on 'many sound principles . . . that should not be changed'. These are both meant to tap tradition-mindedness. Henley managers corresponded to the control group of American executives that Schein studied: 88 per cent of Schein's businessmen agreed with the first proposition; 58 per cent with the second. Schein's MIT faculty showed a much lower percentage than the businessmen, on the first proposition, and a bit lower

CAREER VALUES

Though our questions on management philosophy were geared only to present attitudes, we asked ex-members to rank eight career values in order of importance to them personally, first as they recalled them to have been prior to Henley, and second as they now felt them to be. The eight career values were drawn from a similar question used by Moment at the Harvard Business School with members of the Advanced Management Training Program (Moment, 1966). The replies ranked as shown in *Table 20*.

TABLE 20 *Eight Career Values: Rank Order Pre- and Post-Henley**

	Pre-Henley	Post-Henley
Opportunity to show what I can accomplish	1	1
Intellectual problem-solving	2	2
Interesting job, minimum disturbance	3	5
Stable, secure future	4	6
Freedom from supervision	5	4
Opportunity to be creative	6	7
Work with people	7	3
Helpful to other people	8	8

* The mean scores show that these differences, while interesting, are not significantly different statistically. Responses also showed a greater spread in the Post-Henley scores, indicating a tendency to 'individualize' the responses, making them more heterogeneous. This seems to indicate that whatever 'party line' there may have been on career values was in the outer world of the organizations, not in the Henley course.

on the second. Interestingly, Henley ex-members in the Private Sector corresponded more to the MIT faculty levels for the second proposition than they did to the American businessmen, whose responses more closely approximated to the British Public Sector types.

Another somewhat comparable item is one of Schein's 'attitudes towards people and groups'. Over half of the Henley ex-members agree that 'the average worker in industry prefers to avoid responsibility, has little ambition, and wants security above all', as compared with 44 per cent of the American control group of business executives and 30 per cent of the MIT faculty. As in the American samples, the men actually in industry agree with this proposition more than those only theoretically or abstractly concerned. The Henley Private Sector businessmen agreed 59 per cent of the time, compared with 46 per cent of the Public Sector members.

Though the data are fragmentary, they lend empirical support to the impression that British managers more frequently prefer clear hierarchies of authority and have less positive images of the workers' motivations than do their American counterparts. However, it is also impressive that, by and large, there is a fairly high degree of correspondence between the two groups in many of the elements of management philosophy. This corroborates the findings of Haire and his colleagues (Haire *et al.*, 1966).

'Opportunity to show what I can accomplish' and 'intellectual problem-solving' were the career values most frequently ranked at the top by Henley men, both before and after the course. The most conspicuous change, overall, was in the wish to 'work with people rather than things or ideas'. If one thinks of the list as a top cluster of three, a bottom cluster of three, and two in between, the value of 'work with people' rose dramatically from the bottom cluster to the top one. The desire to be 'helpful to people' remained at the bottom, and the wish for a 'stable secure future' moved down into the bottom cluster of three, along with 'creativity' and 'helpfulness'.*

DEVELOPMENT FOLLOWING HENLEY

As we have already indicated, the transition from Henley back into the member's organization was often an unexpectedly complex process. While many of the members were going to new jobs within their organization, and saw the Henley experience as a directly relevant preparatory event, individual experience varied considerably in this. Even for the 10 per cent who indicated that they felt that the course had direct relevance, the process of applying their new insights was not uniformly smooth. The following comments illustrate this problem, which, though relatively infrequent in its intense form, seems fairly widespread as an element in the post-training situation:

> 'The course helped me to clarify my ideas about what is wrong in the organization in which I work. It is frustrating not to be in a position where I can do anything about them . . .'

* The top three values are the same for Harvard and Henley managers following the course – to 'show what I can accomplish', to 'use intellectual problem-solving abilities', and to 'work with people'. Then the differences emerge. The Harvard people next rank 'an opportunity to be creative' and 'an opportunity to be helpful to other people', with the more 'security-orientated' items at the bottom. The Henley members – probably reflecting British managers generally – rate the security items 'stable and secure future', 'freedom from supervision', and 'minimum disturbance' higher than the creativity and helpfulness items. 'Creativity', as will be indicated below, is a value that is markedly different for those who developed a great deal at Henley and for the rest. The former moved it upward into their *second* position, while the non-developers or limited developers kept it in their bottom cluster.

Comparisons like these must be taken cautiously because of the limitations of the instrument and of the statistical patterning of response, but they are suggestive. Also interesting, in looking at the breakdowns by organization, is the place of the Bankers in relation to other kinds of manager. In the American sample the Bankers resemble the other business managers very closely. In the British sample they are different, giving even higher value to the security items, and placing a correspondingly lower emphasis on intellectual problem-solving.

'. . . frustration at not being able to apply the contents significantly.'

'. . . in establishing standards of management performance which it is particularly difficult to get accepted in my present company . . .'

'. . . the frustration resulting from the reluctance of some more senior officers to accept some of the techniques learned on the course which could be applied to our own organization.'

'. . . I can [now] see mistakes in the organization and control of my company, and I am alarmed . . .'

One man indicated that his boss had expected him to change even more than he had, and another admitted that he felt some surprise that the firm had not changed more while he was away undergoing what he felt to be rather profound changes in himself. In some cases, the changes in the member and in the firm were felt to be in opposite directions, making for new incompatibilities:

'While I was on [the course] the situation in my company deteriorated to such an extent that for some time afterwards I regretted being away.'

'. . . I found that an absence of three months had substantially altered my job relations to other staff . . .'

'. . . It took me away from my factory at a critical time and I found it difficult to get back into line . . . because of a sudden change in top-line control while I was at Henley.'

These are minority experiences, and represent possible dangers to be watched out for rather than the general pattern. The challenges faced by these people are somewhat different from the mainstream of challenges, which correspond fairly closely to the role-characteristics of senior managers towards which the College's course is directed. Therefore it is not surprising that their response patterns are different as well. Two such variant patterns – displaced development and diverted development – will be mentioned:

Displaced Development refers to the pattern in which the man, sensing frustrations in his work situation of the kind described, chooses to develop his new capacities outside the work situation. Examples of this are the man who, feeling frustrated at not being able to find scope for his newly awakened managerial abilities in his organization, turned to community activities and began organizing and administering a range of community associations. Another man, who clashed over management policy with his boss after taking the course, lost out, and was sacked. In his next job he determined not to take work so seriously, and put most of his energies into home and family life, seeing work as too much of a 'rat race' and 'dog-eat-dog' situation.

Diverted Development refers to the pattern in which the individual felt blocked or frustrated as in the previous pattern, but rather than de-emphasizing work and career as a channel for personal development in favour of some other form of activity, instead sought a new employer. As we have indicated, this is mainly a Private Sector pattern. The data suggest that where an ex-member encounters frustrations in exercising his developing capacities following Henley, and where he does not divert his development into a new channel e.g. by changing employers, his dissatisfaction rises.

These patterns which are minority patterns, have a place nevertheless in the overall picture of career development patterning. In the chapters that follow the major patterns will be described through the use of a more complex form of analysis which aims to show how these various elements of background, attitude, and career performance fit together.

Managers and their Careers

PART THREE

Managers and their Careers

Chapter 8 · Types of Managerial Development Pattern

The development of a typology of managers is a major goal of research in this field. The utility of such a typology is both descriptive, in the sense of classifying the wide range of managerial jobs and styles one observes, and predictive, in the sense of indicating more accurately which managers are likely to be capable of development in mid-career and which not.

One of the most striking findings of some recent research on managers is that there is no single pattern of managerial development: there are several. Employing organizations are likely to benefit by recognizing this diversity which exists within all of them. While it is a familiar enough observation that men may rise to the top of organizations through a variety of functional channels – personnel, finance, production, etc. – it is less well understood how differences of orientation to the organization yield contrasting styles or strategies of career development that may cut across these formal classifications.

There are many combinations which can produce effective partnerships, management teams, boards, and so on. Barna summarized the research consensus as follows:

'The attributes which characterise the most suitable businessman have scarcely been explored by research, but certain conclusions are beginning to emerge. First the personality of the successful businessman does not conform to any single pattern but shows great variation. Indeed, a successful firm appears to contain people of differing personality who stimulate and correct one another. Secondly, attitudes as well as abilities are important, and in many instances overwhelmingly so . . . Thirdly, the personal characteristics and attitudes which make for success in one line of business are not the same as those required for another . . . Fourthly, the qualities required are only partly inborn. In part they are the result of training and experience . . . Fifthly, a few people in key positions are capable of transforming the outlook and efficiency of a large organisation . . . The successful businessman recognises social wants and he creates new means, or more efficient means, to satisfy them. He is orientated towards his market and not towards his product, his techniques of production, or his organisation' (Barna, 1962).

Barna's general observations on typologies are borne out by more recent research by such people as Schein (1965), who indicates the complexity of career development moves and orientations as they affect aspirations and performance, and Jerkedal (1968), whose findings indicate the importance of the fit between the individual manager and his organization as a determinant of performance. Jerkedal's conclusions are partly derived inferentially, since he finds less correlation than expected between changes under the impact of a management training programme much like that at Henley and personality factors alone – e.g. attitude set, intelligence, flexibility. He advocates evaluation in terms of the specific organizational goals. Hesseling's (1968) work reinforces this and adds an observation on the importance of considering age as a variable. Perhaps a clearer statement of the need to study the personal qualities which are developed in a training programme, as they find expression subsequently, is reported in the studies described by House (1968). House points out that while McClelland and Miner have shown that leadership training programmes increase social skills and capacities of individuals to develop managerial competence within bureaucratic organizations, there are some findings (Fleishman, Harris, and Burtt, 1955) that indicate dysfunctional consequences of leadership training. We have already indicated this sort of thing in the previous chapter, when we pointed out that for some ex-members their training meant an increase in frustration and dissatisfaction, and that, for those unable to deal with this within themselves or their organizations, diverted or displaced development patterns might result.

The relevance of these observations and many more for the point of view we are presenting here is that we would argue for a new kind of typology – one based not only on personality types (e.g. introverts – extraverts; thrusters – sleepers; authoritarians – democrats) or only on social and environmental factors (e.g. social class of origin, type of organization) etc. Each of these typologies and others that can be derived explain a certain amount of the pattern and leave a good deal unexplained. There is much to indicate that a typology ought to be not only multidimensional, but also diachronic, i.e. based on criteria taken through time.

A managerial type based solely on response to training may not encompass differences in subsequent adjustment to the job. A type based on early history, education, type of job experience, and firm might not predict as much of subsequent behaviour as it might if some indication of reaction to the programme were included.

We propose, therefore, to develop a typology of managers that has two criteria: first, it must relate to the central issue of the research, namely development at mid-career; second, it must make sense in terms of recognizable career patterns on all relevant dimensions through time.

DEVELOPMENT AT MID-LIFE

Consider first some of the issues relating to development at mid-life.

An examination of the literature shows that there is very little by way of either detailed research or theory that contributes to the understanding of the processes with which we are concerned. Most of such research as there is on the period of life which interests us is 'off target' in one sense or another. Most of the theory, for example, pertains to earlier life stages where there is an assumption of biological forces of development acting as the moving focus around which reorganizations occur as the individual develops. Most of the research of a careful empirical kind relating to life processes at mid-life, i.e. from 35 onwards, documents the progressive decline in psychological as well as biological powers. This work, whether based on experimental methods (e.g. Welford et al., 1963; Talland, 1963; Bondy, 1966) or on clinical methods rigorously applied (Neugarten et al., 1964), indicates a general decline with ageing. Many of the capacities specifically associated with the managerial role – scanning printed materials, vigilance, memory, speed, accuracy – are negatively correlated with the ageing process. Many of the precise skills which are called more than ever into heavy demand by senior roles are in a state of gradual decline from the late thirties or early forties. Most of the writings on this issue, other than the more conceptual treatises such as those included in Soddy's cross-cultural mental health symposium, Men in Middle Life (Soddy, 1967), do not systematically relate the process to external demands of social roles, particularly the kinds of changes in roles that are normally expected at this time. Belbin and associates (e.g. Belbin, 1958; Belbin & Downs, 1964) have concentrated on the issue of retraining persons who, in middle age, are seen as beings if not on the decline, at least as rather set in their ways. They have emphasized the issue of unlearning set ways as a prerequisite in making new learning possible, and advocate 'activity training' methods.

In another tradition, the importance of unlearning – or as Schein puts it (following Lewin) 'unfreezing' – established attitudes as a condition for personal development in adulthood has been emphasized by the devotees of the T-group method (Schein & Bennis, 1965). This type of group resembles the syndicate in being leaderless, and the method utilizes group dynamics but concentrates on the problem of fostering insight into one's personal style of relationships without providing a group task directly related to the specific work roles of the participants. Schein emphasizes, in this, the importance of removing the individual from his normal role and environment with their constraints and pressures. Considerable evidence is accumulating about the effectiveness and utility of this kind of group process for the purpose described, and particularly among people of the middle age-groups (Schein & Bennis, 1965; Bradford et al., 1964).

From the psychoanalytic tradition, a relevant point of view is advanced by Jaques, and a variant of it by Erikson. Jaques argues that at mid-life there is a developmental crisis which reactivates an earlier 'depressive' dilemma of personality development. According to how the earlier crisis was resolved and what resources are available in dealing with the reawakening of it in mid-life, the individual may enter a period of relative stagnation from a creative point of view (i.e. revert to a depressive 'position') or he may undergo a creative renaissance. Jaques (1965) demonstrates these two possible outcomes in the works of great creative artists and writers, comparing their productivity prior to the mid-life crisis, at, say the age of forty, with their situation after this age. Erikson's formulation is similar in deriving from psychoanalytic conceptions of the nature of personality development through a period of successive crises, the resolution of each of which is determined in part by the modes of resolution of prior dilemmas. On the other hand, he assigns a somewhat different emphasis to the dynamics of the particular life-cycle crises which people at mid-life may be experiencing. In moving through these periods and working through the process that Maslow (1962) refers to as 'self-actualization', the individual has to come to grips with somewhat different focal preoccupations at different stages. After having worked through, in some degree, the earlier issues of 'basic trust', 'identity', and 'intimacy', men in the Henley age-group come to grips with issues of 'generativity', which may be spurred, as Jaques suggests, by an awareness of death and the depressive force that this awareness may entail. Erikson goes on to add later stages of life in which there is a greater preoccupation with wisdom and justice. His actual investigations, however, have tended to concentrate more on the earlier phase of 'identity', and we have little to tell us what factors may be assigned weight in the social environment for harnessing the forces of generativity and wisdom so important for the senior manager's role, particularly when seen as a counter-weight to the actual biological forces of decline (Erikson, 1968).

The view set forth by Erikson, which is echoed in a larger framework by the discussants in the Soddy symposium, while very congenial to our way of thinking, is exceedingly difficult to apply in a piece of empirical research. Though our own work may be seen as an effort in this direction, it is far from what might be required by way of rigour or definitiveness. It is merely suggestive. Be this as it may, how can the perspective be stated, and the evidence contributing to its elucidation set forth?

The perspective we would hold is that men at the age drawn upon by Henley are concerned with issues of generativity, by which we mean how they can be most effective in the exercise of their personal capacities. They wish, in varying degrees, to develop themselves and to take on roles of greater responsibility and challenge. This may be due to an inner drive of ambition, a counter depressive reaction to awareness of impending death, conflicts associated with still unresolved issues from earlier stages, or whatever. Some of it may be thrust upon the individual by his superiors and he may enter into a new experience which has developmental consequences relatively passively or even reluctantly. Such individuals may nevertheless in favourable circumstances undergo an 'awakening' of personal interest in developing and in undergoing some degree of change.

The important central conception here is one of *crisis*. It is hypothesized that unless there is a sense of crisis – some kind of important turning point – development is much less likely to occur. The actual studies of life crises have approached the issue from three perspectives, all of which are present in some degree in the population studied. One approach, largely used by clinicians, selects crises that are relatively unexpected and unwanted and have the character of a traumatic unsettlement for the individual – disasters, surgical operations, accidents, bereavement (Lindemann, 1944; Caplan, 1964; Tyhurst, 1958; Janis, 1958). For some men, being selected to go to Henley may have a faint element of this in it, since it unsettles many of their routines in life and they go more or less in spite of their own wishes. A second approach to the study of crisis is one which emphasizes the developmental potential of ordinary role transitions – getting married, graduating from university, being promoted to a new type of job (Rapoport, 1963). This conception is very close to the Henley one. As members ideally are moving into more senior general management roles there arises the need to reorganize their ways of thinking and behaving. The third approach, exemplified by Jaques's and Erikson's frameworks, emphasizes the inner workings of the biologically maturing person, with its necessary psychological concomitants. The most studied of these sorts of crisis are the early ones – of childhood and adolescence. However, that such a crisis occurs at mid-life is now generally accepted. Henley members are all involved in the psychobiological types of crisis by virtue of the age-group from which they are recruited, though they may differ in terms of how central this crisis is to them at the actual point of coming to Henley. What is not well understood are the conditions which make for different kinds of outcome to the mid-life crisis. Jaques's study of the creative products of gifted artists gives some insight into the problem. We are concerned here with the kind of outcome which contributes to the development of the man's occupational competence as a senior manager.

We now move to the second criterion governing our typology of managers, namely how to discover the types of empirically valid developmental pattern observable in managers at this stage.

THE METHODS FOR CONSTRUCTING A TYPOLOGY OF DEVELOPMENT PATTERNS

The types are constructed from items of information in the survey that are intercorrelated. From all the possible types, we are concerned with those which are linked to development as a manager. The variables highly correlated with perceived development are shown in *Table 21*.

TABLE 21 Correlates of Perceived Development

(Variable reference number in parenthesis)*

	As both Person and Manager	As Manager Only	As Person Only
Post-Henley Career	Henley experience found 'directly relevant' to job (63)	'More involvement with others from different specialisms' (80) Many changes of employer (67) Job change from specialist function to general (272)	Deals with problems by 'self-expression' (270) 'Work environment 'insecure' (99) 'Work problems dealt with by strong action by man on top' (97)
Henley Experience	Actually got from Henley: 'Increased understanding of relations between own organization and the environment' (26) 'Increased understanding of self' (29) 'Ability to handle new situations' (28) Aspect of Henley useful: 'personal development' (41) Most valuable staff contribution *not* 'none of above' (50) While at Henley 'worked hard' (57)	Initially wanted: 'Increased understanding of manager's role' (16) Actually got: 'Increased understanding of manager's role' (25) Initially wanted: 'Improved ability to work with others from different organizations' (18) Actually got: 'new knowledge' (30) Values 'syndicate method' (32) Values 'career advice' (54) Values 'self-appraisal' (52)	Initially wanted: 'new knowledge' (21) Actually got: 'Increased ability to work with others with different outlook' (27)
Pre-Henley Attitudes or Experiences	Main reason: 'assess potential' (3) Main reason: 'earmarked' (6) Initial reaction: 'enthusiastic' (13) Main reasons *not* 'pure chance' (2)	Main reason: 'Fill in areas of weakness' (4) Secondary reason *not* 'sabbatical' (7)	
Personal Characteristics	Wife's education: 'attended technical college' (185) Self-description: 'moody' (212)	Self-description: *not* 'cautious' (191) 'ambitious' (188) 'rebellious' (216) 'competitive' (192)	Father did *not* work for local authority (123) Pre-Henley 'Private Sector' (273) Pre-Henley employer *not* Public Sector (276)
Early Background		Mother's satisfaction: 'don't know' (130)	Main academic interest in school 'natural sciences' (152) Main academic interest in school 'engineering and applied sciences' (154)

* (All variables listed have coefficients of correlation ·25 or better. See Technical Appendix I.)

The information in the survey was coded into a total of 300 items. A correlational matrix was formed on the basis of correlations between each item and all the others. From this, a method of analysis based on the McQuitty Hierarchical Linkage technique was employed (McQuitty, 1960). Forty clusters were delineated. Of the forty, thirteen contained variables correlated with development as a manager or development as a person or both. The thirteen clusters were named as follows:

1 Ambitious/Creative
2 Restless/Hard-driving
3 Environment-oriented
4 Accommodating
5 Uncritical
6 Dogged
7 Humanistic
8 Conflicted
9 Venturesome
10 Manipulative
11 Fulfilled
12 Alienated
13 Climbing

The clusters were used as a basis for developing scales on which individuals were rated, and to ensure that none of the scales were superfluous the relationships among the scores were first studied by constructing an intercorrelational matrix of the scale scores. The intercluster correlational matrix is shown in *Table 22*.

The low level of intercorrelation is expected, given the fact that the clusters were arrived at by the McQuitty method, which aims precisely at producing separate clusters.

None of the clusters are sufficiently intercorrelated to make it obvious which may be grouped together, yet there are sufficient low-level correlations to make it desirable to attempt a further reduction of variance. Accordingly, a factor analysis was performed.

FACTOR ANALYSIS

The thirteen clusters related to development represent trait complexes which may be combined in a large number of different

TABLE 22 *Henley Study: Interchuster Correlation Matrix*

	1	2	3	4	5	6	7	8	9	10	11	12	13
1 Ambitious/ Creative													
2 Restless/Hard- driving	0·126												
3 Environmental	0·145	0·018											
4 Accommodating	0·080	0·032	0·026										
5 Uncritical	0·034	−0·009	−0·009	−0·002									
6 Dogged	−0·034	0·005	0·050	0·006	0·049								
7 Humanistic	0·015	0·112	−0·004	0·067	0·000	−0·010							
8 Conflicted	0·148	0·089	0·054	0·026	0·031	−0·089	0·033						
9 Venturesome	0·177	0·031	−0·030	−0·045	−0·015	−0·050	−0·013	0·121					
10 Manipulative	0·032	0·049	0·057	−0·030	0·023	0·040	−0·113	0·020	0·120				
11 Fulfilled	−0·048	−0·137	0·049	−0·120	0·039	0·034	−0·045	−0·019	−0·083	−0·077			
12 Alienated	0·035	0·021	0·022	−0·047	0·034	0·007	−0·045	−0·063	−0·092	0·037	0·042		
13 Climbing	0·114	0·008	0·135	0·045	0·110	−0·017	−0·015	−0·036	0·068	−0·065	0·080	−0·012	

ways. If one seeks to use clusters as a basis for 'typing' individuals and their careers, one would prefer a smaller number of traits which overlap as little as possible.

To this end, we scored individuals on the scales derived from each of the thirteen clusters and performed a principal-components form of factor analysis, with varimax rotation. Four factors emerged based on the thirteen clusters. The factors comprise a nexus of traits – some personal, some environmental – and they group together elements through a member's entire life career. The point of this is to view a man *in* his career as a single complex rather than, as is more conventionally done, to separate the men into different personality types, or social or managerial types, and then relate the types to selected dependent variables such as re-action to the course or subsequent career pattern.

The following matrix shows the interrelationships among the thirteen cluster scales, according to four major factors:

TABLE 23 *Principal Components Analysis: Orthogonal Factor Matrix*

(Varimax)

Cluster		I	II	III	IV
1	(Ambitious/Creative)	·3997	·1131	·0927	·0582
2	(Restless/Hard-driving)	·2040	—·1310	·1277	·1393
3	(Environment-oriented)	·1281	·1694	·0608	·2191
4	(Accommodating)	·1312	—·0182	·2069	—·0480
5	(Uncritical)	·0139	·1925	—·0855	·0544
6	(Dogged)	·0770	·0157	—·0488	·1549
7	(Humanistic)	·0240	—·0706	·3433	—·0175
8	(Conflicted)	·2816	·0080	·0357	—·0643
9	(Venturesome)	·3512	—·0190	—·0891	—·1878
10	(Manipulative)	·1968	—·1496	—·2614	·1244
11	(Fulfilled)	·1773	·2985	—·0856	·0383
12	(Alienated)	·0277	·0445	—·0557	·2636
13	(Climbing)	·1098	·3398	·0863	·0334

Factor I accounts for the greatest amount of the variance and 'loads' most heavily on cluster 1 (Ambitious/Creative), 9 (Venture-some), 8 (Conflicted) and 2 (Restless/Hard-driving). Because of the characteristics of these clusters – which will be described in the next chapter – we term this pattern *Metamorphic*. This term, based on biological analogy, suggests a process of transformation in manager–environment relations. The developmental process, where it occurs in members scoring high on this factor, is one of transformation of a fundamental kind.

Factor II, which accounts for the second greatest amount of variance, loads most heavily on cluster 13 (Climbing), cluster 11 (Fulfilled), and cluster 5 (Uncritical). The impression this communicates is one of an orderly advance within an organizational structure which is fundamentally accepted as given and with which the manager lives quite happily. We term this type of developmental pattern *Incremental*, because it seems to show a growth pattern which is cumulative, advancing stepwise without major transformations.

Factor III loads most heavily on cluster 7 (Humanistic), negatively on cluster 10 (i.e. *not* Manipulative) and cluster 4 (Accommodating). This is a factor which may be termed *Humanistic* because it conveys the sense of 'people-oriented' and *un*-ruthless attitudes and behaviours.

Factor IV loads most heavily on cluster 12 (Alienated), and cluster 3 (Environment-oriented). As this conveys the impression of the sort of manager who prefers to work at the periphery of his organization, perhaps feeling unhappy with many elements of the internal structure and functioning of the organization and preferring to interact with people from other organizations, we term this the *Tangential* factor, recognizing that many managers may develop at the edges of their organizations, being perhaps rebellious or even antagonistic towards things going on at the centre. This and the other factors will be discussed in the following chapters.

When the clusters were used as scales by developing a scoring system for the component variables, a correlational analysis was done which showed that six of the thirteen clusters were correlated with a sense of having developed as a manager as a consequence of Henley (variable 61). These six are:

Cluster 1   Ambitious/Creative (correlation coefficient ·27)
Cluster 3   Restless/Hard-driving (correlation coefficient ·23)
Cluster 5   Uncritical (correlation coefficient ·11)
Cluster 6   Dogged (correlation coefficient ·16)
Cluster 8   Conflicted (correlation cofficient ·11)
Cluster 13 Climbing (correlation coefficient ·14)

These are the clusters that load very heavily on factor I (Metamorphic), factor II (Incremental), and factor IV (Tangential).

It is not surprising, therefore, to find when one scores the individuals for the factor scores, and correlates factor scores with development as a manager, that only factors I, II, and IV correlate with development as a manager. This is summarized in *Table 24*.

TABLE 24 *Coefficients of Correlation of Development as a Manager with Factor Scores*

Factor	Correlation Coefficients
I	·23
II	·20
III	·01
IV	·15

Factor III, the Humanistic factor, relates to development as a person but *not* as a manager. As development as a manager is central to this work, we shall give a detailed account of factors I, II, and IV in the next three chapters, devoting a chapter to each factor. As factor III is of considerable interest in itself, however, we shall give a brief account of it, displaying the clusters that load most heavily on this factor and discussing the type of manager who scores high or low on it. In addition to its intrinsic interest, this will provide an indication of how one reads cluster scores and how one thinks about factor scores, so that the next three chapters may be somewhat easier going. First a note on how to read the clusters.

A note on how to read the clusters

The clusters represent groupings of highly intercorrelated variables. The McQuitty Hierarchical Linkage method of developing these clusters is a relatively simple way of grouping the intercorrelated variables without making too many assumptions about their properties. Beginning with any given variable, the total array of available variables is scanned for the one most highly correlated with it. The two are shown as linked at the first level of closeness, no matter what the actual correlation coefficient is, though where the coefficients become small the variables are not presented as clustering. Then the two most highly intercorrelated variables are combined and their mean scores used as a single score, whose correlations with all other variables are again scanned to form a second-order linkage. Once a given variable is used in its most highly correlated cluster, it is not used again in other clusters though it may, of course, be related to variables in other clusters less powerfully than to those in its own cluster.

Thus, one reads the cluster below as follows:

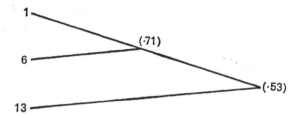

Variable 1 is most highly correlated with variable 6. The two of them together form a variable which is more highly correlated with variable 13 than with any other variables in the array.*

THE HUMANISTIC DEVELOPMENT PATTERN (FACTOR III)

As indicated, members who scored highly on this factor did not tend to feel that they developed as managers, whatever they may have felt about their personal development, which sets Factor III somewhat apart from the others. This is not to say that none of the members who scored highly on this factor felt that they developed as managers. Many did feel this, but the statistical tendency overall is for a high score on this factor to be irrelevant to the sense of managerial development. If a man scoring high on the Humanistic factor felt also that he developed very much as a manager it is probably because of other aspects of his attitudes, background, and behaviour, for example his level of ambition or his acceptance of and by the organization for a more senior role.

There are three clusters that predominate in this factor: The *Humanistic* cluster, the *negative* end of the *Manipulative* cluster (i.e. the un-manipulative), and the *Accommodating* cluster. These clusters, 7, 10, and 4, will be presented in that order.

---

* In the cluster diagrams, correlation coefficients will be shown in parenthesis. No signs will be shown on the diagrams, but the captions will be worded in such a way as to reflect the directions of the correlations. The types of correlation coefficient used are described in Appendix II.

The Humanistic Cluster

This is a 'people-oriented' cluster and fits well with the human resources (McGregor's Theory Y) approach to management. The cluster itself relates development as a manager and development as a person with variable 185 – wife attended technical college. The fact of having married a wife with some form of higher education seems to go along with an interest in persons and personal development, and this feature is correlated with the rather minority

Cluster 7 *Humanistic*

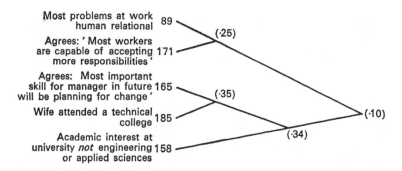

viewpoint of management philosophy that 'the most important objective in an organization is to facilitate the development of its employees as individuals'. This trait, when combined with others that make for success as a manager, is found to correlate with the increased tendency to delegate responsibility when there is a rise in status, and a corresponding increase in the time spent at home for family-oriented leisure activities, by contrast with the more general tendency to spend more and more time on work.

There is a tendency for this pattern to be associated with higher education (see *Table 25*).

This is a derivative, to some extent, of the tendency for more highly educated individuals to marry people of a similar educational level. However, the clustering with the other traits is a product of the relationship between higher education and general managerial and life values.

TABLE 25 *Education in Relation to Humanistic Orientation*

(Percentages scoring in each category)

	Graduates	Non-Graduates
Low scores (Quintiles 1 and 2)	19	38
Medium score (Quintile 3)	24	23
High scores (Quintiles 4 and 5)	57	39
TOTALS % =	100	100
N =	(72)	(503)

An analysis of the distribution of these scores by type of organization shows a tendency for Public and Private Sector managers to score higher than either Bankers or Nationalized Industry managers, particularly the latter. This is shown in *Table 26*.

TABLE 26 *Employing Organization in Relation to Humanistic Orientation*

(Percentage scores in each category)

	PI	B	NI	PS
Low scores (Quintiles 1 and 2)	36	30	48	27
Medium score (Quintile 3)	19	35	23	30
High scores (Quintiles 4 and 5)	44	36	29	44
TOTALS % =	99	101	100	101
N =	(300)	(82)	(87)	(103)

Given the heavy technological emphasis in the Nationalized Industries, and the tendency for technologists not to be 'people-oriented', this finding is consistent with a good deal of the literature on occupational values. Sales managers are highest in their scores

MCD—L

for this cluster, and research scientists followed by production managers lowest – also consistent with the general picture.

The Manipulative Cluster

People who score high on the Humanistic cluster tend to score low on the Manipulative cluster, and vice versa. As we are terming the factor as a whole the Humanistic pattern, this cluster must be interpreted in its obverse form. That is, people with a high score for the Manipulative cluster tend to have a low score on the Humanistic factor.

This is a small cluster of five variables, with one (154: main interest at school, engineering and applied sciences) correlated with development as a person.

Cluster 10 *Manipulative*

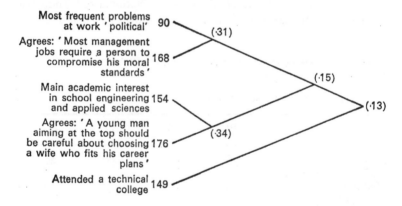

This cluster does not relate directly to development as a manager, though it is interesting to note that some members who had an early interest in engineering and applied sciences felt that they benefited as *persons* from having attended a course. The relationship between this variable and development as a manager seems to take the form of a U-shaped curve, with high and low scorers on the cluster showing a high frequency of feeling that they developed as managers while intermediate scorers are lower. These tend to be men who have since their early days been troubled by the problems people get into with one another, as indicated by their declared sensitivity to 'political' problems in their work environments. They have a rather cynical attitude toward their careers, feeling that advance means compromise of moral standards and that if one wishes to advance one has to calculate on using everything at one's command to do so, even one's wife.

The highest 'Manipulative orientation' scores are found, as one might predict, among the Nationalized Industry members, with the Private Sector managers following them in second place. Forty nine per cent of the former and 44 per cent of the latter fall into the top two scoring quintiles, as compared with 27 per cent of Bankers and 28 per cent of Public Sector managers. Along the same line, the production managers show the highest scores, with sales and marketing men in second position, while accountants and general managers (often Civil Servants) are very low on this scale. The cluster scores show no relationship to age, but do relate to education. Those having no higher education tend to score highly on 'manipulativeness'; 39 per cent of those having no higher education, compared with 3 per cent of university graduates, are in the top quintile of scores on this cluster.

The Accommodating Cluster

This cluster relates to development through the correlation with two specific variables – main reason for being sent to Henley 'to

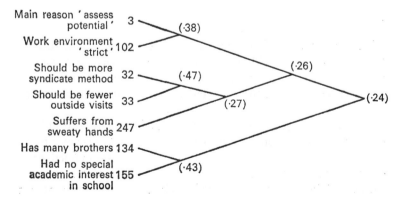

Cluster 4 *Accommodating*

assess my potential for senior management roles' and 'should be more syndicate work at Henley'. However, the overall cluster scores do not correlate significantly with development as a manager.

This is the sort of person who works in an environment which he sees as strict and where he feels to some extent on trial and uncertain of where he stands. This is important to him. He found that at Henley he could make a place for himself within the syndicates, which he heartily endorses as a method of work. He is the sort of person who takes his cues from the outside world, is not particularly self-propelled by inner drive as with many of the Metamorphic types, and a good deal of his energy goes into finding out where he stands with those in his environment and into staying in line. He shows symptoms of the stress that this conformism entails in his reports of suffering from 'sweaty hands'.

This is a pattern which scored very highly most frequently among sales managers – 60 per cent in the top two quintiles as compared with under 40 per cent for the other occupations and groups, but lower among Public Sector members than the others, though the differences here are not statistically significant. There is no relationship of Accommodating tendencies to the member's age. Members who had higher formal education and completed their courses of studies at university or technical college rather than leaving earlier did show significantly higher scores on this cluster scale than did others. Fifty six per cent of university graduates and 57 per cent of technical college graduates scored in the top two quintiles as compared with 40 per cent of university attenders who did not graduate and 37 per cent of non-attenders at institutions of higher education.

SUMMARY

We have sought to develop a typology of managers that reflects the reality of managerial personalities and careers as our questionnaire responses indicate them to be and is at the same time relevant to the central issue of the research: development as a manager at mid-career.

Through a process of correlational analysis, hierarchical linkage analysis to form clusters, and factorial analysis to discover principal components, a set of four types of manager was defined, each giving particularly heavy emphasis to a sub-set of the thirteen clusters of intercorrelated variables relating to development. Of the four factors – the Metamorphic Development Pattern, the Incremental Development Pattern, the Humanistic Development Pattern, and the Tangential Development Pattern – only the first, second, and fourth were found to correlate significantly with development as a manager. The third factor relates more to a sense of development as a person, but is not significantly related to development as a manager. Those individuals, comprising most of the group who felt that they developed as persons and as managers as well, are distinguished from the others by scoring highly on factors I, II, and IV.

Because of the wish to concentrate in particular detail on the three factors which correlate with development as a manager, they are set aside to be dealt with in the next three chapters. The fourth factor, the Humanistic, was briefly described in this chapter, but is not pursued further in this context.

Chapter 9 · The Metamorphic Development Pattern

Metamorphosis means literally 'transformation'. The biological sciences have provided descriptions of forms of life that develop though a process of transformation from one stage of life, or one form of existence, to another. In human development there are a number of examples which seem to parallel this type of development, though as with all analogies there are of course limitations. The most dramatic examples in the human sphere are probably those associated with what are known as 'conversion' experiences. These are found in religious and political life, and perhaps less frequently in the professional lives of managers and administrators. This does not mean that dramatic changes of belief, value, or behaviour pattern are lacking. Indeed, the point of designating this chapter and the factor it describes as the 'Metamorphic Development Pattern' suggests that there are sufficiently notable examples of major transformation among the Henley members as a consequence of their training to allow qualified usage of the designation. Indeed, this is the factor that accounts for the greatest amount of variance in the questionnaire responses, and one may infer from this that it reflects more than other patterns the experiences and concerns of Henley ex-members who consider that they have developed as managers – in so far as we can determine them from this type of survey instrument.

Perhaps it would be best to set forth the relevant clusters and some illustrative cases vignettes before going on to the question of exactly how one may use the notion of a metamorphosis as a major career pattern of members going through the College. Certainly it is the intention of the College to provide such a transformation where it is required. Are the members who show the highest scores in this factor the same sorts of people the College aims to assist in undergoing the transformations necessary to pass from middle to more senior managerial roles? We shall return to this after setting forth some of the findings.

Factor I is most heavily concerned with four clusters:

Cluster 1 the Ambitious/Creative cluster, which receives a weighting of ·39

Cluster 9 the Venturesome cluster, which receives a weighting of ·35

Cluster 8 the Conflicted cluster, which receives a weighting of ·28

Cluster 2 the Restless/Hard-driving cluster, which receives a weighting of ·20.

Other clusters that participate quite heavily in this factor, though they are more involved in other factors, are the Fulfilled (cluster 11, which is more deeply involved in factor II) and the Manipulative (cluster 10, which is more deeply involved negatively in factor III), and, to a lesser extent, the Accommodating and Environment-oriented clusters, both of which are more deeply involved in other factors, though they play a fairly active role in this pattern.

We shall first describe the clusters which are most heavily involved in this factor: clusters 1, 9, 8, and 2, and then give some vignettes of managers who show high scores in this factor and some who show low scores, so that what we are talking about may be given some substance.

The Ambitious/Creative Cluster

This is the sort of manager who sees himself as expressive and creative in dealing with challenges which confront him as his career develops. Members with many of these characteristics neither see themselves as concerned with security as a career value, nor do they enter or stay in work environments which they could consider dull. They are healthy and energetic and view positively the burdens of responsibility which tend to go with more senior positions.

The individual variables in the cluster which correlate with development are 13 ('enthusiastic' about being nominated to go to Henley) and 192 (self-description 'competitive'). When the cluster scores are used to rate individuals on the whole cluster, the correlation with development as a manager comes through dramatically, significant at the 1 per cent level.

The classification of individuals on this dimension also produces dramatic correlations with type of employing organization and with the type of occupational specialism the member had prior to

Cluster 1 *Ambitious /Creative*

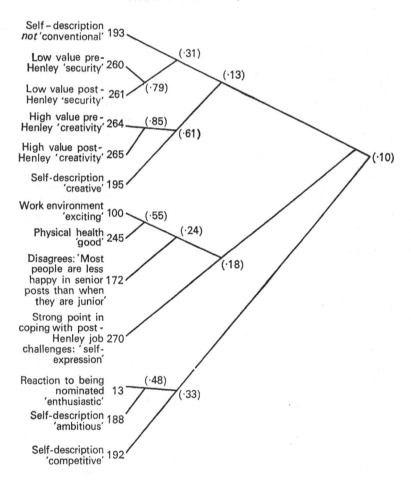

coming to Henley, but not with age or with educational level.* *Tables 27* and *28* show the patterns that correlate:

TABLE 27 *Employing Organization and Ambition/Creativity Scores*

(Percentages in each category)

Scores on Ambition/ Creativity	PI	B	NI	PS
(low) 1	13	21	15	29
2	16	30	17	22
3	24	12	28	15
4	17	18	15	17
(high) 5	30	18	25	17
TOTALS % =	100	99	100	100
N =	(300)	(82)	(87)	(103)

This table indicates that the high scorers on this dimension are to be found more frequently in the Private Sector than elsewhere, with Nationalized Industries second. Bankers and Public Sector managers are conspicuously lower scorers on this cluster of traits.

From these figures it would seem that the ambitious-creative pattern is one which is modal for Private Sector men, but the reverse for men in the Public Sector. Nationalized Industry men are squarely in the middle, and Bankers are more like Civil Servants in this dimension.

Managers coming from production and research are higher in this dimension, perhaps the former emphasizing the 'ambitious' part of the syndrome, and the latter the 'creative' part. Sales managers seem to be bimodal in this, with one large group about average, and another group very high in it. The accountants, too, are slightly bimodal, having an average peak, but with their second peak on the low end. Pre-Henley generalists, who tend to be Public Sector men on the whole, are low in this, as might be predicted from the previous table. The 'other' category is mixed (all

---

* In other words, men who score high in ambition/creativity are much more likely to be found in certain organizations than in others and more in certain occupational specialisms than in others. Age or educational level have little to do with it, except in the case of the very youngest group where there was found a rather high proportion of members who responded in the ambitious/ creative pattern; for all other groups the scores were randomly distributed.

other types: personnel, management services, military, etc.) and, as one would expect, distributes itself somewhat randomly.

TABLE 28 *Occupational Specialism and Ambitious/Creative Cluster Scores*

(Percentages in each category)

	Production	Research	Sales	Accountancy	General	Other
(low)						
1	11	16	7	21	25	22
2	17	21	11	16	23	31
3	22	15	32	29	13	24
4	17	15	19	19	20	7
5	32	34	31	16	19	16
(high)						
TOTALS % =	99	101	100	101	100	100
N = *	(149)	(62)	(81)	(58)	(171)	(55)

*The total sample is 4 larger here than in the previous table, from which the 4 Trade Union managers in the sample were omitted, the group being too small in number to form a separate organization. They are included here in the residual category of 'other'. Incidentally, the Trade Unionists split on this, with two in the highly ambitious/creative categories and two at the other end of the scale.

The Venturesome Cluster

It would seem that people who score high in this dimension are particularly talented and high-flying individuals who take risks which may carry them into insecure situations. The staff at Henley see this sort of person as a 'top' manager and they seem to be similarly regarded in their employing organizations, where they are highly rewarded financially and where they are satisfied, even where there is insecurity in their positions.

This cluster, used to scale individuals, does not produce a significant correlation with a sense of development at Henley as a manager. The three variables which link this cluster to development (99, 273, and 276) are all correlated with a sense of development as a person, but not as a manager. This may be because so many of these men are high-flyers whose mettle has already been tested in their jobs and who do not feel that Henley provides them with this sort of benefit.

There is a strong tendency for members with high scores in the Venturesome pattern to come from the Private Sector, and to have come up from production or sales specialities. Younger

Cluster 9 *Venturesome*

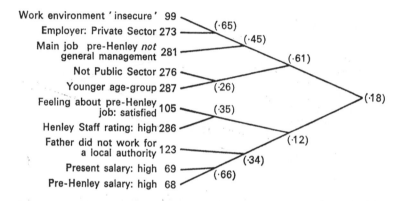

Work environment 'insecure' 99
Employer: Private Sector 273 (·65)
Main job pre-Henley *not* general management 281 (·45)
Not Public Sector 276 (·61)
Younger age-group 287 (·26)
Feeling about pre-Henley job: satisfied 105 (·35)
Henley Staff rating: high 286
Father did not work for a local authority 123 (·12)
Present salary: high 69 (·34)
Pre-Henley salary: high 68 (·66)
(·18)

members also tend more to score highly on Venturesomeness than do the older members, and less educated members to score more highly than do the more educated. *Table 29* gives specific information on how Venturesomeness relates to employing organization:

TABLE 29 *Venturesomeness, by Employing Organization*

(Percentages)

Scores on Venturesome cluster	PI	B	NI	PS
Low (1 + 2)	11	75	38	98
Med. + High (3, 4, 5)	89	25	62	2
TOTALS % =	100	100	100	100
N =	(300)	(82)	(87)	(103)

Venturesomeness is most conspicuously a Private Sector orientation, and most antithetical to attitudes of members in the Public Sector.

The Conflicted Cluster

Cluster 8 *Conflicted*

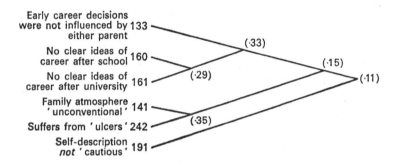

This clustering of items suggests a background not orientated to a management career and from which the youthful individual emerged lacking role models or any other guidelines about the future. In such a situation, *ad hoc* decisions tended perhaps to be made on impulse. The strains of this general pattern are seen in the prevalence of 'ulcers'. Within this particular complexity, however, this kind of person seems to have developed well and been promoted – perhaps through success at 'crisis' management.

Though the cluster links to development via a negative correlation with the self-description 'cautious', there is only a very low correlation between high scorers on the scale derived from this cluster and development as a manager. There is no correlation between members high on this dimension and type of employing organization; nor is age correlated. Those who did not finish university, and sales managers, are relatively high on this scale.

The Restless/Hard-driving Cluster

Here is another type of 'thrusting' pattern, where advance may be accomplished by leaving one situation for another that is more favourable. It portrays the sort of person who does not stay to work through details, but moves on from challenge to challenge,

Cluster 2 *Restless/Hard-driving*

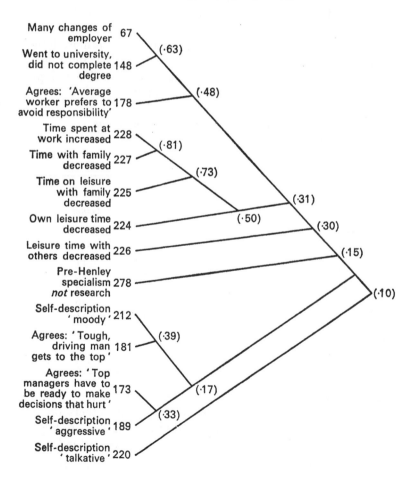

and often strength to strength. This is the pattern that Watson (1958) has termed 'spiralling', and the type of manager that Jennings (1954) calls 'mobi-centric'. The picture is one of a somewhat moody person, who often works at the expense not only of family life but of his own personal leisure and social enjoyments. Psychologically fairly ruthless, he feels that the competitive world of management careers is one of 'dog eat dog' and is rather contemptuous of workers, whom he thinks lack ambition – and he does not mind saying so!

There is no significant relationship between the type of employing organization and this set of characteristics, though there is a limited tendency for persons with it to be found in the Private Sector; nor does it correlate with age or education, though there is a slight teddency for younger men and men with more formal qualifications to score higher in this dimension.* The most highly significant relationship among the variables examined is with pre-Henley specialism. *Table 30* shows the pattern.

TABLE 30 *Pre-Henley Specialism and Scores on the Restless/Hard-driving Cluster*

(Percentages)

Restless/ Hard- Driving Scores		Production	Research	Sales	Accountancy	General	Other
(low)	1	8	76	6	10	11	5
	2	11	5	11	14	10	24
	3	28	2	26	26	32	24
	4	30	2	23	38	26	25
(high)	5	24	16	33	12	21	22
TOTALS% =		101	101	99	100	100	100
N =		(149)	(62)	(81)	(58)	(171)	(55)

The differences here are statistically significant at the 1 per cent level. Research managers are much lower than others on this Restless/Hard-driving syndrome, and sales managers are higher, with production men and accountants running close behind. Some

* The latter tendency is countered by the stability of research managers, which counters the tendency among other graduates.

types of generalist, probably the non-Public Sector ones, are also quite high on this dimension.

While the cluster is linked to development as a manager through two of its fourteen variables – 'moody' and 'many changes of employer' – the dimension defined by the cluster as a whole does not correlate with the sense of having developed as a manager as a consequence of Henley.

VIGNETTES ILLUSTRATING HIGH AND LOW METAMORPHIC DEVELOPMENT SCORES

When the clusters combine to form a factor – the *Metamorphic Development Pattern* – appropriate weightings are applied to each, to produce scores.

The distribution of scores is shown in *Figure 2*.

Figure 2 Distribution of Factor I Scores: Metamorphic Development Pattern

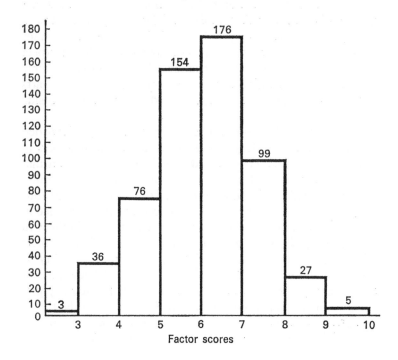

A few vignettes follow which will give some substance to the figures and charts illustrated, giving a comparison between a few members who score very high on Metamorphic growth patterns and a few members who score very low on this factor.

Examples are taken at random from among the five highest and three lowest scorers to represent the two extremes on this factor.

A High Scorer on Metamorphic Development: 506

506 came to Henley when he was 40 as an engineer responsible for a functional department in a Nationalized Industry. He was a man from the North of England, son of a skilled worker in a smallish industrial firm who was rather dissatisfied with his job. He indicates that both parents, however, were very keen on his improving his own position and gave a good deal of positive help and encouragement. He was the only son, having one sister. He describes the family atmosphere as warm, secure, and united. He attended a technical school and left school at about 15 to obtain further technical training and a course on work-study on a part-time basis to achieve his qualifications as an engineer. From a very early age he had a clear idea about what he wanted to do, though he says now that he did not expect to go as far as he has in fact done. In addition to his academic interests in technological subjects, he was interested in the arts and social sciences at school, and had a good many outside interests.

506's organization sent him to Henley, he thinks, to 'broaden him', and as a secondary reason to 'fill in areas of weakness in management skills'. He was enthusiastic when he learned that he was going to Henley, and had specific things in his mind that he wanted from the experience. He initially wanted four things from the list provided in the questionnaire: a 'chance to compare and evaluate my experience with those of others in different organizations', an 'improved ability to work with others of different outlook and experience', an 'improved ability to handle new kinds of situation', and 'increased knowledge of myself as a person'. Of the four he felt that he 'actually got' the first three, though not the fourth. In addition to the things he initially wanted, however, he got two other things not envisioned from the start: a 'better understanding of the relation between my own organization and the wider environment', and 'new knowledge, specific skills such as writing reports, chairmanship, and public speaking'.

He repeats his feeling of not having learned as much about himself as a person as he would have liked when answering the question about how the staff contribution could have been more helpful. He selects 'help in self-appraisal' as the main thing here, and states that 'the lack of critical appraisal on a systematic basis led to a lack of awareness' of himself and of how he was functioning. He also expressed the wish for more follow-up contact on a regular basis, e.g. an annual weekend.

He considers, in retrospect, that most of the Henley programme was about right, wanting only more outside visits, and more experience in public speaking. He worked very hard while at Henley – when he was working – but he feels that the total time spent at Henley could have been more efficiently used. On balance, he feels that he got 'not very much' as a person from the Henley experience, but a 'great deal' as a manager. He made the definite decision to go into general management instead of functional management, and this for him was a major life-decision made as a consequence of the course at Henley. Given this, he feels that the course had direct relevance to his subsequent work and cites 'better understanding of the need to coordinate others – managing through people not simply by direction' as a major kind of insight. He feels that the course in future should have more case studies, more management-union relations, and specific studies toward personal development, e.g. through individual projects.

Since leaving Henley, 506 has had a promotion and a change of employer, but within the same Nationalized Industry, which has been accompanied by a major salary rise – from the £2,000–3,000 bracket to the £4,000–5,000 bracket. He has increased in managerial responsibilities across the board: in terms of the number and magnitude of decisions taken; participation in planning, delegation; and interaction with various kinds of people, both inside and outside the firm. He feels that the nature of his job has changed completely. Engineering now comprises only one of many specialisms with which he has to deal, forming about 10 per cent of all his work. He now has to deal with commercial and administrative functions of various kinds, and controls a large staff of all grades and specialisms relating to the industry. A good deal of his work requires negotiation with unions, customers, and staff. He enjoys all aspects of the work and has strong views on how things should be done. He feels that he is not always as tolerant as he might be with his staff, and reckons that he is for the most part ahead of them because of his Henley experience in his ways of thinking about management, but often has to change his approach rather rapidly in order to take into account where his staff are in their thinking. He is only 'moderately satisfied' with his job, but feels that it is 'exciting'. He would like to make more changes than he feels possible in the face of the constrictions on him, despite his rise in status. He notes that, while in some ways he has more freedom now than previously, in other ways his present position is more restrictive.

Since his promotion, he actually spends less time at work because of the great amount of overtime he used to do, and more time with his family and in community affairs.

As to his personal life, 506 is married, has two children, and his wife does voluntary work in women's organizations; he considers himself 'adaptable', 'ambitious', 'competitive', 'cooperative', 'creative', 'dominant', 'efficient', 'energetic', 'harddriving', 'intuitive', 'loyal to an organization', 'middle-brow', 'outgoing', 'physically strong', 'rational', 'self-sufficient', 'talkative', 'unconventional', 'volatile', and 'witty'.

The Henley Directing Staff remember him as an engineer who was 'on the ball', bright, alert with a good sense of humour and fun, popular with his syndicate, congenial, and well liked. While he was seen as a 'great enthusiast', he was not felt to be a very ambitious and hard-driving type, one who would go to the very top. He seems to have succeeded in keeping this aspect of his personality fairly covert. The staff considered that he grew a little while at Henley.

A High Scorer on Metamorphic Development: 1148

1148 came to Henley at the age of 40 from a post as head of a scientific research group in industry. He was one of two children of a professional family which he describes as 'warm', but 'unconventional' and 'insecure'. The marriage broke up when he was in his teens, but by then he was well launched on an academic career and had a fairly clear idea by the end of secondary school what his career was going to be. He knew that he wanted to be a scientist, and that he wanted to be a manager of scientists in industry. He says that it is only recently, however, that the managerial part has become much more prominent, and the scientific part less relevant.

When he was nominated, he felt that it was done primarily to give him a sabbatical experience, and secondarily to broaden him. He was 'keen but diffident', and had only a rather vague idea of what he wanted from the course. He chose four from the list of things initially wanted: 'complete break', 'chance to compare', 'improved ability to handle new situations', and 'increased understanding of myself as a person'. Of these he felt that he actually got all but an 'improved ability to handle new situations', but he indicated that, in addition to the initially intended ones, he got 'an improved ability to work with others of different experience and outlook'. In response to the question about what he found especially useful at Henley, he says: 'I feel that it has given me a better understanding of other people's problems, and it has given me a chance to compare myself with men whom their employers have thought worthy of sending on a three-month managers' course.'

He feels that the staff were helpful with private advice and with self-appraisal, but would like to have had even more of this and more 'direct teaching'.

At Henley he worked 'moderately hard' and both he and his wife found the residential character of the course 'quite disturbing'. He is one of the few men in the sample who is married to a professional wife who is also employed (though only part-time) in a senior capacity. In the end, he felt that he got a 'fair amount' of development from the course, both as a person and as a manager. As a manager he feels that he got 'a much clearer appreciation of macro-economics and of the transitions between science, technology, and management'; as a person he felt that he benefited by 'being able to work at my own pace in a group, several of whom were rather slow'. This may be taken broadly to mean that he gained self-assurance and formation of an identity which allowed him to recognize his own differences and to behave in a variant rather than a group-conformative manner.

Some of his suggestions for Henley and the future are 'common' ones, e.g. more didactic inputs; however, he also made some rather distinctive suggestions, mainly in the area of change. He felt that more should be taught on the 'effect of science and technology on changes in the economy, and on the effect of changes in the educational system on the type of people now entering society in important positions and who will affect the community within the next 20 to 30 years'. In general he wants more emphasis on the future 'and desirable changes to make the future'.

Since leaving Henley he has had a rise in salary and a slight increase in responsibility, but it would be fairer to say that the nature of his work has changed more than is reflected in any change in title or position. Whereas he was head of a research unit, he is now head of a department charged with 'development', or bridging the gap between research and its practical application.

He describes the difference between his post-Henley and pre-Henley jobs as follows:

'My present job differs from the previous one in two major ways: first I have lost the day-to-day administration of a large research group (behind which I could hide when I didn't want to do a particular job), and instead I have a small team of young men working with me and learning (as I am learning). Secondly, the scope of the job is much wider. It embraces products and technologies of which I am crassly ignorant, whereas (in retrospect) in my previous job I knew a lot about the technical aspects of the work and understood the details of what my contacts were doing.

I have not yet come to terms with these changes, and am sure that my greatest difficulty will be to establish the easy collaborative conditions which are essential if the transition from team-leader to "general" manager is to be successful.'

He describes the work, and his own strengths and weakness in coping with its new challenges in the following terms:

'My job, at present, involves the bridging of the gap between science, technology, and marketing. I work in a research department and try to achieve the commercial exploitation of the work in progress. This is difficult and requires the cooperation of a surprisingly large number of people within the organization to which I belong and other organizations . . . Cooperation must be willing and cannot be forced on the people. I have had this task but a brief time and all I have so far is weaknesses: no doubt, when I've made every mistake (once only I hope), and recognize them as mistakes it will all seem easy and I'll be full of strength.'

In his kind of work, problems are technical, intellectual, and human relational (the intellectual being felt to be most irksome); and problems are dealt with by 'consensus with colleagues'. He regards his work environment as 'warm', 'exciting', 'united', and 'unconventional'. While he was very satisfied with it in his pre-Henley position, he declines to indicate his current state of satisfaction because he feels the situation is still very much in flux – 'not sufficiently well established yet'; at present 'worried'.

As mentioned above he is married to a professional wife who is engaged in work while at the same time raising two children.

He describes himself as 'adaptable', 'aggressive', 'competitive', 'cultured', 'energetic', 'fun-loving', 'hard-driving', 'loyal to an organization' (while with them, he adds), 'rebellious', 'talkative', and 'unconventional'. He chose as top three values both pre- and post-Henley (though rearranging them within the top three), 'intellectual problem-solving abilities', 'creativity', and 'interesting job with minimum disturbance'.

Staff members recall him as a 'very high-quality brain', a bit of a 'polymath', very able, a bit arrogant, and somewhat intolerant of others.

A High Scorer on Metamorphic Development: 1314

This man came to Henley at a fairly young age, 34. He was at the time responsible for manufacturing standards, for the development of new brands, and for the improvement of existing ones. He was moderately satisfied with his pre-Henley job, but felt that he was sent as a matter of 'pure chance' primarily, and secondarily to 'broaden' him. He was 'enthusiastic' about having been nominated, and had specific things in his mind that he wanted from the course, based on the information in the brochure. He checks four of the nine things as 'initially wanted': 'chance to compare and evaluate experiences', 'improved ability to work with others', 'improved ability to handle new situations', and 'new knowledge and skills'. He indicates that he got all of these things with the exception of the 'improved ability to work with others', and adds 'complete break', 'better understanding of managerial role-requirements', and 'increased self-understanding' as unexpected positive gains, with the latter indicated as of 'greatest personal value'. He felt that especially useful in the course was 'the opportunity to come into contact with able, interesting, enthusiastic managers of differing environments and backgrounds'. He did not find anything particularly 'unhelpful', but suggests that the staff contribution could have been of greater value in help with 'self-appraisal', and 'direct teaching'. He worked very hard at Henley, and both he and his wife (like 1148) found the fact that he had to be away so long in a residential course 'quite disturbing'. Like 1148 he is married to a graduate, who directs, on a part-time basis, her own small business, while raising three children.

1314 feels that he benefited a 'great deal' both as a manager and as a person; as a manager through 'the experience of chairmanship'; as a person by 'assessment of one's colleagues, and by analysing a successful and an unsuccessful presentation'. He would like, in future, for Henley to have less emphasis on the collective syndicate work, and 'more concentration on private study and report writing, individual projects and small-group projects'.

Since leaving Henley, 1314 has changed his job twice, and has had a promotion and a change of employer. He has gone into a branch of the industry which he likes better, involving the running of a new factory. 'This is a new appointment in a new industry. Decisions are required much sooner and are more critical; short cuts in one's thinking and reasoning processes are necessary. New manufacturing processes have to be learnt.' The particular problems and requirements of the industry and of the products of the factory 'take up his efforts', and he is concerned with a range of problems in cost-control, and trouble-shooting. He feels that the new situation presents a 'tremendous challenge'.

One of the interesting things about 1314's pattern is that he seems to have undergone a transformation which was largely covert – a kind of 'sleeper effect' of the course. While he was at Henley, the staff remember him as a rather quiet and well-behaved chap, 'not terribly dynamic; public-school type; nice quality; good manners; delightful social gifts; quiet front; never lost his temper', all very laudable traits but no great sense of thrust or turbulence as in the case of 1148; and the staff did not think that 1314, unlike 1148, developed at the College. In 1314's case this was going on underneath, and his exterior calm belied an inner set of concerns about himself and his career.

In commenting on this aspect, he says:

'Since Henley I have been quicker to adapt to new situations because I am no longer afraid and uncertain of tackling unusual problems and giving decisions. Henley, combined with my previous experience, has given me the confidence to assume responsibility and to make decisions when required, and to profit from mistakes. This is because Henley teaches you that above all if you are a manager, then "the buck must stop on your desk". You therefore *must* concern yourself with situations to a depth whereby you have all the facts necessary for you to make a personal decision whether on the advice of others or not.'

He now considers himself to be 'adaptable', 'ambitious', 'competitive', 'efficient', 'loyal', and 'outgoing'. He reports major shifts in his values, for example with 'an opportunity to be creative' going from seventh to second place; 'interesting job, minimum disturbance' going from fifth to first place; and 'relative freedom from supervision by others' from eighth to third. This would seem to indicate a general increase in values related to personal fulfilment and conditions to allow this in the work, with the 'helpful' and 'stable' elements moving downward to the bottom of the value hierarchy.

A Low Scorer on Metamorphic Development: 312

312 came to Henley relatively late, at age 47, from a large local authority. He feels that he was sent for general broadening, and was enthusiastic about coming to Henley, having specific things in mind. He wanted a 'complete break', a 'chance to compare and evaluate experiences' and 'contacts'. He feels that he got all three, no more. He indicates that the most useful parts of the course to him were 'visits' to outside organizations (of which he wanted more) and 'contacts'. He felt that the staff contribution was most helpful in 'self-appraisal', and he wants even more of this. He felt that he worked 'moderately hard' on the course, and got 'not very much' out of it either as a manager or as a person. He suggests more trade union representation on the courses in future. The staff considered him to have developed a little, and to have been undistinguished as a member.

After leaving Henley, he had no changes on job or of employers, but a modest pay rise brought him up out of the £2,000–£3,000 to the £3,000–£4,000 bracket. The only increase mentioned in managerial responsibility is the amount that could be done by machine aids. He characterizes his job as 'secure', 'exciting', and 'warm' and average in other respects, but does not indicate his degree of satisfaction or dissatisfaction with it. He indicates that he dislikes that aspect of his job which limits his participation in the determination of policy, because other than discussing the plans with the chairman of the local government committee concerned, 'I cannot present my own views to the party group who determine ultimate policy.' He indicates that, since Henley, the nature of his work has not changed, but 'I have found a greater confidence in expressing my own points of view. This feeling of confidence has been brought about by contacts with people in other types of work in large-scale organizations. This means of contact and exchange of views is one of Henley's attractions.'

This is a man who came from a small business family which he characterizes as 'secure, permissive, conventional, and united'. He himself describes his personal traits as 'calm', 'cautious', 'conventional', 'cooperative', 'idealistic', 'loyal', and 'reserved'. He is a family man whose pattern of life has remained very stable following Henley, as have his personal career values, which place at the top 'an opportunity to work with people', 'an opportunity to be helpful to people', and 'relative freedom from supervision' with 'accomplishment' and 'creativity' very low.

A Low Scorer on Metamorphic Development: 1106

1106 came to Henley a bit later than many, at 43. He was a section head in a Ministry. He considered that he had been nominated for Henley 'for having done a good job', and as an indication, secondarily, of having been 'earmarked' for a more senior post. He was 'keen but diffident', and had only a vague idea of what he wanted from the course. The three things chosen were 'chance to compare and evaluate', 'better understanding of senior managerial role requirements', and 'better understanding of the relations between my own organization and the environment'. He considers that he got what he expected and that the main thing that was useful in the course was the chance to compare standards of 'competence' to be found at comparable levels in men from the different kinds of employing organization. The major staff contribution for him was 'help in self-appraisal'. While at Henley, he worked moderately hard and considered that he got 'not very much' either as a person or as a manager from the course. He thought that many aspects of the syndicate work were 'platitudinous'. He considers that subjects needed sharper definition, and that some, notably the handling of computer technology, needed to be improved. The staff felt that this was an undistinguished member and that he developed little.

Since leaving Henley, he had had one change of job, a promotion within the same organization, and moved up from £2,000–£3,000 to the £3,000–£4,000 range. He is now in charge of a number of small planning groups. This requires the fitting together of the work of a number of different subsections, and he finds it difficult to accept the very different levels of competence and drive that various people have in contributing to this overall task. In fact, he indicates, as a general weakness of his in making this transition to a more senior managerial job, being 'unable to accept the inevitable unevenness in the capability of staff to do work that appears necessary, or to completely accept a role of directing as opposed to doing'. He indicates that he finds the new job fascinating, having always managed to like his job, but finds that he dislikes attending so many committee meetings which have no profitable outcome, and also the degree to which people in his working environment sometimes adhere to rigid terms of reference, inhibiting a freer exhange of ideas. He considers, overall, that his work environment is insecure, exciting, and permissive, and is very satisfied with it, as he was prior to Henley.

This is the son of a skilled worker employed by a South of England local authority. He had one sister, characterized his family environment as warm, secure, conventional, and boring, and attended a grammar school before leaving for service in the RAF.

He is a family man, married with three children, whose wife works full-time as a secretary. He considers himself to be 'adaptable', 'cautious', 'conventional', 'cooperative', 'efficient', 'idealistic', 'loyal', 'nervous', and 'reserved'. The course has not affected the distribution of his time or his values. His value profile does not differ as markedly from the high metamorphic types as one might expect from the personal trait descriptions, in that he values 'creativity', at the top of his list, with 'intellectual problem-solving' and 'interesting job with minimum disturbance' in the top three positions – all intrinsic job characteristics. Perhaps the most distinguishing point is that 'opportunity to show what I can accomplish' comes fourth, and 'opportunity to work with people rather than exclusively with things or ideas' comes seventh – rather than in the top three positions – and 'security' comes fifth, rather than in the bottom three.

SUMMARY

The vignettes illustrate the picture derived from the cluster and factor analyses. The high scorer for Metamorphic development is one who has the described personality traits, a somewhat more 'off-beat' background, including marginality and perhaps foreign extraction or difficult early familial experiences. These have produced a pattern of striving and of dissatisfaction both with self and with one's environment, which when coupled with a high degree of competence and creative drive results in a thrust to improve the situation. This dissatisfaction may, as in the case of 1314, be covert, occurring behind the façade of a well-mannered public-school type – but on the whole the pattern is closer to the surface and recognized by the staff.

In contrast, the low scorers tend to come from more conventional and placid environments, to feel relatively satisfied with their lot despite things about it which they do not like, and to be content with an improvement in their capacity to function within the situation in which they find themselves. They are somewhat more fatalistic about things – 'it's the nature of local government' that one can't get one's views expressed at the policy-making levels of the political party in power – and to have lower standards for what they will acccept in a situation.

The high scorers are the kinds of people Watson described as 'spiralists', Jennings as 'mobile managers', and Willings as the managers who emphasize the creative artistry of management rather than its science. While this type of developmental pattern would seem likely to be found among the kinds of manager described by Moment and Zaleznik as 'stars', no direct correspondence is indicated, and it is likely that 'stars' may be found among managers in the other developmental patterns as well. The hard-driving high Metamorphic is likely to use management sciences as a tool for mastering situations rather than an end to be mastered for its own sake, and his urge is to form new creative syntheses in the situations he encounters.

Chapter 10 · The Incremental Development Pattern

Incremental development suggests a growth by a different process from that which characterized the Metamorphic pattern. Rather than a picture of change, transformation, reorganization, and so on, one gets a picture of step-by-step cumulative development in which new elements are added to old to increase the total by a relatively more straightforward process of addition. The steady advance, the increase in capacities without fundamental change in underlying organization, these are the qualities which bespeak Incremental in contrast to Metamorphic development.

The three clusters most heavily tied in with Incremental development provide the motif of the overall pattern. These are: cluster 13 (Climbing, loading ·33); cluster 11 (Fulfilled, loading ·29); and cluster 5 (Uncritical, loading ·19). There is a degree of External-orientation (loading ·17) together with a tendency towards acquiescence as indicated by the *negative* correlation with Restless/Hard-driving traits (loading — ·13), but both of the latter tie in more closely with other factors. The three clusters most centrally involved in this factor will be described, and then vignettes presenting illustrative cases for high and low factor scores for the Incremental pattern of development.

The Climbing Cluster

This cluster groups the members' reports on the recognition they have received from their organizations in terms of increased managerial responsibility. The items used to measure increase in general management responsibility are found to be highly inter-correlated, so that men who are found, for example, to increase their participation in long-term planning are also highly likely to have increased their involvement with others of different specialities, etc.

Those scoring high on this cluster, which clearly measures the 'climb' up the general management ladder, are found to indicate that they consider that they developed as a manager as a consequence of Henley. This lends validation to the variable of self-assessed development. The correlation is statistically significant at the 1 per cent level.

There are no statistically significant differences in general management Climbing scores by specialism or by employing organization, though Civil Servants occur rather more frequently

Cluster 13 *Climbing*

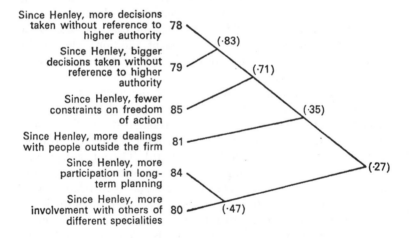

in the higher-scoring groups than do others, presumably because of the higher correlation between advance in rank and increase in general administrative responsibilities in the Civil Service than in other organizations, where men may move up by way of consultancy, or other staff roles.

There is a tendency for people who score as high climbers to be more highly educated and to have come to Henley at an earlier age.

The Uncritical Cluster

The impression created by this cluster is that people who score highly on it are 'uncritical' and accept the organization in which they function on the organization's terms: his organization sent him for reasons of its own – it had 'earmarked' him or wanted to 'assess' him. Whereas many ex-members criticize the staff for not enough direct teaching, this type of man accepts the staff as

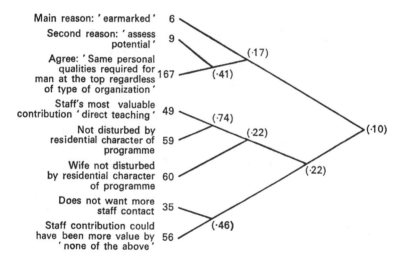

Cluster 5 *Uncritical*

teachers and indicates that direct teaching was their main contribution. The members who score high on this accept the residential character of the course, and indicate that their wives do as well. They accommodate cheerfully to the demands of the system and do not ask it to be different. In the training situation, as in the work situation, the authorities are accepted on their own terms; the uncritical members like it this way and do not wish to come closer to the revered figures themselves.

The 'uncritical' cluster is not correlated with 'development as a manager', though the variable 'earmarked' does on its own. It does not carry sufficient weight in the cluster as a whole to carry the correlation of the whole dimension represented by the cluster.

The same is true of the other variables examined age: of attendance at Henley (though there is a tendency for the older ones to be more uncritical); education, specialism or employing organization (though Bankers have more high scorers as more uncritical than others); and Private Sector members and Public Sector members, whose patterns for this cluster have much more in common with each other than either has with the other groups. Both are lower than the other groups on the *uncritical* end of the scale, and higher than the others on the critical end.

The Fulfilled Cluster

This is a very large cluster (18 variables) which will for ease of reading be presented as two sub-clusters, the first representing a sub-cluster mainly made up of traits representing recollections of the childhood family environment, and the second representing more contemporary assessments.

This is a picture of stable, contented happiness and fulfilment. It links to a sense of development as a person, via variable 152, 'main academic interest in school: natural sciences', but not to a sense of development as a manager; so it is only present as an

TABLE 31 *Scores on Fulfilment Cluster, by Type of Employing Organization*

(Percentages)

	PI	B	NI	PS
Low scores (Quintiles 1 and 2)	41	30	35	28
Medium	22	17	18	27
High scores (Quintiles 4 and 4)	36	54	47	45
TOTALS % =	99	101	100	100
N =	(300)	(82)	(87)	(103)

Cluster 11 *Fulfilled*

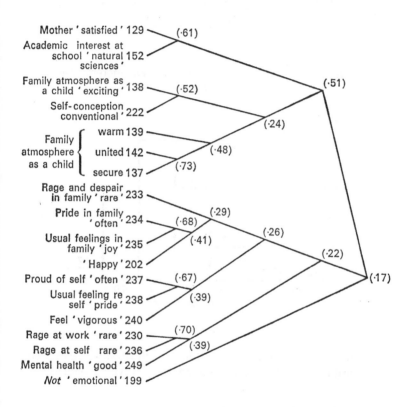

important component in the Incremental development factor to provide the element of stability, which is important to the general picture of the solid organization man who can be relied on to be steady, dependable, even-tempered, and constructive. It is not correlated with any age, educational, or occupational groups, though accountants and general managers are higher on it than the others, particularly 'research' members. Bankers tend in greater proportion than the others to score highly on this cluster, while Private Industry members are lower, as is shown in *Table 31*.

The distribution of factor scores, derived from the individuals'
weighted cluster scores, is shown in *Figure 3*:

Figure 3 Distribution of Factor II Scores: Incremental
Development Pattern

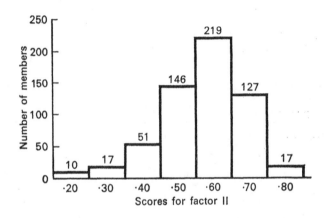

From the top 17, and the bottom 10, illustrative cases were
selected at random. Vignettes based on their individual data follow.

A High Scorer on Incremental Development: 115

115 came to Henley at age 34 as a section head concerned with
exports in one of the large Private Sector chemical companies.
He thinks that he was sent first of all to broaden him generally,
and secondarily to fill in his areas of weakness in management
skills. He is an arts graduate, son of a North of England small
businessman, and has a family background that he describes as
very secure.

When 115 was nominated to go to Henley, he was enthusiastic,
but had only a rather vague idea of what he wanted from the

course. The three aspects he chose to emphasize were the same three that he felt he got out of the course, namely 'chance to compare', 'better understanding of senior role', and 'better understanding of organization-environment relations'. He considers that everything in the course was 'about right' and that especially useful were 'direct teaching on finance', 'discussions on delegation of responsibility and accountability', 'opportunity to compare myself with other managers', and 'opportunity to exchange views with Civil Servants and Bankers'. The only criticism was about the amount of time spent on biographical and other reviews. He felt that the staff were most helpful through their direct teaching and that they could have done more of it.

He considers that he worked 'moderately hard' at Henley and developed 'a fair amount' both as a manager and as a person. The benefit as a manager was felt to be in relation to an increased awareness of financial matters; and as a person in relation to an increased self-confidence coming from the opportunity to compare himself with similar people in other organizations. The staff remember him as someone who was of very high calibre intellectually, whose opinion people in syndicate would be interested in, but who did not have high leadership drive. He was not thought to have developed at Henley.

115 made two suggestions about the future at Henley: first that there ought to be a greater emphasis given to the topic of marketing (he felt that this was considered undesirable as a topic), and second, that topics should be closed with a greater degree of indication as to which solutions were better, or 'right'. Usually he felt the topics were left hanging, and this was obviously something which he personally did not like.

These experiences, with attendant increase in self-confidence, led to a feeling that this was all directly relevant to his career, and he moved first into a larger supervisory job of a group of overseas subsidiaries, and then to an even larger job within the company which related to personnel services. With divisional directorship, he showed marked increase in salary, moving from a pre-Henley level of £2,000–£3,000 to a current level of £5,000–£6,000.

He describes his post-Henley career as having encountered success in pressing the company's expansion into the European markets, opening markets for his company's products in ten different European countries, and supervising the formation and functioning of the subsidiary companies, rising to become deputy to the overseas director of the company. He says:

'The main change has been an enormous broadening of responsibility and authority . . . it has brought about greater responsibility for technical, financial, and personnel matters across Europe, and particularly for long-term planning – 10 years or more. The size and complexity of the task have required greater delegation downwards and have shown, I think, the value of the discussions at Henley on this subject. One of the main difficulties is the considerable involvement in human/personnel matters in the various subsidiary companies, and the reconciliation of theoretical, organizational, and efficient solutions with practical and humanitarian considerations.'

He describes his work environment as average in every respect, except that it is unusually exciting. He is a married man, with one child and a graduate wife who works part-time. He describes himself as 'adaptable', 'calm', 'cooperative', 'efficient', 'happy', 'intellectual', 'loyal', 'rational', and 'witty'. The amount of time spent on work has increased, and correspondingly the amount of time spent with his family has decreased. He is moderately happy with his situation, and did not change his values at all from his pre-Henley hierarchy, which put 'chance to work at an interesting job', and 'intellectual problem-solving abilities' on top, 'creativity' third, and 'stable future', 'work with people', and 'helpful', eighth, seventh, and sixth respectively.

A High Scorer on Incremental Development: 145

This is a man who came to Henley at age 42 as a manager of an O & M unit responsible to the managing director of a group of companies.

He indicates only the reason that was told to him for having been sent – 'to broaden me generally' – and says that he was enthusiastic and had specific things in mind. He chooses four things that he wanted from the list of ten suggested possibilities: 'chance to compare and evaluate', 'better understanding of senior role,' 'better understanding of organization–environment relations', and 'improved ability to work with others of different background'. He states that he got all four, plus a 'complete break'. He does not consider that there was anything unhelpful about the course and does not indicate any way in which the staff could have been more helpful. 145 feels that he worked 'very hard' at Henley and had benefited 'a fair amount' both as a manager and as a person. For the future, he says: 'nothing specific, other than incorporating into courses such material as keeps abreast with developing management techniques and services – operational research, data-processing, etc. – which I imagine is in fact already happening.' This is a man whom the staff considered average in calibre but who grew a lot at Henley.

He says that his Henley experience had general relevance to his subsequent work. His promotion to head of the O & M section had come prior to being sent to Henley, so he had no subsequent changes of job or promotion, only job enlargement and increase in salary commensurate with it. Except for sheer number of decisions and delegation, he indicates a general increase in the managerial responsibility which he has experienced and indicates that the most frequent problems are economic/financial, though the most irksome ones are human-relational. He likes his job, which is seen as 'a never-ending challenge over a wide range of the organization's activities', and his strength as the 'confidence people have in us, based on satisfaction with past results. If we fail on a job we shall not be invited to look at another one!' He sees his work environment as average in most respects, but more secure and warm than most, and more unconventional (in the 'one-off' nature of each job).

145 describes himself as 'adaptable', 'calm', 'creative', 'loyal', 'methodical', and 'rational'. He shows no change in his career values, and rates 'creative' first, 'chance to use intellectual problem-solving activities' second, and 'chance to work at an interesting job with a minimum of disturbance' third. At the bottom of his list are 'opportunity to show what I can accomplish' eighth, and 'stable secure future' seventh.

A High Scorer on Incremental Development: 706

This is a local government man, who moved up from assistant to a deputy director's post. He came to Henley rather late, age 43, but considered that there were good reasons – first, that he was earmarked for a more senior job and, second, to broaden him generally. He was enthusiastic about being nominated, and had specific things in mind which he wanted from the programme. He indicated four things that he wanted: a 'better understanding of the senior managerial role', an 'improved ability to work with others of different experience and outlook', an 'improved ability to handle new situations', and an 'improved understanding of the relation between my own organization and the environment'. He feels in retrospect that he got these benefits from the course and others as well – including a better understanding of himself and a complete break (which he notes was a prerequisite).

Looking back at his experience at Henley, this man felt that most elements in the course of studies were about right, except that he would have liked more experience with public speaking and less with report-writing and private study. He felt that the main thing about the experience which he found useful was 'that it took one out of one's work and into an atmosphere of "management" where one could take stock of oneself and one's job and made one always ask "Am I doing what I should be doing to do my job properly?" ' He considered this as directly relevant to his job, even though he does not consider that he developed as a manager very much.

He did not find anything 'unhelpful' at Henley, and felt that the main benefit he had received from the staff was in social mixing. He felt that he worked 'moderately hard' and that in the end he developed 'a great deal' in consequence of the experience as a person, but 'not very much' as a manager. This was important to him because most of the problems in his job are technical and are handled by technical expertise, but the most irksome problems are human-relational and it is for these that he found the Henley experience directly relevant.

In responding to the question about suggestions for the future, he says that 'the curriculum did not appear to me to be important, although much of it I enjoyed; the benefit of the course was in the chance to take stock of oneself and given the opportunity of being able to do this in the Henley environment'.

On leaving Henley he was moved up from the number three position to the number two position in his local government organization, and given a pay increase from the £2,000–3,000 bracket into the £4,000–5,000 bracket. He indicates that there were general increases in managerial content to his job, and that the most irksome problems were concerned with human relations. He describes his work environment in superlatives – as exciting, warm, permissive, and united – but rather average for conventionality. He is very satisfied with his job, as he was prior to the course.

Looking at his personal background, he was the only child of a Welsh family which he describes as warm, secure, conventional, and united. His father was a clerk in a religious order, and he indicates that his own choice of career was not influenced by his parents. He was a scholar, and went to grammar school and graduated from university with an engineering degree. He had had a very clear idea of what sort of career he wanted from his schooldays onward.

This is a man who values an opportunity to show what he can accomplish and the autonomy to do his work relatively free from supervision. He describes himself as 'ambitious', 'aggressive', 'competitive', 'cooperative', 'efficient', 'energetic', 'happy', 'hard-driving', 'intuitive', 'lazy', 'loyal', 'pedestrian', 'quiet', 'rational', 'rebellious', 'reserved', 'ruthless', 'self-sufficient', and 'tense'. He is a family man, with two children and his wife is a full-time homemaker.

His Henley experience, according to his own account, seems to have tempered his rebelliousness with a modicum of humility. He says: 'Certainly now the job never overwhelms me. Sometimes it seemed to before because I had the common failing of believing that no one could do certain parts better than others (and this is doubtful). I have not the time to do it and have to trust and delegate. I am therefore better able to perform my proper task of management.'

The Henley staff recall this man as follows:

'. . . two years older than the rest of the syndicate; grew a lot here. I took to him – he seemed a good influence on the rest of the syndicate . . . had moved around quite a bit before he came to us – in fact, he applied for and got another job while on the course, but did not let this interfere in any way with his work here. A good friend of the College and a great family man . . . always comes to Open Day with his wife and kids . . . did not have a lot of strong competition within the syndicate – most of the others were a bit weak – so he may have been shining possibly in a rather weak team, likeable, forthright.'

A Low Scorer on Incremental Development: 854

This was a man who was second in command of management services in a Private Sector firm when he came to Henley at the age of 37. He felt that he was sent primarily to broaden him, and secondarily to indicate that he had been earmarked for a more senior position. He was keen but diffident about going, but had specific things in mind which he wanted from the course. The three things indicated as 'wanted initially' were 'improved understanding of senior managerial role-requirements', 'improved ability to work with others with different experience and outlook', and 'useful contacts'. He felt in the end that he had got the second two, but not the first. In addition, he felt that he did get a 'chance to compare and evaluate my own experience and attitudes with those from other organizations'. He felt that most of the course was 'about right', but wants less syndicate work, and more experience in public speaking and writing. As 'most useful' about the course he mentions 'contacts at the time', and 'subsequently the fact that I have been to Henley'. He indicates that the staff were most helpful in relation to social mixing, and that they could have been more helpful in giving 'career advice'.

He worked 'moderately hard' at Henley, felt in the end that the course has contributed to his development both as a person and as a manager 'not very much', and that 'it had little or no direct relevance to his subsequent work'. He suggests for the future that there should be 'more awareness of and tuition in modern management techniques, and more case studies; less aimless syndicate discussion'.

While 854 received a promotion and salary increase following Henley (from the £2,000–3,000 to the £3,000–4,000 bracket), he did not show any increase in participation in his firm's policy-making or planning, and actually experienced a drop in the amount of dealings with others outside the firm (though, in keeping with his move to become head of management services, he was able to make more and larger decisions without reference to a senior authority). However, in making his move, he experienced a sharp change in his feelings about his job and his firm. He changed from being 'very satisfied' with his work to being 'very dissatisfied'. While he does not tell us what the trouble was, he reports that though the most frequent problems with which he was faced were 'technical', the most irksome ones were 'political', and that he is 'dissatisfied with organizational changes and the manner of changing jobs'.

The limitations of a questionnaire study do not allow us to infer what went on here, but the kind of man with whom we are dealing is one who describes himself as 'emotional', 'hard-driving', 'intellectual', 'self-sufficient', 'unconventional', and 'witty'. He is divorced. His first three career values are: 'chance to use intellectual problem-solving abilities', 'opportunity to work with people rather than things or ideas', and 'opportunity to be creative', and these did not change as a consequence of Henley. One may speculate that under different circumstances this man might have fallen on the Tangential or Metamorphic development pattern, but as things were he shows up as low on incremental development.

A Low Scorer on Incremental Development: 1143

This is a man who came to Henley at the age of 38 from a scientific post in a government department. He felt that he had been sent as a matter of 'pure chance', and secondarily because of a 'vague consciousness that I might be more effective in administration away from research'.

He himself was nevertheless enthusiastic about being nominated, though he had 'very little idea' of what he wanted at the time. He lists as 'initially wanted' nothing very specific; but under 'actually got' he indicates 6 out of the 9 categories provided.

He reports that he worked 'very hard' at the beginning of the course, gradually diminishing, and that in the end he felt that he developed 'not very much' either as a person or as a manager. He would have liked more contact with staff, more talks with outside visitors, and more private study. While he checks 'none of the above' as elements in the staff role that were helpful contributions, he indicates five of the six categories provided (all but 'social mixing') as ways in which he would like to have had the staff help more. He adds to suggestions, the following:

> 'A general analysis of situations as they arose and how they might arise during course of discussions – e.g. What was this part of the course trying to do? How was it failing to succeed? What could we do to improve it?'
> 'DS who can analyse and influence, rather like tutors.'

Both he and his wife found it 'very disturbing' to have him away so long on a residential course – and this is understandable when one notes that his wife is a professional person herself engaged in part-time work outside the home. This type of situation tends to make it more difficult for the husband to be away for an extended period.

Nevertheless, he notes that in one way at least the course was of *direct* relevance to his subsequent work – namely in relation to job evaluation. He changed the kind of work he was doing rather radically, moving into the recruitment and administration of scientific personnel for his agency, and along with this an increase in some administrative responsibilities but not others. As his pay rise was very modest, this was essentially a 'sidewise' move.

He describes the general atmosphere of his employing organization as somewhat 'insecure' and 'divided' and is only 'moderately satisfied' (though he was 'moderately dissatisfied' previously). He has had to travel more in his new job, and has experienced frustrations in his work primarily in relation to human problems – resulting in rather frequent feelings of rage and despair, and a number of psychosomatic symptoms reported (sleeplessness, backache, insufficient energy). He says:

'What I dislike is that I am supposed to deal with jobs, but the problems that arise are from people.'

He feels critical of and frustrated about the organizational problems he faces in trying to adapt an organization to 'requirements which it was not created to cope with' and 'people who have been promoted too far or whose expertise is out of date'. He also criticizes the recruitment machine, which was not designed to do the job he has to use it for, and his superiors 'who are themselves under strong pressure'.

He describes himself as 'aggressive', 'cultured', 'emotional', 'intellectual', 'moody', 'sensual', and 'witty' – and was very critical of the questionnaire (often correctly).

SUMMARY

The high Incremental Development Pattern gives heavy emphasis to a steady career advance within an organization, towards which one is fundamentally accepting. This is accompanied by a happy and fulfilled personal and family life and a considerable impression of stability.

The impression one gets from the vignettes is of people who take a great delight in seeing their organization function well.

They like to see the wheels going around smoothly, the machine functioning efficiently, and they tend to take great pride in overcoming obstacles to this in a calm, rational, and unflappable way. They are known, in their organizations, to be men who can make things work within an existing framework, and tend to be given jobs that require persistence, ingenuity, and compatibility with others. These men, while not impressing staff and others who meet them as 'balls of fire', are the kind who wear well and frequently turn up later on in very responsible posts which they have obviously earned by dint of their steady and dependable thrust in the direction the organization requires.

There are overtones of Burns and Stalker's 'mechanistic' as contrasted with 'organic' qualities, bearing in mind that these are career patterns and not organizational structures that we are talking about. However, the man who is high on Incremental development patterning is not necessarily rigid, or conservatively minded. He often prides himself on being 'creative', and values this in his career. The main thing about him is that he accepts the framework and functions within it, accepts the people in it and negotiates amicably with them, accepts difficulties and hurdles and gradually wears them down through persistence, ingenuity, and personality.

The low scorers on this dimension show the obverse pattern. They may be critical rather than accepting of their organizations so that their efforts to change a situation or to advance in it are doomed to failure by virtue of miscarriages of performance which seem to belie their underlying competence. They may have difficulties with others, and at the same time lack the creative efficiency of the Metamorphic types which helps enterprises to forgive a good many foibles.

Chapter 11 · The Tangential Development Pattern

This developmental pattern is in a sense anomalous, in that the people who score high on this factor and who tend to feel that they developed as a manager as a consequence of Henley are predominantly people whom one might not have expected to show such a pattern on the basis of prior characteristics. They tend to have been 'buried' in rather impersonal organizations. They tend to feel that they were nominated as a matter of 'pure chance'; they came from work environments from which they felt alienated, and yet from the College experience they somehow emerged as from a chrysalis to take a new interest in their environments and their own potential in relation to it. Unlike the Metamorphics, however, they accomplish this by seeking a peripheral role for themselves whereby they can develop more or less in spite of their organizations. They may take up a position on the boundaries of the organization, and find outer-directed functions which benefit their organizations and themselves. In these functions and relationships they find new kinds of satisfaction and reward.

Some writers on organization have noted the importance of outer-directed roles. Miller and Rice (1967), for example, have pointed out that some organizational members – notably sales managers – have more to do with members of outside organizations than with their own. The managers described here develop by an increase in environmental awareness and interaction which provides them with an escape from their previous roles, buried deep within bureaucratic structures. Conversely, men who score low on Tangentiality tend to be ones who were already very active and effective, needing no 'bringing out'. While less spectacular on developmental scores, the low-scoring Tangential type shows less development because he is already highly developed – a 'high-flyer' – clear to all to be *en route* to the top.

The loadings on factor IV – the Tangential Development Pattern – are as follows:

·0582 (Creative/Ambitious)
·1393 (Restless/Hard-driving)
·2191 (Environment-oriented)
— ·0480 (Accommodating)
·0544 (Uncritical)
·1549 (Dogged)
— ·0173 (Humanistic)
— ·0643 (Conflicted)
— ·1878 (Venturesome)
·1244 (Manipulative)
·0383 (Fulfilled)
·2636 (Alienated)
·0334 (Climbing)

The main clusters involved in this Factor are the *Alienated* and the *Environment-oriented*, followed by a fairly high negative loading on *Venturesome* (which as a cluster is more heavily involved in

The Alienated Cluster

Cluster 12 *Alienated*

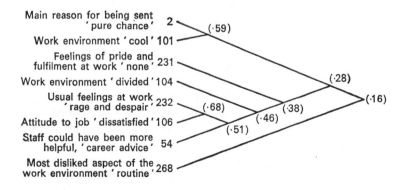

factor I), and *Dogged*. These three clusters – Alienated, Environment-oriented, and Dogged – will be described and then the factor itself will be illustrated with case vignettes.

While the first variable in this cluster, 'pure chance', as a perceived reason for having been nominated, is negatively correlated with development as a manager, the cluster taken as a whole is not correlated with development. The overall impression the cluster gives is of a type of person who is trapped in a work situation which he finds very uncongenial and from which he does not know how to escape. He smoulders with 'rage and despair', dislikes it, and would have appreciated help from the staff about how to manage his future career given this situation.

This cluster is not correlated with age or educational achievements, nor does it relate to a particular specialism. However, there is a marked tendency for this to be a Public Sector pattern, as is shown in *Table 32*.

TABLE 32 *Alienation Cluster Scores by Sector*

(Percentages)

	PI	B	NI	PS
Low (Quintiles 1 and 2)	38	47	28	26
Medium	28	26	16	21
High (Quintiles 4 and 5)	34	28	55	52
TOTALS % =	100	101	99	99
N =	(300)	(82)	(87)	(103)

The Environment-oriented Cluster

Three variables in this cluster correlate with development (63 – Henley *directly* relevant to subsequent job; 216 – 'rebellious'; and 26 – actually got from Henley 'a better understanding of own organization in relation to the wider environment').

The impression that one gets from this cluster is of the sort of person who is like the restless/hard-driving type, somewhat dissatisfied. He may see himself as 'rebellious', but unlike the more mobile and active Metamorphic, this type of manager prefers to stay in his organization rather than to move out. He may become more interested and motivated when he realizes an opportunity to work at the margins, where his organization interacts with the larger environment. This is the area of his interest at Henley, and for which he found direct relevance after the course. Unlike high scorers on the 'restless' cluster, people who score high on this cluster are not 'thrusters'. However, they are not 'lazy' sleepers. This is the kind of 'sleeper' who shows overtones of active discontent with his situation. As with the ambitious/creative types,

Cluster 3 *Environment-oriented*

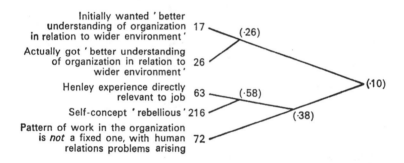

value is placed on creativity, but the massive bureaucratic character of their environment leads them to feel that creative change of the environment is impossible. They discover another way to realize their personal value of creativity, looking outward rather than inward in their organization. High scorers in this cluster tend to indicate that they spend an increasing amount of time at work. The difficult character of relationships sustained by the alienated type is also seen in family life. A degree of dissatisfaction is expressed in family life and this is the category of member whose wife tends more than others to go out to work. No causal inference about this is made on the basis of this data. This type of person may have grown up in a more permissive family atmosphere in which the mother worked, and consequently the man himself may show more understanding and sympathy with this wish in his wife.

There are indications of the validity of this line of thinking in that people who report that their organizations are the type indicated in this cluster also indicate that their mothers were happy with their occupations and that they had a permissive early home environment.

Environmental-orientation is very highly correlated (1 per cent level) with development. It does not correlate with age or degree of formal education or with pre-Henley specialism. It does correlate very significantly (1 per cent level) with type of organization (*Table 33*).

T ABLE 33 *Environment-oriented Cluster Scores, by Type of Employing Organization*

Environment-oriented	PI	B	NI	PS
Low (Quintiles 1 and 2)	11	27	9	17
Medium	38	29	31	32
High (Quintiles 3 and 4)	52	44	60	51
TOTALS % =	100	100	100	100
N =	(300)	(82)	(87)	(103)

The scorers on environment-orientation, as defined in this cluster, are skewed toward the high end. Within this framework the Bankers are relatively low, and Nationalized Industry members relatively high.

Venturesomeness has already been described as highly involved in factor I, the Metamorphic Development Pattern. It should be noted, however, that it is negatively related to this factor so that a high Tangential developer is low on Venturesomeness. He is, however, high on Doggedness.

The Dogged Cluster

This is clearly the hard-working, unspectacular type of developer, whose career pathway shows effort and conformity to well-established patterns and practices of his work environment. There is a correlation between scoring high on this cluster and the sense of having developed as a manager as a consequence of Henley.

High scores are more frequently found among members who were sent to Henley at a somewhat older age and, among the more highly educated members, more of those who are high scorers on Doggedness tending to be among the graduates who were sent to

Cluster 6 *Dogged*

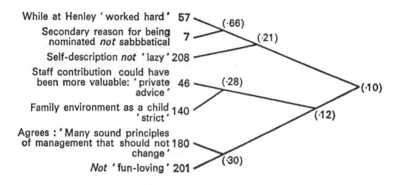

While at Henley 'worked hard' 57
Secondary reason for being nominated *not* sabbbatical 7
Self-description *not* 'lazy' 208
Staff contribution could have been more valuable: 'private advice' 46
Family environment as a child 'strict' 140
Agrees : 'Many sound principles of management that should not change' 180
Not 'fun-loving' 201

(·66) (·21) (·28) (·12) (·30) (·10)

Figure 4 Distribution of Factor IV Scores: Tangential Development Pattern

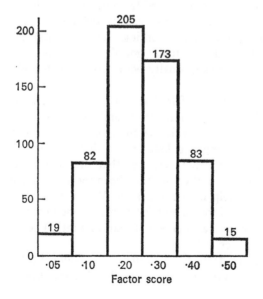

Henley. More Bankers score highly on this cluster than do members from other sectors, but the differences are not statistically significant.

VIGNETTES ILLUSTRATING HIGH AND LOW TANGENTIAL DEVELOPMENT SCORES

The factor scores were computed for each member, and a distribution of scores plotted, as shown in *Figure 4*.

Two from among the 15 highest scorers and two from among the 19 lowest scorers were chosen at random to illustrate the extremes at both ends of this development pattern.

A High Scorer on Tangential Development: 554

554 was a Public Sector man working in a Government central office, who came to Henley at the age of 42. He felt that he was sent to 'broaden him' and to assess his potential for a more senior position. He was 'keen but diffident', and 'rather vague' about what he wanted from the course. He indicated that he wanted a good many things by ticking six out of the nine suggested (other than 'nothing very specific') and indicated that in the end he actually got all those plus a seventh. The only ones not ticked finally were 'complete break' and 'useful contacts'.

In the course he felt that most of it was about right, but would have liked more talks and discussions with outside visitors. He felt that this was the most useful part of the course to him – 'meeting and listening to distinguished visitors from many different fields'. He felt that the staff were helpful in 'social mixing', and could have been more helpful with private advice and help in self-appraisal. While at Henley he worked very hard, and in the end felt that he benefited as a manager a 'great deal', and as a person a 'fair amount'. The impact of the course was general.

He moved from headquarters to a regional office where he became a regional deputy controller. He says that 'some of the work is similar to my pre-Henley job, but the general character of the work is entirely different – dealing with a widespread staff instead of staff concentrated on one site at a central office. Considerably greater expenditure of effort in "throwing one's personality about" to gain confidence and liking of staff. Many problems of accommodation and organization . . . solutions have been in compromises, but generally I feel I have made a marked contribution by personal drive and adaptability toward finding quick solutions and establishing harmonious relationships with new colleagues'.

His change was accompanied by a general increase in managerial responsibilities, and he has had a modest pay rise within the Civil Service scale. He has increased his satisfaction from 'moderate' (pre-Henley) to 'very satisfied' now, though his usual feeling at work is described as 'moderate satisfaction'.

554 is a family man, with two children and a wife who is a full-time homemaker. His new job has allowed increased time at home, despite more time spent on work. He regards himself as 'adaptable', 'creative', 'aggressive', 'efficient', 'hard-driving', 'highly strung', 'idealistic', 'loyal', 'reserved', and 'tense'. He experienced slight value shifts as a consequence of Henley – with an 'opportunity to work with people' moving downward from first to third position, and 'an opportunity to be creative' moving up from second to first position.

Some of the doggedness comes out in his attitudes towards much of the work he described, when he indicates how much he 'dislikes' some of the social occasions he has to attend, when 'time is spent all out of proportion to what is gained – if anything'. He wants to get on with the job, and enjoys having been given the chance to expand into a more environmentally oriented job, though he chafes under some elements of it.

A High Scorer on Tangential Development: 119

119 was a Principal in the Civil Service, sent to Henley at age 36, in his opinion as a matter of 'pure chance', secondarily possibly as 'compensation for not having got something else'. He was 'keen but diffident', and had only a very vague idea of what he wanted from the course. Initially there were three things: 'chance to compare', 'organization-environment', and 'self-understanding'. He feels that he actually got these three, plus 'complete break', 'better understanding of the senior role',

'improved ability to handle new situations', and 'new knowledge' (chairmanship). He feels that most of the course was about right, but would like to have more outside visitors, more informal contacts among members, and less report-writing. The thing he found 'especially useful' was 'knowledge of how groups work and react to each other and to innovation'. He felt that there was too much emphasis on 'set pieces' of presentation which tended to become stilted and to him 'unhelpful'. He would have liked the staff to do more direct teaching.

119 worked 'moderately hard' at the College, and in the end felt that he got a 'fair amount' as a manager and as a person. As a manager he felt that he gained 'skills in the art of persuasion, particularly in the field of innovation. I know how difficult it is to write simply enough for others to understand'. He would like in future to have 'more teaching content in such fields as decision theory, economics, statistics, and group dynamics'.

Since leaving Henley he had a transfer within the Civil Service on being promoted, and receiving a pay rise. He has had an increase in managerial responsibilities almost across the board, and considers that the course at Henley has had general relevance for him. The most irksome problems (though not frequent) are political. Most frequent are technical and economic/financial. He regards his working environment as secure, exciting, and permissive, but divided. Since having taken the course and received his promotion, he has moved from being 'very satisfied' to being 'moderately satisfied'.

119 was the only son of a school-teacher's family who describes his early family life as warm and united but insecure. He moved about a bit in his youth, and was always interested in academic work, thinking originally that he might teach, but later at University thinking more in favour of the Civil Service. He is married to a graduate who works part time outside the home.

He considers himself to be 'adaptable', 'calm', 'unconventional', 'cooperative', 'creative', 'cultured, 'efficient', 'happy', 'hard driving', 'idealistic', 'loyal', 'methodical', 'outgoing', 'strong', 'poised', 'quiet', 'rational', 'self-sufficient', and 'sensual'.

Since Henley, he has increased the amount of time he gives to community activities, particularly the church, and indicates that he regards a successful marriage as more important than success in work, reporting 'joy and fulfilment' in family life, though occasional rage and despair and only moderate satisfaction in the work situation.

His values changed, with the course – and he indicates a rise in the wish to be helpful to others (from the fourth to first position), a drop in the 'opportunity' to show what I can accomplish from first to third, with 'creative' rising from sixth to second, and 'minimum disturbance' dropping from third to sixth. Since leaving Henley, he seems to have come out considerably, rising into a 'senior' Civil Service job, participating in training, drafting new legislation and seeing it through, writing articles for publication, and generally becoming more active. He says that among the challenges he has most enjoyed are: 'bringing on subordinates and giving them useful experience', battling against complacency, being responsive to new or unorthodox views, working *through* people and getting them to move out of the accustomed 'timelessness' of the Civil Service. He feels that there are a number of problems in this – questioning the *status quo*, keeping up standards, counteracting the movement of people out of his section, making integration and communications efforts, and having to force himself to be patient with incompetence, of which he sees a good deal.

A Low Scorer on Tangential Development: 248

248 perhaps illustrates the pattern by giving its other extreme. He was a divisional manager of a major building and construction firm in the private sector, who was sent to Henley at age 36 – he felt to 'broaden' him, and secondarily as a sabbatical. He was 'enthusiastic' but had little idea of what he wanted at the time. He mentions only two things – 'chance to compare' and 'understanding senior role requirements'. He says that he got 'useful contacts, and a complete break as well as a chance to compare', but did not improve his understanding of the senior role. On the other hand, he saw as most useful 'the realization that widely different industries and organizations have similar problems'. He would like the staff to give more help in self-appraisal, and do more direct teaching. He did not work at all hard in the College, and felt that he did not at all benefit as a manager. The staff, though they considered him to be a top manager in his future potential, considered that he grew only a little while at the College. He urges, for the future, more case

studies, less 'vague' syndicate work, particularly in the second half of the course. After leaving the College he had a change of job and a change of firm, and a large rise in salary – from the £2,000–3,000 to the £4,000–5,000 bracket. This is reflected in an overall rise in managerial responsibilities, and he is moderately satisfied in his work, which he characterizes as having a 'warm' environment.

The change he experienced was an unusual one. He indicates that he was fortunate in having a considerable private income, so he was able to throw up his job in large-scale industry, with its highly competitive environment, and join a smaller firm in a pleasant part of the country at an initially lower salary. He has since found himself with more personal responsibility because of the smaller scale of the business. He is now the managing director of the firm, and enjoys the work partly because he does not have to spend the same proportion of his time in 'internal political battles' as he had to do when he was with the large organization.

This is a man who describes himself as 'calm', 'cautious', 'lazy', 'quiet', 'reserved', and 'self-sufficient'. He has sustained his values, which emphasize creativity, work with people, and a chance to use intellectual problem-solving abilities.

A Low Scorer on Tangential Development: 337

This man also illustrates the situation where a man does not consider himself to have developed largely because he is already of surpassing excellence in his field, and consequently a low scorer on tangential development. He came to Henley at the age of 38 as a sales manager in a highly technical science-based industry. He came because he asked to be nominated, and was enthusiastic and had definite things in mind that he wanted from the course. The three things he wanted, and got, were: 'break', 'understanding of senior role', and 'self-understanding'. He wanted, but did not get, 'useful contacts'. He feels that the most useful thing he got out of the course was 'the rest', then 'the financial management aspects'. He did not find anything 'unhelpful', considers that the staff contribution was not valuable to him, and suggests that they join in discussion more. For the future of Henley he suggests: 'a good deal more emphasis on management as a science and less as an art. Nothing like enough made of computers in this context'.

He did not work very hard at Henley, found being away from home 'quite disturbing', as did his wife, and in the end he felt that he had developed 'not very much' as a manager and as a person as a consequence of the course.

On leaving Henley, he felt that it had 'general' relevance for his work as he underwent two changes of job and two promotions rising from the £4,000–5,000 bracket of income to the £8,000–9,000 bracket. He showed an increase across the board (except for contacts with people outside, which were always very high as a sales manager, and machine aids) in the indicators of managerial responsibility. He does not consider human problems to be the most irksome he encounters, though they are the most frequent. He sees economic/financial problems as the most irksome, and these are solved by strong action from the man at the top.

He characterizes his work environment as out of the average only in being 'warm', 'permissive', and 'exciting', and in being 'unconventional'. He is moderately satisfied with his job now, as he was prior to Henley.

After leaving Henley he found his role enlarged, first to taking charge of the market development organization of his company, and then to becoming general overseas sales manager for the major portion of the world. His job has been to revitalize the companies overseas, many of which in the more far-flung parts of the world have been allowed to run down.

The 'action-orientated' thrust that had characterized this man's career is seen in how he describes the part of it following Henley and leading to his present position:

'When I was running the market development organization in the firm this affected the functioning of product and market planning, commercial division, personnel division, education division, sales promotion division, and internal EDP. During this period I was chairman of the New Product Committee. This involved a whole new aspect of our company's activities, and I had to learn fast and make many changes – principally by introducing Marketing to Research and Development. It was new, difficult, stimulating, and eventually boring: too abstract and too little power to effect what one could clearly see needed to be done.'

This man's background resembles that of the 'ambitious/creative' type, and indeed his score on this factor is very high –

just under the very top group selected to represent the development pattern. He comes from a family in which the father was a clerical worker, and the mother died when he was very young; he characterized the household as 'insecure', 'boring', 'cool', 'permissive', 'unconventional', and 'divided'. He had a brother and a sister, and they moved about several times in his youth in the north of England. He was sent to a boarding school, and left it with no idea of his future career, and did not go to university.

He is married now, with three children, and tends to express 'happy' family feelings. He has definite views, and tends to agree very strongly with strong leadership opinions and at the same time with humanistic views of the organization and its workers. His self-descriptions include: 'ambitious', 'aggressive', 'competitive', 'creative', 'dominant', 'emotional', 'idealistic', 'impetuous', 'intuitive', 'lazy', 'loyal', 'moody', 'rebellious', and 'volatile'. His career values were a rather unusual combination. Usually members who value highly, as he does, the 'opportunity to show what I can accomplish' are venturesome and place 'security' low on their list, yet he places it very high – in first position both before and after Henley. Indeed, this man shows at least two kinds of conflict – between security and personal achievement values, and also between his familistic values (expressed in terms of the areas from which he derives greatest happiness and satisfaction) and his world-travelling promotional role. These conflicts may account for his high score on psychosomatic complaints – heart beating hard, trouble sleeping, nervousness and tenseness, all sorts of aches and pains, backaches.

This would seem to be a highly successful person who emerged early under his own steam, developed very much on the metamorphic lines in his organization, but sustained in the course of it a number of conflicts that, while adding to his 'drive', may have also taken toll of his personality.

SUMMARY

It would seem that the high scorers on this factor are people who were, prior to Henley, buried in a large bureaucratic organization that they disliked. They tended to be 'sleepers', but not the fixed lazy type or the type whose values made the 'sleeper' orientation congenial; in fact, they tended to emphasize 'creativity', but their environments limited their possibilities for realizing this value. While they score highly relative to other managers at Henley for alienation, it must be remembered that this is really a very muted phenomenon among the Henley men, who are selected and sent as a form of investment by their firms. They may be rebellious, critical, and dissatisfied, but they are rarely alienated in a very deep and destructive sense. These men felt that they developed as a consequence of Henley, particularly when their organizations offered them an opportunity for a change of job. The opposite polar types, the low scorers on Tangential Development, are men who had been very successful already, who were in a sense 'stars' at Henley, but who did not necessarily feel that they developed at the College. They were destined for the top, Henley played some kind of a role in this advance, and they indicate various things that they got from the experience, but it did not 'bring them out' in the same sense as it did for the men on the high-scoring extreme.

PART FOUR

Findings and Implications

Chapter 12 · Henley and the Future

ADAPTING A DEVELOPMENTAL COMMUNITY

At this juncture in its development, the Administrative Staff College faces a challenging situation. It has a tradition of both pioneering spirit and effective leadership in the development of managers at mid-career. For more than fifteen years, until the advent of the British business schools, it faced little competition. Within the last decade, however, there has been a proliferation of new forms and techniques of management and to some extent distinctive methods of management training. More firms now recognize that education and training can increase the effectiveness of a manager by adding to his knowledge and his range of skills. On the other hand, there is by no means a consensus about the best combination of approaches and methods for effective training. This lack of consensus is particularly marked in relation to the task of developing managers from the middle levels for more senior positions, much depending upon the assumptions made about the nature of the task of development and the nature of managerial work and the processes by which managers in their mid-thirties best learn.

As Andrew Life pointed out in an earlier chapter, the guiding conception in 1948, when the College was founded, was based on the notion of the fundamental difference between specialist and general managership, with the College serving the function of assisting managers to make the transition. Specialist managers could and usually did learn their art through didactic methods of instruction. To the extent that the specialist skills were scientifically based, they could be taught by recognized authorities. General managership, on the other hand, was seen as involving the development of such qualities of character as sound judgement, insight, self-confidence, and the capacity to weigh up diverse information in making decisions. Heuristic methods were deemed more appropriate for these goals, and the method of work involving group discussions under a member–chairman seemed both innovative and sound. There has been a good deal of subsequent research, such as Abercrombie's demonstration of the value of the group-discussion method as a way of improving the judgement of medical students (Abercrombie, 1960), and the work of the proponents of training-group methods. Heuristic methods, it would seem, have value both in situations where management theory and science are relatively undeveloped and in situations where the development of the manager as a person is an integral part of the task of enabling whatever there is of the science to be practised.

SOME CHARACTERISTICS OF THE STUDY OF CAREERS AND HENLEY

The study reported here was based on exploratory interviews with a wide range of managers, nominators, and trainers and on a survey conducted in 1967 of 576 managers who had attended Henley between 1960 and 1966. In summarizing the findings, it must be kept in mind that many of the suggestions made by the managers in the survey were products of the particular circumstances of their own training experience, the climate of opinions and dominant issues of the times, the state of the course at Henley and so on. Many of the things against which they reacted have been subsequently changed – partly in response to the study itself, and partly as a part of the normal development of the College in response to the challenges facing it. These adaptations will be described below, after some of the salient findings have been indicated.

The study from which these findings emerge is exploratory with evaluative elements. It is exploratory in the sense that it brought approaches and questions hitherto untried into a new situation, under a rather general mandate to search for meaningful problems and issues that could be illuminated by research of this type.

No particular hypothesis was put forward, no particular topic for investigation was pressed. The pivotal point was a general increase of knowledge relating to the changing role of senior managers and to the place of a training experience such as that provided at Henley. It was assumed that any contribution to knowledge in this area would also contribute to the efforts at evaluation already under way at the College, and that evaluation based on scientific knowledge was more useful as a basis for action than evaluation based on haphazard opinion or impression.

As an evaluation study, it must be said that the design and execution of the research have many deficiencies. There is no measurement of 'before' and 'after' training characteristics of the relevant population. There are no control groups. There are no measures of tested reliability, only a survey instrument constructed on the basis of exploratory interviews. There are very few collateral sources of information about the managers studied that can help to assess the validity of their answers, e.g. the appraisals of their superiors, their colleagues, or their families.

The fact that the focus of the research was on 'growth' or 'development' in relation to Henley made it particularly important that the measurement of the dependent variable 'development' should be valid. There is some evidence that the individual's self-appraisal can be a risky basis for measuring this kind of dependent variable. Individuals who have a 'one-shot' experience, such as a training course, have been found to be prone to indicating that they benefited by it. This is found true almost irrespective of the kind of experience – a religious group meeting, a psychiatric hospital experience, or an educational experience. One can usually count on about half to two-thirds of the population indicating that they benefited by such an experience, apparently in response to a general human need to feel that a life experience has done one some good. It should be noted, however, that it is not only destructive or traumatic kinds of experience that arouse negative reactions. The consumer and entertainment fields offer many illustrations of negative responses, even to stimuli which are *intended* to please. So it may be said that a positive response, such as the one found among Henley members, does not prove the superiority of Henley methods to other forms of training, but it does indicate a basic level of acceptance that might have been lacking. Even the best-intended and enthusiastically propagated programmes may fail to rouse this basic level of support.

Furthermore, the assessment by the individual of the value to him of his own training experience may be thought of as having special merits. While one cannot attach much importance to the exact percentage of people who say they benefited (as one would want to do if this were the kind of evaluation study that assessed whether the College's programme was better or worse than some other), one can accept the judgement of the individuals about whether they consider they benefited from the course as being in a sense a 'true' appraisal. It has what is generally described as 'face validity'. That is to say, if the individual feels that he has developed as a manager as a consequence of Henley, one may say that he is the best judge, up to a point. There is an element of managerial role that only the manager himself knows about, and this is part of what each manager feels when he makes his own self-appraisal. Of course, there is also a part of the managerial role, perhaps the most important part to the organization, that depends not on what the person himself thinks, but on what his subordinates and employers think. While we have no direct evidence on either of these other sources of assessment, we do have indirect evidence of the latter in the form of reported promotions and increases in managerial role-responsibilities. Assuming that the respondents – being senior managers and Henley ex-members and therefore inclined to answer honestly – did in fact give valid answers to such questions as whether they now took larger and more decisions without reference to higher authority, one finds that managerial increase (as measured by our 'climber' cluster and scale) is indeed correlated with a sense of having developed as a manager. This provides one form of 'criterion' or correlational validity check. Another form of criterion validity check is the correlation of members' appraisal of their own development and the appraisals made of them by the Henley staff. The members' own evaluations were more predictive of subsequent career success, as one would expect, because by the time they were sent the questionnaire they had the advantage of hindsight, which was not available to the staff in rating the men's performance while at Henley.

We therefore feel a fair degree of confidence in the validity of the dependent variable – the judgement of the person that he developed as a manager in consequence of Henley. We have, in this context, learned quite a bit about this development, both in terms of its process and in terms of different types of developmental pattern that may be observed to occur at mid-career.

At the outset, then, it is clear that we have not been doing the sort of evaluation that aims at indicating whether the College at Henley is better than other colleges. This is, in the circumstances, impossible to assess. We take the College as 'given', and ask, first, whether some parts of its programme are felt to be more effective in terms of its goals than other parts, and, second, whether some kinds of people in some kinds of environments respond differently to it from others. This is what may be referred to as a *process* evaluation.

There are many obstacles in the way of undertaking a more experimental form of evaluation. For example, control groups might be required, so that a group of managers sent to Henley can be matched in terms of age, background, and personal characteristics with other groups whose members may consist of those given no training outside the company or those attending institutions characterized by a preoccupation with management techniques presented didactically. However, methodologically, there are many complexities and difficulties in the way of establishing and studying such control groups.

Similarly, longitudinal studies would be necessary, involving the collection and analysis of data about the life-histories and behaviour of those attending courses at Henley and those in the control groups. Conceivably these studies could continue for thirty years or more, from the time members left the College at the end of a session.

In addition, greater precision will have to be developed in the measurement of the relevant variables, such as pre- and post-Henley attitudes and behaviour, and this will call for very close collaboration with enterprises.

FINDINGS

In response to the first question – about the relative effectiveness of different parts of the programme – the most impressive finding has to do with the need felt by members to have a greater element of didactic or expository teaching incorporated into the programme. This does not mean that the centrally important 'participative' or 'heuristic' elements of the programme were not appreciated. The suggestions of members and their patterns of response to questions asking about which part of the programme benefited them suggest that the wish for more expository components of the programme is 'in addition to' rather than 'instead of' the participative syndicate elements. The core elements of removal from the ordinary round of work pressures, mixing in an accepting 'community' with others of different background and viewpoint where the lid could be taken off one's normal inhibitions for a free critical exchange of views, are still held to be of central importance. The members' wish for more didactic inputs does not mean that they wished to become technically expert at these new methods. They regarded them as tools of management and not the essence of management. They felt the need to know more about the technical details of many new developments in management science from authoritative experts if they were to make the most intelligent use of them as tools.

Another component of the programme that was emphasized as deserving more explicit cultivation has to do with the whole area of personal advice and career guidance. As we have indicated, there is a relationship – as postulated by the earliest founders of the College – between development as a manager at mid-career and development as a person. Development as a person is something that is left to a largely implicit aspect of the programme. Taking time out for reflection and integration of experiences, general broadening, the challenge of new ideas and questioning of one's habitual thoughtways, etc. are all well recognized as significant, though not part of a formal curriculum. On the other hand, there is another component of more active effort, something close to counselling, which many members report as important. The opportunity to talk freely with someone not in one's usual 'system' of judgement and power – the political system of one's home organization – is important to many members. This is a time when many try to sort out the meaning of their life-experiences up until this point, a process that is facilitated by the kind of personal communication that paradoxically is often lacking in one's usual personal network of relationships, which might be upset by the unburdening that may be entailed. New forms of insight and of personal values may emerge from this and many members ask for more of it as part of the explicit programme.

Still a third element seems wanted, though by implication only; that is, the element of continuity between the college's training programme and the subsequent experiences in the employing firm. Part of this is implied in what the members say in their questionnaire, and part from what others say about them. Many members who considered that they developed at Henley and whom the staff considered to have developed, expressed feelings of frustration at not being able to apply their new knowledge and insights to their organization. Some, of course, leave their employers when this happens and others seek to develop in roles peripheral to their organizations. Most, however, smoulder in discontent. There are also instances where success comes too rapidly. A man returns from Henley with the feeling of new competences and he is pressed into more responsible and demanding roles more rapidly than he may feel ready for. This form of discontinuity, while more agreeable in some ways, may also be stressful for the developing manager. In relation to the differences among the managers and the extent to which these might affect their developmental potential, there were a number of issues of initial interest. Are younger members more likely to develop than older members? Private Sector members more than Public Sector? University graduates more than non-graduates? The earlier members more than more recent ones, given the existence of so many new alternative courses? Do Trade Unionists have enough in common with other managers to be able to benefit from taking the same course?

The first results of the survey indicated that, while all of these questions may be answered to some extent with the information from the survey, they did not provide the basis for the most meaningful differentiation of types of manager and types of managerial career. Each of these items – age, education, employing organization, etc. – contributed a little to explaining the developmental patterns observed, but they were far from adequate to explaining the diversity of career patterns found among ex-members. It is true, for example, that ex-members sent in their thirties tend to indicate more frequently than those who were sent when they were over forty that they developed as managers as a result of Henley. On the other hand, there were many instances contradicting this tendency. The same is true for the other items mentioned. It is more interesting to indicate the different ways in which each item affects developmental patterns, rather than simply to show a statistical tendency for the item to be related to development.

Take education as an example. There is no correlation between level of education and the assessment of having grown at Henley. Instead there are indications of the different ways in which people with different types and levels of education used Henley. The group, for example, who had *no* formal higher education is found to be associated with a working-class background (father's occupation more frequently manual labour), and tended to characterize their early family background as 'boring'. These members tended not to have had a clear idea of their career objectives when they were in school and they seem to have fallen into two groups, those who were simply interested in 'English' and those who were interested in 'applied sciences'. Members from this sort of background are often found in the Banks, and least frequently in the

Civil Service. They tend to have undistinguished careers at Henley and, following Henley, to return comfortably to their organizations, which they see as 'secure'. Their values include an emphasis on the importance of a 'clear-cut hierarchy of authority' and on the importance to them personally of security. The kinds of problem they find most irksome are those involving considerable intellectual challenge, and it is here they feel most acutely their lack of higher formal education. However, since they emphasize more the human relations elements in their work and their family situations, this is unlikely to create acute conflicts for them.

The university-educated managers may be divided into two subgroups, those who completed their degrees and those who did not. The latter is a very interesting group, though proportionately small. These members tend to have come from families that moved around a good deal when the member was young and to recollect their early family environments as being 'cool', with the father satisfied with the work he did but the mother perhaps less so. This sort of person tends to have had a career exhibiting a good many elements of turbulence and conflict, but where it is accompanied by creativity he seems to experience considerable success, embodying the Metamorphic type of career pattern. There is a tendency to move about and to change employers if sufficient scope is not offered, 'spiralling' upwards to better jobs in other firms. This group enjoyed the highest salary level pre-Henley, perhaps using Henley in some ways as an experience that rounds off the uncompleted university experience of the past. While this type of person continues to rise following Henley, he does not easily find personal happiness in his career success. Though he tends to be married and to have many children, he often feels a sense of despair about himself and his life. We get some idea of the kinds of turbulence that may be involved for such a member at this stage in his life-career, when we consider that the members in this subgroup indicate the greatest degree of change in values relating to their personal career while at Henley; following Henley, despite their movement upward, they also indicate the greatest tendency to take advantage of their seniority, to take more time off for their homes and families, and to be less wholly embedded in their work than previously. Often their wives work outside the home, a situation that may have various determinants and consequences for them. Whatever the case, these members do not sacrifice managerial advance for their new pursuit of family and leisure values, but use their career success to make the latter possible. Their personal turbulence would seem to be a product in part at least of the feeling that they had given themselves too much to the career aspects of their lives and that they now seek to restore a balance, finding it not always easy to do so.

Those members, more numerous, who graduated from university with a degree are characterized by a more democratic orientation than the other groups, disagreeing more frequently, for example, with the proposition that a clear-cut hierarchy of authority is the cornerstone of a well-functioning organization. In contrast to the non-university group, this group values most highly – rather than finding it most irksome – 'the chance to use my intellectual problem-solving abilities'. At Henley, the graduates were less interested than others in cultivating their skills at writing reports and at public speaking, presumably because these were skills they had already cultivated. This type of manager tends to be sent to Henley at a slightly earlier age than non-graduates, and tends to be on the increase in recent sessions.

Perhaps as interesting as the level of education is its emphasis. The arts and humanities graduates had a less clear idea than the others about the line of career they would pursue after university. They worked less hard while at Henley and changed their values in the direction of de-emphasizing the intellectual problem-solving elements. They wanted fewer outside visits as part of the course, and, following the course, they felt a greater degree of satisfaction than other sub-groups.

In contrast, those who emphasized the physical sciences did well prior to Henley in terms of salary, but following Henley they experienced more dissatisfaction. This would seem to stem from their dislike for administrative tasks, and their preference for keeping their identity as scientists. Among the Henley group, as has often been found among creative scientists in other studies, e.g. of Nobel prizewinners, the element of loneliness in their backgrounds is marked. They characterize their early family environments as 'insecure' and 'unconventional' and show considerable unhappiness in their subsequent lives, despite their conspicuous career success.

The engineers and applied scientists, including those who went to a technical college, are the most conservative. They disagree more than others with the proposition that 'the most important skill for managers of the future is planning for and controlling change'. They are also, particularly the technologists, disillusioned with the requirements of management as distinct from their more technical work, and agree more than the other groups that senior managerial jobs 'require an individual to compromise his moral standards'. On the other hand, these sub-groups appreciated the increase in freedom associated with movement upward, and changed their personal values more in the direction of wanting to be 'helpful to people'. The technologists particularly found the Henley experience 'directly relevant' to their subsequent job requirements and suggested that the course should provide even more experience with public speaking, which is not surprising, given the tendency for technologists to have been more taken up with non-verbal activities and relationships.

The differences between sectors, including the Trade Unionists, are also interesting. Though we found the differences were not as high as we had initially expected – with certain types of Civil Servants resembling certain types of Bankers and certain types of Private Sector managers more than they resembled their colleagues of different personality and career style in the same sector – there are some differences which are characteristic of these sub-groups and they are interesting to note. The Civil Servants, for example, are sent to Henley at a slightly later age than the other groups, they come from a relatively higher social class and educational background, and they tend to have certain characteristic attitudes, values, and patterns of career development. They tend more than members from other sectors to characterize their work environment as 'secure' and their own feelings about their jobs as 'satisfied'. On the other hand, they tend to have a lower salary level both pre-Henley and post-Henley than do members from other sectors and experience a relatively small number of promotions following Henley.

The Civil Servants at Henley suggested less report-writing, for obvious reasons, and, though they developed as managers in proportions comparable to other groups, felt that they did not develop so much as persons. Their career values de-emphasized the authoritative elements, disagreeing more than others, for example, with the proposition that 'it is more important than ever today that the man at the top should be a bold leader more than a skilled administrator'. They give a very low rating to the career value which is ordinarily rated very highly by industrial managers, 'A chance to show what I can accomplish'.

Civil Servants are a bit less enthusiastic about being sent, a bit more inclined to feel that they were chosen as a matter of 'pure chance', a bit more likely to describe themselves as 'idealistic' and 'cooperative', a bit more conservative in their overall management philosophy.

The Trade Unionists, only four of whom returned questionnaires out of a total of eight who attended the course during this period, are an interesting group. Obviously, with so small a sample one cannot make confident generalizations, but some observations seem so sensible and probably valid that they ought to be mentioned because of the very great interest in the possibility of bringing together managers and trade unionists within a single course. Some of the differences are obvious. The Trade Unionists come more from working-class backgrounds than do the others; one-fifth of the others had skilled or semi-skilled workers as fathers; three-quarters of the Trade Unionists. All of the fathers were employed by industrial firms, compared with less than half of the fathers of the other members. They had less formal education than the other managers, and while at school tended to occupy themselves more with sports and extra-curricular activities than with academic subjects.

The career values of the Trade Unionists differed markedly from those of other members. Whereas members overall placed 'an opportunity to be helpful to others' at the bottom of their hierarchy of career values, the Trade Unionists placed it at the top. (This value shifted downward slightly for the Trade Unionists following Henley, to third position, while overall it stayed on the bottom.) On the other hand, 'an opportunity to work with people rather than things or ideas only' rose from second to first position for the Trade Unionists, emphasizing the human interaction with a task orientation. This rose for the members overall from seventh position pre-Henley to third post-Henley. While for members generally 'an opportunity to show what I can accomplish' is the paramount value both pre- and post-Henley, for the Trade Unionists it is of much less significance and drops from fourth to fifth position. Similarly 'intellectual problem-solving', placed second both pre- and post-Henley for members generally, starts fifth and drops to seventh for the Trade Unionists.

The Trade Unionists worked hard at Henley and were in general more disposed to accept the course as it stood, giving fewer suggestions for revision. On the other hand, they did not feel that, as managers, they benefited as much from the course as did the others, and they indicated less direct relevance to their subsequent work. They felt more than others that their jobs following Henley did not provide scope for changing things around very much. Their salaries did not change greatly, and were at the low end of the scale. They showed the lowest increase in managerial responsibilities and a relatively high degree of dissatisfaction, though paradoxically also a relatively high feeling that they achieve pride and fulfilment in their work. They do feel that their work environment is 'divided' and that they must absorb considerable conflict. This is reflected in a relatively high incidence of symptom formation, e.g. 'heart beating hard', 'insomnia', 'tenseness and nervousness'.

Their managerial philosophy puts a stress on the human factor, the importance of group decision-making, a faith in the workers' capacity to take on more responsibility and a certain cynicism about top managers (top managers are willing to take decisions that hurt others; they get ahead through knowing the right people; they take decisions that make them compromise their moral standards).

In other respects the Trade Unionists resemble other managers. They feel, as do the others, that they have something important to contribute to the course by virtue of their special experiences and interests. Like other specialists, they feel that they 'give' something to the others. In their case they are less sure about what they get back, this being complicated by the difficulty they experience in putting into practice the things they learn at Henley because of their own organization's limitations.

Given that each of these items – age, education, sector – explains only a small amount of the variance in development, we proceeded to carry out cluster and factor analyses of the responses. We found that most of the variance could be explained by three factors, representing three patterns of managerial development. These three types of manager are quite different from one another in terms of the way they orientate themselves to their organizations and the kinds of people they tend to be, with respect to both personal traits and managerial philosophy and values.

The first type of manager, the type that characteristically displays the developmental pattern we have termed *Metamorphic*, is the sort of person who is ambitious, creative, little concerned with security, willing to take risks and to deal actively with new situations in such a way as to change them or to change his own ideas if appropriate, so as to bring about new creative syntheses. This is the sort of member who, if he cannot change a situation or himself so that he can function better in it, is likely to change his organization. He is often a very energetic person who communicates a sense of competence and leadership and therefore his moves outward are often also moves upwards; hence the term 'spiralist' for people scoring high on that sub-cluster of the Metamorphic type.

The second type of pattern is the one termed *Incremental*, because development seems to be by cumulative steps along a given track or channel. This sort of man tends to orientate himself to his organization in a more accepting way. Essentially, he wishes to advance within a structure, without being strongly impelled to change it. He is more likely to be willing to change himself to do what is required by the organization rather than to seek to change the organization. When associated with managerial competence, this type of career is characterized by steady advancement accompanied by a good deal of personal satisfaction and happiness.

The third type, the *Tangential* development pattern, is characterized by the manager's tending to taking up a position of dissent in relation to this employing organization. He is dissatisfied with many elements in his work environment, tends to find it cool, divided, and excessively bureaucratic, and experiences considerable frustration. Nevertheless, if he also possesses a constructive orientation and appropriate levels of competence, this sort of a manager may develop notwithstanding his feeling of opposition or antagonism. By making explicit to himself his disagreement with the situation in his organization, he may be able to take up a role peripheral to it and thereby serve both the organization and himself. Working in relation largely to members of other organizations, he provides a valuable boundary function for his own organization and is able to develop even with, or almost because of, this modicum of distaste he feels for his own organization and its way of functioning. Where the individual is tied into an organization which is in fact dull and routine, impersonal and bureaucratic, he may be able to find a measure of both personal and managerial fulfilment in peripheral roles. Sometimes the rebelliousness or sense of protest is functional for the organization, and a man who expresses this, under appropriate conditions, is pressed to set things right by moving into a responsible position. His career pattern may assume at that point the character of the Metamorphic developer.

A THEORY OF DEVELOPMENT

Development seems to occur through two basic processes: accumulation and transformation.

Accumulation is the addition of elements to a system already functioning in a stabilized state, without changing the structural properties of the system.

Transformation is the process of change in the structural properties of the system itself. The transformations possible are many, ranging from fission – which involves the separation off of a part of the original system to form a new second system – through to a reorganization of the internal elements of the system without appreciable change in the properties or values of the elements themselves.

Development may be described in systems of all kinds and its determinants and consequences assessed (Emery, 1969). The languages of different disciplines describe these processes differently. In our study of whole careers as units we have used the terms Incremental and Metamorphic. The Tangential Development Pattern seems to represent a special case of the transformation process, in that the development comes about not within a stabilized structure through the accumulation of similar units, but by partly rejecting the stabilized structure and developing through the accumulation of new elements tangential to rather than within the given structure.

Most developmental theory concerning individual human beings concentrates on childhood. We have indicated earlier why, in a complex and rapidly changing society, it is important to begin to develop conceptions of development that extend through adulthood. Erikson's theory, which is a life-cycle theory, would seem to state that development takes place by accumulation within stages, punctuated by transformations at critical points of growth that are determined 'epigenetically' by the nature of the biological organism. The theoretical problem arises when one considers critical points of transformation that are not biologically imposed, either by the thrust of a growing organism or by the deficits and perceptions of deficits of an organism in decline. Attention is only now beginning to concentrate on structural properties affecting the developmental process in adulthood (Cogswell, 1968). The kinds of developmental node with which we are concerned are those presented by transitions in work role, broadly speaking by the transition from functional managership to general managership.

A dynamic conception of development would postulate a condition of turbulence and reorganization attendant on a major transition. Old information, and old structures and interrelations, have to be disturbed and new ones developed. This involves work, psychic work, often of a very intense kind, often accompanied by resistances, struggles, conflicts, and difficulties as old arrangements are abandoned and new ones forged. Elliott Jaques has presented a conception of the motivating force underlying this process when it occurs at 'mid-life' – namely the awareness of death as a real eventuality for the individual. This creates a psychic process which reactivates earlier dilemmas of a 'depressive' nature, which the individual then works to resolve, the transformations taking either a creative form or one that is sterile.

Examining the Henley situation specifically, we have a series of adults approaching the mid-life period who differ in their intrapersonal dynamics and in their organizational situation. Some have the capacity to react to most critical transitions, whether internally or externally activated, by a creative transformation, others less so. Some are moving from a specialist role to a general-manager role which requires a major transformation of role behaviour. Others may be making a different kind of move. The pattern of a man's career is thought of as emerging from the interaction of the individual with his social environment. The Metamorphic pattern is one in which the environment allows a major role transformation and the individual is able to reorganize himself to take advantage of this. The Incremental pattern is one in which, for reasons of environment and/or individual proclivities, the pattern is more one of accumulation than reorganization. The Tangential pattern is one in which the organization does not provide scope for transformations, but the individual creates them on the margins of the organization.

What is the role of an educational institution that aims at providing a transitional experience within a long-term developmental *evolution*? From our information it would seem that the institution fulfils quite different functions for different person–organization combinations. For those who are of the Incremental type, it provides information that assists individuals to grow within a given structure which does not change. For those who are involved in the Metamorphic type of development pattern, the contribution is more one of providing help with the reorganization process. For those involved in the Tangential pattern, it is some of each, with quite a strong emphasis on the factors that go with the transformation process.

What is involved in the transformation process? This is more difficult to grasp immediately, for it is the accumulation process that fits the formal didactic methods of lectures and communication of expert information. These are the methods used by traditional schools and colleges. Ashby has noted that Scottish undergraduate education has been based on them, on the assumption that the accumulation of knowledge was what was wanted in the general liberal arts education, as contrasted with later phases of development in the professions which called for educational methods of a different nature:

'There was no effort to superpose character-training on the formal teaching or to cultivate the qualities of leadership . . .' (Ashby, 1966).

The Hale report on university teaching methods accepted that the didactic method, notably the lecture, may be appropriate for adolescents, because as Erikson (1968) has pointed out young people in this stage of life are 'searching for some inspiring unification of tradition or anticipated techniques, ideas and ideals' to help them to decide upon a future occupation in which they can achieve their aspirations. The Hale Report has proved to be only partly correct. Student reactions against the formal didactic method, among other things, indicate that the theoretical assumptions which were used to rationalize it were unsound or at least incomplete. While many students wish to attach themselves to a revered exemplar and to internalize the information which he imparts in a rather accumulative way, many wish to reorganize quite fundamentally the structure of teaching and learning. For some students, it is the incremental or accumulative method that is wanted and is effective, while for others this is unacceptable or felt to be inadequate. The students who are rejecting the didactic methods are doing so in a way that is involving them in a struggle of wills and values with the authorities. The educators who side with them do so partly on the basis of substantive agreement about the need for reforms in the educational system, partly because they see the creative and developmental potential of learning through conflict.

Returning to the adult situation of Henley members, where paradoxically there is pressure toward greater structure and didactic input at the same time as the reverse pressures are coming from younger learners, the same basic formulation seems to hold. For some, it is mainly by accumulative gains that they develop, for whatever combination of personal and environmental reasons. They either accept the basic structure within which they are functioning and see the way toward advancement within it by simply accumulating competences, or they are so limited in their competences at the start that what they want at this stage of their development is to accumulate skills. The managers who are of the more Metamorphic type, on the other hand, wish to engage in a more active process of learning, one that involves the give and take of criticism, the reconceptualization of themselves and their relations to others, the reformulation of many ideas and ideals, some of which may have been quite affectively loaded for them, as in the stereotypes they may hold about members of other kinds of organization, the Government, the trade unions, etc. For this kind of transformation, an environment is required in which criticisms and conflicts can be resolved creatively rather than pursued destructively. This means the building up of trust, a protected environment where sanctions and reprisals of a lasting or irreversible type will not occur and where reconstruction can take place. In biological metaphor, this means an environment in which both catabolism and anabolism can occur (with a breaking-down and a building-up phase). The environment of a community – where members are out of their ordinary work situation, where the sanctions of the 'real' workplace are absent and where a member-centred rehearsal work-group (syndicate) takes its place – is aimed at this goal. Within this framework specific new techniques – more highly structured and active than some of the older ones – may find a compatible setting for effective applications e.g. the Group Feedback Analysis (GFA) (Heller, 1969) and various modifications of management gains, multi-dimensional grids, and T-groups. It is possible that new techniques of an intensive group-interaction type – 'D-groups' to coin a term – may be developed.

The earlier assumption of the 'developmental community' at Henley was that for most purposes the men had a sufficient accumulation of information and experience to engage directly in the transformation process, but this is no longer so. Some need a phase or component of accumulation as a prerequisite to the transformation process. It has become a necessary though not sufficient condition for the transformation. Sometimes the process rests on Incremental development only. Sometimes, where there are environmental limitations, a person who might have Metamorphic potential is able to develop only by taking a Tangential tack. The College cannot control for these variations in circumstance, but it can allow for differences in requirements and for differences in response pattern, and is so doing. These provisions, in the form of changes in the organization and work of the College, are the ways in which it is adapting to changing circumstances and hence towards a more effective type of developmental community.

In the Survey we included open-ended questions requesting ideas about the future role of Henley, as well as questions about the role of the Directing Staff and the learning situations provided for members. In general, the Henley members found the programme of studies rewarding, but where criticisms were given they tended to take the form of suggesting more structure in the staff roles and more technical inputs in the direction of the didactic approach, these suggestions tending to be associated with certain types of manager.

In their answers many members expressed a desire for more knowledge about economics, planning, and the applications of computers, through the medium of lectures. Considering that the members were at Henley between 1961 and 1966, when Economic Development Councils, mergers between computer companies, and recurring balance-of-payments problems were topical, their desire for knowledge in these fields is intelligible, especially since so many members subsequently moved to roles concerned with planning and forecasting. In this respect members might be regarded as voicing an enterprise view of the developmental task which Henley ought to be discharging.

The desire on the part of some members for the role of Directing Staff to be more clearly defined and 'visible' might be regarded as a reflection of current practice in bureaucratized organizations, anxieties about 'invisible' activities of the staff, feelings that the Directing Staff were not being fully utilized as a potential learning resource, and confusion about the role identity of staff members. Here again, one can detect the possible influence of institutions using the didactic approach where, for example, one has expectations about the competence of individuals who are described by their status as Assistant Lecturer, Lecturer, Senior Lecturer, and so on, and by their specialist competence in, for example, law, marketing, and accountancy. At Henley, however, staff members responsible for syndicates simply have the appellation of 'Directing Staff', usually abbreviated to DS, without the identifying tags of status and specialization.

Even before the first questionnaire had been despatched, Directing Staff on their own initiative had invited a consultant to attend their discussions on staff roles. These discussions continued for more than a year and were given further point by members' responses to the Survey. In these discussions, the various components within the DS role were elucidated.* The *specialist* components related to the knowledge, expertise, and experience of the DS which might be put at the disposal of an individual or syndicate as a resource relevant to the task of a group or to its maintenance as an effective working group. On the other hand, the DS would have to exercise his own discretion as to whether it would be appropriate to put these resources at the disposal of the syndicate, in the light of the learning objectives of the task set. This situation might arise, for example, in relation to the skills of chairmanship required in different syndicate situations.

In addition, one could identify an *executive* component in the role, linked to the administrative responsibility of a DS for a subject and its long-term development in the course and to the authority derived from representing the College as an institution.

In contrast to the specialist component, there could be a *consultative* component through which the DS attempts to help the individual or syndicate to find effective methods or solutions to their own problems without imposing a solution of his own.

This DS behaviour corresponds more closely with the heuristic approach and is at the same time illustrative of the *teaching* component of the DS role, which relates to the different ways in which the DS can use his skills and knowledge.

Having isolated these components of the DS role, the College reviewed its staff resources and systematically augmented them to fill in areas of weakness and to achieve an improved overall balance. It also extended experiments with the use of staff whose primary commitment was to research, but who could be made available in a consultative role to syndicates, while giving more

* Harold Bridger conducted this work (Coles & Bridger, 1969).

encouragement to DS to undertake research and development projects on sabbaticals.

Some members wished to see an extension of the specialist component of the DS role and more giving of personal advice on career matters. Others felt that the staff had been of no help at all to them. This matter of criticism raised many complex issues, some of which the staff discussed with their consultant in considering desirable role and curriculum developments. There were, nevertheless, some inhibitions in the way of discussing all the criticisms raised by members. For example, criticisms directed towards the staff role and the associated methods of working could be interpreted as the projections of managers as they experienced the turbulence of personal disorganization and reorientation. The criticisms might also represent a residue of resentment, often latent and unrecognized, at having to give up the old ways of behaving which were known and comfortable.

In considering the specialist component of the DS role, the staff felt that they could perhaps proffer more readily their expert knowledge whenever syndicates were in doubt. The staff also concluded that colleagues possessing appropriate knowledge should be used more in future to make specialist contributions to the course of studies.

The criticism of the Directing Staff role further underlined the desirability of making members more aware of the executive and development responsibilities of DS. One simple example of a step by the Principal in this direction was to hand over the chairmanship of the second half of each plenary meeting to the DS responsible for administering the subject, who also determined its content and specified the task of the syndicates. Awareness that some members disliked the relative formality of the plenary meetings at the end of each subject, though in retrospect many came to value them highly, led the staff to experiment with new forms of plenary meeting. On several occasions, the chairmen of syndicates took the responsibility for deciding the form of the meeting and conducted it themselves from the platform. On other occasions, for example in the field of industrial relations, a national authority was invited to share the platform with the Principal and to comment on the written and oral reports from each syndicate. There were other experiments too in the design of tasks for syndicates.

The findings of the Survey, that different types of manager responded well to different types of learning situation, led Directing

Staff to question whether the fullest use was being made of the learning situations presented by syndicate work. Successful experiments had already been carried out by one member of staff with questionnaires which focused attention on individual and group behaviour, and it was decided to extend their application to all syndicates at regular intervals during the session, in the belief that members would become more sensitive to the impact upon others of their own behaviour. At the same time, Directing Staff agreed to extend the process in the opposite direction and to combine reviews of syndicate work with reviews of the course in order to supplement informal feedback by formal group discussions. Besides representing a practical example of joint consultation, these review periods demonstrated the value of extending one's information system as a device to improve decision-making by reducing the degree of uncertainty.

The problems of making business decisions under conditions of uncertainty, which had previously been treated by discussions in syndicates, now received further attention, from which the staff evolved an executive management exercise with supporting lecture–discussions. Besides providing yet another form of active and, to some extent, heuristic learning situation, the exercise, which had been under consideration from 1965 onwards, enabled members to use on-line computers for the purpose of comparing the outcome of decisions based on different assumptions, and introduced them to the practicalities of simulating the activities of a business.

During 1968, the College and the Industrial Training Research Unit (ITRU) of University College London collaborated in a further examination of the behaviour of syndicate members in decision-making situations in the exercise, training members as observers and feeding back the results of their observations to their syndicates. This represented another attempt to make fuller use of syndicate activities as learning situations, to introduce experiment into course content and design, and to involve members in an activity from which they could learn more about the practical problems of behavioural science research from working with social scientists themselves.

Linked with this activity, the ITRU invited volunteers among members to take a battery of psychological tests, covering facets of intellectual ability and personality. Here again, the feedback principle was followed of offering a private consultation with the psychologist to every member who took the tests, the occasion providing a further opportunity for the individual to obtain information about himself which could, if necessary, assist him in recognizing his own values and abilities and in relating them to the career pattern he might pursue upon returning to his enterprise. These tests provided information confidential to the Unit about the personality characteristics of members which could be used to predict syndicate performance as a group in the executive management exercise.*

In a later stage of the project, in 1969, experiments were carried out in the structuring of syndicates for the exercise, using data derived from the work of the ITRU, in order to test hypotheses and predictions about group behaviour and performance.

The College also took note of members' comments on areas in which they would have valued further instruction. As one response, the College began to offer short supplementary courses on quantitative analysis which adopted a basically didactic approach. In this way it was able to maintain the primary form of the main course and yet meet specialist and optional needs. The College was also aware, not least from members' comments and from nominators, that many senior managers of an older age-group would welcome the opportunity to bring themselves up to date on the changing managerial scene, which in many instances had already been studied by their subordinates at Henley. As a response, the College mounted its first three-week General Management Appreciation Course in September 1968 to meet this particular need.

The College, then, is a changing institution, the findings of its own research being related and in many instances applied to the role of its staff, the design of new learning situations for its members, and a dynamic adaptation of its objectives.

The College has, in a sense, undergone a developmental experience not unlike that of its members in mid-career, with research to some extent playing a role in relation to the College similar to that played by Directing Staff in relation to their syndicates. The basic kernel of Henley's special contribution – the

* As the research developed, it was found that members were keenly interested in participating in the psychological testing and receiving the feedback information. This checks with the expressed wish of ex-members of the survey for more personal insight and counselling. The actual tests used by R. M. Belbin and his colleagues measure different psychological traits or factors than those of the current research, but it is expected that ultimately the findings and insights of the two pieces of research will be related to one another.

recognition of the interdependence of personal growth and managerial competence and the contribution to be made by group work in carefully structured syndicates – is something that was recognized in advance of its time; it is not likely to be changed hastily because of the prevalence and popularity of other aims and modes of training. While many of the members asked for more structure and technical input, they also indicated that they derived more benefit than they expected from personal guidance and advice, and from the unanticipated value of being away from the working environment with the opportunity to reflect upon their own personal development as well as upon the problems of their enterprise.

THE COLLEGE AND SENIOR MANAGEMENT

As managers move up to roles which involve increasingly interactions with people and institutions outside the boundaries of the enterprise, so they face situations of greater complexity and uncertainty. Concurrently, they find a growing complexity in the environment in response to technological, economic, social, and political changes, which they can only understand and cope with by a continuous process of self-education.

Sir Noel Hall, when Principal of the Administrative Staff College, recognized this necessity and, as an example of the kind of reflective experience that might continue to be desirable at intervals throughout a manager's career, instituted early on the review course for members who had attended eighteen months previously. Subsequently, the support for a conference specially designed for those who had been to Henley ten years previously, and, more recently, the demand for a conference after five years, suggest that the concept has an appeal to many managers, although others may adopt heuristic principles so successfully that they may feel no need to reinforce personal learning in this way.

Since the findings of our Survey indicate that different types of manager respond to similar learning situations in different ways, there is obviously scope for even closer relationships between enterprises and educational institutions than generally exist at present. At Henley, potential members from the United Kingdom are interviewed at the College before being accepted, but there is as yet no comparable formal stage after the course in which the College and the nominating firm review the extent to which their investment in the member's experience at Henley has been realized. The absence of a formal stage, however, does not preclude a great deal of *ad hoc* consultation on this issue. In terms of personal development, persons akin to those in clusters 1 to 13 of the managerial types described earlier are more likely to gain satisfaction from Henley than those in the cluster represented by type 12, but they then face the risk of having their development blocked within the enterprise if it fails to provide appropriate opportunities for the application of their recent learning. Personal development, if it is then to occur at all, may then be diverted into channels outside – to local politics, professional associations, or charitable work, to name a few.

It is usual for managers in middle age to be concerned with persons in the succeeding generation, as fathers are with their children, and to enlist their aid in the evolution of new institutions, new products, and other creative projects (Erikson, 1968). Given scope, managers at this stage of their lives are likely to use opportunities within the enterprise to satisfy this inclination, although some persons may seize the opportunity more avidly than others. We have seen, for example, that the more Metamorphic developers can sometimes achieve spectacular results, although at the risk of being critical and possibly disruptive, and sometimes of changing their jobs. The more Incremental types from one point of view may be safer bets, steadily enlarging their capacities and wherever possible taking on new responsibilities to match them, but they tend to be less creative and imaginative. Those whose developmental pattern is Tangential need to be encouraged in a different way – and require tolerance of a degree of antipathy towards the 'core' elements in the enterprise. Such a manager develops antagonistically to his organization, which serves him as a foil, but in the end he may also serve his organization as he evolves his own style of managerial performance.

The findings imply that one should not just think of managers as they are at a given moment in time. Instead, one should try to imagine the different ways in which managers may change or develop, particularly as one is already working with people who have been selected for their drive or potential. Since we have seen that there are many different aspects of the individual manager's situation, more attention to the identification of these differences may help in the design and choice of more effective training programmes, especially if there is an attempt to obtain an integrated view of the person, his experience, and the career paths potentially open to him.

The more differentiated the conception one has, the better one may succeed in matching the manager with his role in the enterprise, with a better and more gratifying use of his talents from everyone's point of view. To this end there seems to be a strong case for close interaction and cooperation between all parties concerned – the enterprise, the member, and the College.

Chapter 13 · Reflections on the Research

THE MANAGER, THE ENTERPRISE, AND SOCIETY

This has been a research investigation that has been limited in a number of ways – by the nature of the sample and its size, the quality of the research information available from it, the limited supplementary information drawn from members' work environments, and the absence of control groups with which to make comparisons. On the other hand, as compared with many attempts to describe managerial styles and to define issues and evaluate programmes, the research reported here has the merit of being relatively rigorous and objective. The sample represents the total membership of a leading management training institution over a period of several years. The classification of the types of managerial career is based on their measured attributes, not on characteristics that happen to come to the attention of a particular observer or participant in the managerial scene. The analyses and conclusions are not based on a prior commitment to a particular position, but on the weight of systematically gathered evidence. The picture of how Henley members saw the Henley experience in the early 1960s in relation to their careers and how Henley has been working to adapt its programme to a changing environment is now fairly clear.

The question that arises is what can be learned from all this about the more general issues and problems of managers in contemporary society? Here we are on more speculative ground, and, though there is a good deal in the present research and in the research literature generally that is relevant, the information is very fragmentary and any picture to be drawn must therefore be based in good part on a personal integration. This chapter is such an effort; hence the title 'reflections'. What is said here emerges as much from introspection, general observations, and personal conviction as from the technical research findings themselves.

There are three broad spheres of interest that this research touches upon, and in which the College at Henley is involved in the course of its work. These are: the managers and their careers; the enterprises and their functioning; and society as it provides relevant environments both for the enterprises and for their managers. In examining the literature contributed by behavioural scientists interested in management or administration, it seems that some have concentrated on one or another element of this triad; some have concentrated on the interrelations of a pair in the triad; few if any have encompassed all three.

The explicit orientation both of this study as a whole and of this chapter in particular is to attempt a more holistic view, partial as it must inevitably be. The modern manager as he develops within the modern enterprise, which is itself changing in the response to environmental influences in a dynamic modern society, is the focal point – not simply the manager himself as an individual *in vacuo*. Such a focal point requires a synoptic view, one that encompasses a life-long career-perspective, because the functioning of an individual at any given stage in his life in a specific environment becomes less and less adequate as a picture of how he could function at another stage or in another setting. A more comprehensive conception is required of his life-style and developmental style, taking into account how he has functioned in different kinds of environment as well as how he may be functioning in any given one at a particular point in time. The Henley managers, then, were studied from the point of view of providing information about whole 'careers in progress' (White, 1966).

Given this dynamic viewpoint, the research experience can be used to contribute to the discussion of a number of contemporary issues in a way that will be suggestive, even if not conclusive. Three sets of issues confront one another, each grounded in one of the spheres of interest – the manager, the enterprise, and society. In keeping with the overall viewpoint of the research, the issues will be discussed with an 'open system' perspective, examining phenomena within a given sphere in relation to other spheres as well as to itself (Emery, 1969). It is assumed that each of the focal spheres has system characteristics, part of which are directed toward adaptation to the environment and part towards internal system maintenance and integration.

ISSUE I: THE MANAGER – DEVELOPMENT AT MID-LIFE

Managers who come to Henley have in common a background of demonstrated competence and the backing of their organizations. They also share a common set of preoccupations based on their time of life – mid-life – in which the biologically based drives that may have provided the 'steam' for early career development may be diminishing and new goals and motivations may be coming into being. Here the similarities end and differences are apparent. The managers come from different kinds of enterprise, public and private; they have attained their levels of achievement through different kinds of technical competence; they differ in personality values, and life-styles.

The training experience can be taken at least potentially as a critical transition point in their lives – if not from specialist to general managership, at least from one style of life and work to another.

From the individual manager's point of view, the issue is how to use this opportunity to develop at this point. Judging from the responses of managers in this sample, taken together with an overall appreciation of points made in the research literature about the issues and dilemmas prevalent at this stage, it would seem that the managers are concerned with a range of issues that they resolve differently according to their personal orientations and their relevant environments.

The first question is whether or not the individual wants to change and develop, and how much. Though there is a sense in which the statement of Soddy and his colleagues that 'change and development continue without pause throughout life' (Soddy, 1967, p. 4) is true, it is also true that there are great variations in the degree to which individuals have 'open minds' (Rokeach, 1960), and there is a tendency for individuals who have established themselves to get into a rut. They may, particularly those from middle-management groups, have achieved sufficient occupational success to feel established and secure, and they are also likely to be tied in to a family and community life that makes for stabilization for a number of years at this stage. The wish to change and develop is not prodded from within by biological turbulence as at adolescence; nor is it necessarily stimulated externally by a crisis in the occupational or larger environment requiring the mobilization of new resources. When confronted with the induced crisis presented by a training institution of the 'developmental community' kind, such as Henley, the first dilemma faced, explicitly or implicitly, is 'to develop or not to develop'. Only when this issue is confronted can the next issue of 'how to develop' be joined (Tagiuri, 1965; Moment, 1966).

From the evidence available, managers rising into senior positions confront this dilemma with a variety of stances, and seek different kinds of benefit for which they are willing to 'pay' with different kinds of sacrifice – since the gains of development rarely occur without costs. To develop, particularly at this stage of life, ordinarily means to change. Arriving at a given level of competence and achievement has meant commitment and cultivation – certain skills, viewpoints, styles of work, and so on. Even accepting that flexibility may have been cultivated and developed to quite a high level within the occupational role prior to this point, the movement upward into more responsible positions is likely to require a new phase of change that can be facilitated by a developmental experience such as that encountered at Henley (Schein, 1967).

One reaction to this life-option, seen in a relatively small proportion of managers, is to renounce career-development values in favour of a greater emphasis on personal interests. The cluster of experiences, attitudes, and behaviour patterns which characterize this response has been described in Chapter 8 as the *Humanistic* pattern. The emphasis, by managers who choose this pattern, is on enjoyment of life in the round – family, leisure, and personal interests – and if career advances threaten to make inroads into the other areas of life, they are not sought after. It is the non-work areas of life that have the greatest salience, and the notion of becoming totally dedicated to work – becoming a sort of one-dimensional man (Marcuse, 1964) – is unthinkable.

This sort of manager is tolerant of others and content with his own lot, both in his work and at home, but to alter the equilibrium in favour of greater salience and commitment to the job would be regarded as 'selling one's soul' to the job or the company. Such managers tend to be regarded as likeable and valuable to have, in the sense of contributing to the positive emotional tone of the environment, both in their firms and in the training groups. On the other hand, there may be a tendency to regard them as a bit dull and they may perceive themselves the same way. What they gain by maintaining a somewhat detached orientation from the more intense issues of career concentration is a high level of personal satisfaction. Does the manager who, by choice or necessity, opts for a more dynamic developmental pattern in work really prefer the discomforts of dealing with problems, conflicts, decisions, and the other demands of managerial advance, or is he merely rationalizing the inevitable when he says with John Stuart Mill 'better to be Socrates dissatisfied' but with a full appreciation of the complexity of life's challenges than a lesser being who is happy through considering only a more limited range. This is partly a matter of appreciation of complexity, in the sense advocated by Vickers (1968), and partly a matter of personal values, and individual choices must be individually assessed.

At a place like Henley, however, the Humanistic option, whether based on narrow or complex considerations, is not the main option found. In the nature of the case, most of the managers sent to Henley seek to develop as managers and do in fact develop following their training and are given more onerous managerial responsibilities. The issue for them is not 'to develop or not to develop'. They try, and mostly succeed. But the issue is really how best to develop – through what means and in what ways.

For the Incremental developer the central issue seems to be 'how to get ahead within the organization'. For the Metamorphic developer the central issue seems to be 'how to make things work better'. For the Tangential developer, it is 'how to develop more or less in spite of the organization'.

It would be a mistake to assume that the Incremental developers are necessarily 'organization men' in the narrow terms described by Whyte (1957). They would seem to be individuals with a high achievement motivation in the McClelland sense, who are competent within the framework of their organization and who seek 'self-actualization' in the received framework (Maslow, 1962). Their style is 'convergent' (Hudson, 1966) but this does not imply a necessarily narrow conformism (Walle, 1969). They are often in organizations that they themselves have selected and to whose values they are personally attuned, whether it is a public sector department, bank, or particular business firm. These men have a balanced commitment to work and family, and do what is necessary to make both function well and in an integrated way. They are orientated primarily to improving what exists rather to changing things around fundamentally. This orientation can contribute to a man's success at generalship, for as Ridley observes:

'The pure [general] administrator may by his training be inclined to concentrate on the speedy and frictionless despatch of business at the cost of creative policies' (Ridley, 1968, p. 209, brackets supplied).

This emphasis on smoothness within an existing structure depends for its success on the viability of the enterprise, but where the enterprise is functioning well and stably, this sort of manager gets on well and is rewarded accordingly.

He is one who is able to balance demands of various kinds and come out on top – work and home, technical and human-relational dimensions of the job, etc. His skills are in gaining participation and working through decisions. He is the harnesser of energy, the leader and organizer, the creator of order. The Incremental developer characteristically faces a stimulus such as a training opportunity by taking whatever he can from it to complement his own skills and to fill in for his deficiencies, making new integrations. For him, the observations of Warner and Martin about the executive role seem to hold very well:

'The executive operates in dual worlds – the work of the physical, the predictable, and the known on the one hand, and the realm of the social-political, the relatively unknown and unpredictable, on the other. In order to function successfully, he must be able to perform with skill in both' (Warner and Martin, 1959, p. 12).

The Metamorphic developer is in many ways more interesting as a type, though it would seem that organizations can absorb this type of manager only in limited numbers, and for ultimate success they must either shift their mode of functioning when major changes are brought about, or work in tandem with the more 'convergent' types such as the Incremental developers.

The Metamorphic developer is the more restless, entrepreneurial type, and his natural habitat is the world of private business, though he is not entirely absent from other sectors. Whether driven by dissatisfactions arising from life-long experience of tensions, or by an aggressive approach to deficiencies in their environment, men of this type take quite a different tack in response to the dilemmas posed. Whether it is in their personalities or their work, they are very critical by nature and are rarely content to accept things as received without looking for ways to change them around. They value creativity and derive their main satisfactions from leaving their own imprint on an experience. However, if the situation is not amenable to being 'bent' by them, their inclination is to move on to an environment which is more amenable to their efforts. Some men of this kind make a career of moving from one job to another, leaving when things reach just that state of steady functioning that makes the road clear for the advance of the Incremental type of manager. In some cases, a career of management consulting fulfils this sort of orientation.

In dealing with their personal dilemmas, men of this type must often come to grips with the fact that they are not likely to find personal happiness in the same way as the other managers, who more easily accept situations as they find them. Their involvement in their work has deep personal significance, and while they could not be happy without an active remoulding of their environment, this does not imply that, once a work problem has been solved or a status arrived at, they will then be happy and relaxed. The drive continues, and the hope is to derive satisfactions from harnessing this restlessness in ways that will produce personal satisfaction and effective performance at work.

Where the Metamorphic developer is successful, it is because he has a sufficiently strong capacity for reality-testing, is sufficiently decisive in his tackling of problems, and is sufficiently self-confident and authoritative to pull off a change in the environment; or alternatively to take the risks personally and move on to another work setting. When the firm is able to recognize and make use of his talents, the Metamorphic developer may serve the entrepreneurial requirements of the organization.

In the training situation, managers with the Metamorphic orientation are likely to apply the same critical approach as they apply in work and life generally. What they tend to have to learn is different from the previously described types. Self-confidence is not an issue for them, and if anything they may have to have their 'ears knocked back' a bit. The type of competence for which they are being socialized in the training situation is primarily in the handling of more complex relationships in their own and their enterprise's environment (Inkeles, 1969; Cogswell, 1969) and only secondarily in the interpersonal areas (Argyris, 1962). For men of this type, the tendency is to regard their organizational environments as temporary rather than permanent – either in a structural sense or for themselves occupationally. They are thus more interested in the 'new thing', in innovation and change, and are likely to be alert to revolutionary developments both at work and in the training situation. For such men there is likely to be a high interest in new techniques of learning – the management game, the Blake grid, the Group Feedback technique (Heller, 1969), etc. These new training devices are likely to appeal to this sort of man who does not accept the received and established ways of doing things, but likes participative methods for himself (if not always for his subordinates). Power-sharing on the job for a man of this type is likely to be adopted or not according to whether it is likely to work in achieving some change effect. Whereas the Incremental developer is likely to adopt participative or authoritarian methods according to the policy of his employing organization or his subculture (McGregor, 1960; Barron and Egan, 1968), the Metamorphic type will be inclined to share power only if it is likely to 'work' in the situation towards the ends which he is attempting to bring about.

The issue of how to develop is faced by the Tangential type in yet a different way. He is neither as accepting of his organization – for whatever reasons – as the Incremental developer, nor as forceful in attempting to change things as the Metamorphic type. Usually this combination is found in a large bureaucratic situation where there is a considerable degree of 'coldness' and 'alienation' present but where (as in some Civil Service departments) there is also a degree of attachment to the organization for fiscal, ideological, or other reasons. In such cases the solution described as the Tangential one may arise. This is a minority solution – unlike the two preceding ones; and it is a 'surprising' one, not hitherto given any attention in the literature. Whereas the Incremental solution is familiar enough in the guise of the Organization Man, and the Metamorphic is recognizable as an entrepreneurial type within the industrial bureaucratic structure, the Tangential is less familiar. He may be mistaken – both in his own eyes and in those of the observer – for a 'sleeper', but he is not asleep because of laziness or lack of commitment to career values. It is the kind of 'sleep' produced by adaptive responses to a bureaucratic situation that is impersonal and alienating. The issue for such a manager is how to develop personally and as a manager more or less in spite of his immediate work environment. The training programme provides, for some, an answer. Organizations are not all mainstreams (which one has to accept or be alienated from), nor is it necessary to bring about fundamental changes to experience development and creative satisfaction. In many instances there is a way of dealing with an unacceptable and rigid organization in which one nevertheless wishes to remain, by finding roles at the periphery. As has been described above, this solution may serve not only the individual but also the enterprise. The sort of person involved is one who in any case has tended all his life to remain at the edges of things, neither accepting them nor yet being as competent as the Metamorphic type in influencing and changing them. Yet, where there is the right combination of circumstances – partly a personal awakening to an awareness of possibilities and partly the right situation in the employing organization – a resolution can be found that allows development.

In some instances, the developmental pattern – marginal to the organization though it may have been initially – may, as the organization changes, take on a more central role as margins turn into 'frontiers'. If individuals who have posted themselves there have developed to the point of being able to take up the new challenge when this occurs, the Tangential types may find themselves moving towards the Incremental or Metamorphic styles at a later stage in their careers.

This leads to a consideration of the issues facing the enterprise in relation to these types, for it is clear that the enterprise must deal with developing managers in a multifaceted way.

ISSUE II: THE ENTERPRISE – THE USE OF HUMAN RESOURCES

The enterprise has been given a good deal of attention by behavioural scientists, and some of the most interesting work has been done on the analysis of different aspects of organizational functioning and behaviour (March, 1965; Trist *et al.*, 1963; Miller and Rice, 1967; Pugh, 1963; Woodward, 1965; Etzioni, 1961; Blau, 1962; etc.). The aspect of the enterprise here selected for attention is its use of human resources. This is not to imply that the enterprise has sole responsibility for the development of society's manpower, but only that it is an important function to which this research may have relevance.

Most modern enterprises spend a great deal of time, energy, and organizational resources in the attempt to discover and cultivate the human potentials within their own boundaries as well as seeking to recruit new talent from outside. It can be argued that the degree to which an organization has an effective human resources programme is a good indication of its general efficiency, for no matter how automated or efficient the technical components of an organization, it is its human resources and its matching of human and technical resources that will determine its effectiveness (Emery and Trist, 1960).

The range of enterprises in which Henley managers participate is so vast that research of a much more fine-grained type would be required to analyse the specific matching of types of manager to types of organizational structure within the sample. However, even with the data available, it is clear that there are many processes of managerial development that cut across organizations and apply, if not equally, at least in good measure, to the whole range of enterprises encompassed in the sample. Whether a man comes from a Public Sector organization that depends largely on commitment to social values and satisfaction with security, even if it means a measure of sacrifice of certain kinds of stimulation; or from a Private Sector firm that stimulates competitiveness and creative action, giving high remuneration if not complete security – certain common patterns of response emerge which it would be well for the enterprise to consider.

Enterprises face certain risks in attempting to cultivate their managers' talents. For one thing, the more a firm invests in training its managers, the more effective they may become generally; in certain circumstances this may rebound on the firm if they take their competence elsewhere, e.g. to a competitor. This is one of the risks that must be taken, and most firms have rules of thumb about how much to invest in this kind of effort and at which points in the managers' careers. If the enterprise is large enough, the provision of intra-organizational programmes maximizes the skill-development process at early stages while minimizing the risks which may come from exposure to managers from other firms. Loyalty to the organization is cultivated along with increase in technical capacity.

As the manager develops, and is at the point of rising from middle to more senior levels of management, it seems important both for his technical competence as a manager and for his personal development to allow a period of intensive exposure to managers from other kinds of organization. The importance of this is multiple. It may, of course, jolt him out of a comfortable rut into which he may otherwise settle at a certain level of career success. For some it may be important as a way of providing a human-relational complement to an hitherto technically oriented type of expertise. For others it may be important as a way of placing in perspective what the manager perceives to be both the special competences of the parent organization and its staff and its special limitations. Whatever the particular motivation, both of the manager and of his firm, the organization would expect that a developing senior manager is likely to function more as a whole individual with broadly based information and opinions rather than as a specialist giving only his particular expertise to the job. The organization can reciprocate by viewing him more as a senior man than as 'our finance officer', or whatever. Of course, there are vast differences in this from organization to organization, and between sectors. Nevertheless, the tendency towards what psychologists call 'individuation' is a desirable one for the firm to recognize and cultivate in its rising managers.

The finding that there are three major patterns that emerge as the whole developmental picture unfolds has important human resources implications. Every senior manager sophisticated enough to rise into generalship himself knows that simplistic formulae for assessing managerial potential are inadequate. There nevertheless is a tendency to think in these terms. Is a manager a 'thruster' or a 'sleeper'? Is a manager a 'high-flyer' or not? Is he competent for a senior job or not? The findings reported here provide something more complex than the notion that there is *a* type of senior manager who is worth backing, and at the same time something simpler than the notion that there is a nearly limitless range of individual variation. What, then, are the implications for the enterprise of this awareness?

The answer to this seems to lie in the cultivation of a way of thinking systematically about organizational flexibility that is similar to the way Reddin has suggested that managers think about managerial flexibility, modifying their style to the demands of the situation (Reddin, 1967). If an organization has reached a point where its creative thrust has opened a new line of development – whether based on a new technology, a new social organization, or whatever – it may be that the kind of man that ought to be pressed into controlling posts is the Incremental developer, who will accept the mandate given and develop both himself and his subordinates within this framework. If, however, there is rigidity or failure to adapt in a changing situation, the Metamorphic developer ought perhaps to be given more of a run. This is often difficult precisely in situations of the sort described, because there will be resistances and defensiveness in the situation and the Metamorphic types are often not the most diplomatic in their approach. Tolerance for unorthodox ways, uncomfortable new programmes or projects, and a certain amount of iconoclasm should be made possible in such situations.

The Tangential developer is interesting in another way – also related to the issue of creativity and organizational flexibility. His tendency, particularly when he finds himself in a large impersonal bureaucratic setting, is to adopt a rather critical attitude toward the organization and to dissociate himself from its work in any deep personal sense. He may appear disaffected, and often he is sent to Henley more or less accidentally – as a matter of 'pure chance' – being the only one available. This is the way it seems to him. Behind such a nomination there may, in specific instances, be a more purposeful agenda by the nominators precisely along the lines suggested here. However, this does not seem always or even usually to be the case. What often seems to happen with the semi-alienated manager at a place like Henley is an 'awakening' experience. He learns about other kinds of manager and their organizations, about the boundary functions of organizations generally, and the ways in which they must interact with other organisations in their environment, and discovers that he can remain in his own organization serving it well, even perhaps improving it, while at the same time having most of his interaction with people who are actually members of other organizations. He takes a 'new lease' on his career by moving toward the periphery of his organization, working with the adaptive functions where his organization and the environment interplay, often in what Child calls the 'sociopolitical aspects of the organization–environment relationship' (Child, 1968).

This sort of manager presents a different situation to his organization, compared with the other types. More than the others, he seems to change as a result of the training experience, and while he seems to engage the central tasks of the organization no more than previously, it should be recognized that his moves to the periphery are constructive and useful to the enterprise.

More difficult than this is the recognition of the possibility that such peripheral participation, though useful to the firm in its adaptive functions and therefore recognizable and capable of being rewarded, may in future be of even greater significance. As the environment changes and the internal structure evolves in a way only partly geared to these changes, situations often arise in which there is a shift of emphasis and the individuals working on the periphery become of central importance to the enterprise. A marginal activity is always worth monitoring as a potential new frontier, and managers with this sort of proclivity are therefore worth cultivating as potential leaders if a new direction is struck. The reason why this may be difficult in the short term is that such managers may seem to those who are more centrally engaged as rejecting their own core values and preoccupations, and a kind of mutual rejection or withdrawal may occur which is not optimal from the point of view of making the best use of human resources. Paradoxically, the firm that wishes to encourage innovation and creativity has to encourage its marginal and deviant types as well as its 'pillars' of support for the central organizational values and activities.

Part of this discussion on the enterprises' use of their managerial human resources is interesting in relation to work in the behavioural sciences, much of which has been based on the model of the manager–worker relationship. The concepts of participation, power-sharing, communication, and conflict resolution seem to relate primarily to managers and workers in an organization. The management of managers is a field less well delineated, and it is not clear how much the general principles of organizational behaviour relate specifically to these spheres. To the extent that the study of the training experience is instructive in relation to managerial needs generally, it would seem that managers want not only more technical competence, but also more personal support. They need continuous feedback about where they stand in relation to the organization and its functioning, their superiors and colleagues. They want more scope for applying new ideas and information – and ways of following through with an important developmental experience – by using what they have discovered from this training in their own organizations (Heller, 1969).

The management process, then, is not only learning to use managerial techniques, to make rational decisions, to conduct searches and inventories, etc., but it is also the management of managers themselves. If there is a continuation toward the development of autonomous work groups within larger structures, as seems likely, there will correspondingly arise the problems and issues of their coordination. Matching the right sorts of manager to the right sorts of function will be part of the job; to this will be added the need to match the right sorts of work group and then to keep the work of the different groups integrated. Some of these groups might be seen as small-scale laboratories for the organization as a whole, in which 'risky' innovations are tried out and then, if appropriate, diffused through the larger structure. Some might be conservators of the core functions.*

What has been said has a bearing on management staffing policy within organizations. Staffing policy may be affected by the explicit adoption of management-development strategies that seek to cultivate different types of managerial talent, matching the selection and sponsorship to the overall organizational requirements. Given this strategic orientation, at some points it will be more important to cultivate troublesome or alienated types than the 'fair-haired' boys, whereas at other points the reverse may hold. At most times, some sort of blend of managerial types is wanted, and this requires a tolerance for differences in managerial style, and the search for effective complementaries rather than 'carbon copies' of an approved model. Some organizations institutionalize roles that will keep alive dissent and innovation. Innovative programmes are embodied in Research and Development units, though these are mostly at present technological in nature rather than organizational or social-psychological. An example of a role which institutionalizes dissent in a devil's advocate form is the role assigned to some assistants to general managers in banks. In such a role a young manager, who plays the 'devil' for his boss, reacts as critically as possible in a mock argument over the merits of a proposal being put up, e.g. for a bank loan. By so doing, he both cultivates in himself critical acumen which will be useful in senior roles and also serves his organization by performing, in effect, a search for evidence weighing on a management decision. However, the organization can allow only a certain amount of such 'otherwise' behaviour in constricted internal environments, and the developing manager must put the attitude in perspective and not allow it to dominate his own thinking entirely. Such qualifications apply to all the considerations here under discussion, but their importance lies in giving them scope within these limitations.

* Organizational effectiveness, as Morris Brodie argues (personal communication), depends on the optimal balance of innovation and conservation. Too much of either can be maladaptive.

ISSUE III: WHAT VALUES FOR THE POST-INDUSTRIAL SOCIETY?

If one assumes that society is moving into a new era, with changes at work at least as fundamental as those that characterized the Industrial Revolution, it is important to search for clarification as to what these changes are and to gauge their relevance.

The widespread current preoccupation with analysis of the future attests to the relevance of this theme (Wolstenholme, 1963; Kahn and Wiener, 1967; Young, 1968). There are different sorts of dominant image being put forward – aside from the general consensus that there are many possible futures depending on circumstances and on human interventions. The more optimistic ones are embodied in the images of the post-industrial society drawn by Galbraith (1958), Bell (1967), and Trist (1968). More cautious views are held by Michael (1969), and there are some who find ground for very gloomy forecasts indeed (Marcuse, 1964). By and large, the social-science images of the future polarize in the directions earlier marked out by literary observers – Wells with the triumphant image, Orwell the despairing one. It is perhaps most useful in the present context to avoid extreme forms of specula-tion and set one's sights on the nearer future, with the live issues facing today's rather than tomorrow's managers, bearing in mind that tomorrow is and must be a preoccupation to some extent of managers today as well. This more limited scope of inquiry fits with the type of analysis suggested by Andrew Shonfield (1969), who points out that many trends are at work that can be studied empirically providing a more solid basis for research in this field. One wants to use rather more data along with the fantasy, and at the same time not perform mechanical extrapolations of existing trends as though one did not appreciate the complexity of social process (Leach, 1968).

One societal process that seems to be at work is the de-emphasis of production as the central value, displacing it in the post-industrial era by greater emphasis on human and consummatory values. Among the younger generation, the hippies represent a kind of backlash that is occurring against the dominant values of the industrial society, and, though it is unlikely that hippie culture will become dominant in any kind of future society, its message will make itself felt increasingly and it is likely to be incorporated in modified form much more widely than at present (Davis, 1968). The Humane managers of today may become more prevalent tomorrow, and a new version of Renaissance man may replace what Marcuse warns of in present-day man – that kind of uni-dimensionality of character that leads to productivity but not to personal enrichment. The issues that this poses for societal productivity are serious, but not necessarily critical, in an age where wealth can be produced increasingly with the help of technological aids. At present, then, evidence shows that those who emphasize family and leisure activities tend to have to do so at the expense of career advancement, and vice versa; hence our finding that the Humane type of man is not outstandingly successful in his development as a manager. In society in future it may be possible to create new and more productive forms of integration of the work and non-work areas of life. This would seem to be a societal goal worth pursuing (Pahl and Pahl, 1970).

The emphasis in industrial society on individual achievement and competitiveness as dominant career values are likely to give way, in part at least, to an emphasis on sharing, team effort, and cooperation. Outstanding individuals, creative individual decisions, and charismatic leadership will, of course, remain as features of societal enterprises with any degree of spark. However, in reaction against the intense individual emphasis on the one side, and the mass collective emphasis on the other, it is likely that outstanding performance will be nurtured in small autonomous work groups. The creation of these work groups is going on in industry (Herbst, 1962; Emery and Thorsrud, 1966) and to some extent in the Public Sector (*The Sunday Times*, 12 October, 1969). Different types of aspiration may flourish in such groups, and what may be lost in centralization and organizational efficiency may be gained by a reactivation of intrinsic interest in creative task accomplishment.

The post-industrial society will be one that works to remove sources of social inequality based on stereotyped conceptions – e.g. race, religion, social class, or sex. Once again, this trend is based on a mixture of ideological and calculative considerations. A society which is involved in world competition for its existence must use its most talented resources – without giving priority to considerations irrelevant to performance, such as skin colour, accent, or sex. The fact that the evolution of human values reinforces this position makes this trend all the more probable. On the other hand, the conditions imposed by intensive training programmes make it more difficult to incorporate women than men, particularly married women. This is a problem that none of the training institutions have really solved, even those located in the urban centres, but it remains a societal issue with the twin significance of human rights and manpower resources to press for its solution.*

One would then argue in favour of keeping channels open in society for the development of all types of people, and of variant patterns of development. Even more, one would search out and cultivate human resources not at present being adequately tapped. One is aware of the eminence of many leaders who were considered dissidents or rebels in their earlier years. Very rebellious junior Civil Servants have become outstanding Government administrators, and more may do so in the future. Managing directors of large companies have sometimes had an early history of rebelliousness at school and at work, and this pattern may increase in frequency, to general advantage.

The importance of keeping channels open is seen at Henley in relation to the educational background of members. While there is a trend at Henley toward a higher proportion of the managers being university educated, there is still no correlation between level of formal education and development, either as a manager or as a person. This is one of the important research findings. Men who have less formal education find in the course an opportunity to compensate to some extent for limitations in their earlier educational experience. Men who had higher education, but along specialized lines, find in it an opportunity for broadening their understanding, and sometimes for bringing their abstract theoretical ideas 'down to earth' (Brodie and Life, 1969).

The social environment – in organizations and society generally – would seem to be increasingly complex and prone to turbulence (Emery and Trist, 1965). This would seem to call for new attitudes of flexibility and competence in coping with change and diversity.

One of the ironies of the attitude of many of the Henley members who call for more structure in the future training programme is that this is occurring precisely at a time when the younger generation, with their emphasis on change, creativity, and innova-

---

* For an extended consideration of the issues of women in relation to top jobs see Fogarty, Rapoport, and Rapoport (1968).

tion are crying out for more participation and less structure. In a sense both are required, but in different measure for different people, and differently at different times in the career. There is much still to learn about these processes, and they should not be allowed to occur simply as a matter of perpetual action and re-action. It should also be observed that the immediate feelings of individuals in the situation constitute only one criterion on which decisions are to be made. It is not to disparage senior managers to observe that their own wishes for increased structure at a point of turbulence in the throes of a critical status transition are not necessarily more valid than the wishes of young radicals for the loosening of structure at the point in their careers when they are poised to make major life-commitments.

There is a sense in which this discussion is rarefied – not in close touch with the immediate problems of managers and enter-prises in contemporary society. On the other hand, these are tur-bulent times, and changes are under way at a pace that surprises even the most avid futurologists. The contemporary disturbances of young people are to some extent specific to their phase in life, and many of the people who are now most rebellious will them-selves become supporters of one or another element of the estab-lished order. However, their disturbances are instructive, and not without pervasive effect even on those who do not participate in them. Their revulsion against materialistic values, rigidly estab-lished institutions, and individualistic life-styles may increasingly become the accepted basis for the new order, in modified form. What is now defiance as a life-style – among the hippies, beats, and drop-outs drawn from middle-class families – may take on a more positive colouring as society itself becomes more humane and discovers ways of tolerating diverse patterns of living and developing.*

The new managers of enterprises may have something more to teach than they have in the past, for nothing less than a revolution in the management of living is the challenge before us today. The breakdown of rigid boundaries between the enterprise and its environment is not a one-sided process. Influences may be expected in both directions increasingly.

* For some very interesting discussions of the importance of understanding the attitudes of youth for industry of tomorrow see the IBM paper on *Education and Industry* based on a conference held in London in January 1969. In one report, by C. Pastel of France, the importance of this view is brought out in an IBM-sponsored study of student unrest throughout Europe.

Appendix I · List of Variables from the Questionnaire 'Career Patterns and Henley'

(NOTE: + and − signs indicate the two ends of scales. Intermediate categories are not usually shown because these are not included in the coding, although they do appear in the questionnaire. It should be remembered that the positive and negative signs do *not* have any value-judgement connotations as to whether or not certain factors or attributes are desirable.)

What, at the point you first heard about your nomination, did you think your organization had as its main reason for sending you to Henley?

Variable:
2 Pure chance, availability among those eligible
3 To assess my potential for really top management
4 To fill in my areas of weakness in management skills or information
5 To broaden me generally
6 As an indication to me that I had been earmarked for a more senior post

What, at the point you first heard about your nomination, did you think your organization had as a second reason for sending you to Henley?

7 As a sabbatical experience
8 For my having done a good job
9 To assess my potential for really top management
10 To fill in my areas of weakness in management skills or information
11 To broaden me generally
12 As an indication to me that I had been earmarked for a more senior post

What was your own initial reaction to being nominated to go to Henley?

Variable:

13 enthusiastic (+) . . . resentful (—)

What did you initially want to get out of the Henley experience?

14 Complete break from usual work-loads and associates
15 Chance to compare and evaluate your own experience and attitudes with those of others in different organizations
16 Better understanding of senior managerial/administrative role-requirements
17 Better understanding of the relation between own organization and the wider environment
18 Improved ability to work with others with different experience and outlook
19 Improved ability to handle new kinds of situation
20 Increased understanding of yourself as a person
21 New knowledge, specific skills, such as writing reports, chairmanship, and public speaking
22 Useful contacts

What did you feel you actually got out of the Henley experience?

23 Complete break from usual work-loads and associates
24 Chance to compare and evaluate your own experience and attitudes with those of others in different organizations
25 Better understanding of senior managerial/administrative role-requirements
26 Better understanding of the relation between own organization and the wider environment
27 Improved ability to work with others with different experience and outlook
28 Improved ability to handle new kinds of situation
29 Increased understanding of yourself as a person
30 New knowledge, specific skills, such as writing reports, chairmanship, and public speaking
31 Useful contacts

In your opinion do you think there should have been more or less of the following in the organization of the Henley course? (+ = more, — = less)

32 Syndicate method of working
33 Talks by and discussions with outside visitors

Variable:

34 Visits to outside organizations
35 Contact formal and informal with staff members
36 Informal contact with 'opposite numbers' from similar types of organization
37 Informal contact with 'opposite numbers' from different types of organization
38 Reading and private study
39 Experience in public speaking
40 Experience in writing reports

What aspect of the Henley course have you found especially useful?

41 Personal development
42 Experiences at Henley
43 Aspects of Henley curriculum

Have you found anything about the Henley course most unhelpful?

44 Something, but this not specified

In which of the following ways was the staff contribution most valuable to you?

45 Help in social mixing
46 Private advice and encouragement
47 Help in self-appraisal
48 Joining in discussion
49 Direct teaching
50 None of the above

In which of the following ways could the staff contribution have been of more value to you?

51 Private advice and encouragement
52 Help in self-appraisal
53 Joining in discussion
54 Career advice
55 Direct teaching
56 None of the above

While you were at Henley, would you say you worked:

57 Very hard $(+)$ . . . not hard at all $(-)$

Variable:

> *While at Henley did you have much contact with your family?*

58 Yes, a great deal, visits, telephone, writing (+) . . . none at all except correspondence (−)

> *Did you find the residential character of the course disturbing?*

59 Very disturbing (+) . . . not at all disturbing (−)

> *Did your wife find the residential character of the course disturbing?*

60 Very disturbing (+) . . . not at all disturbing (−)

> *As a result of Henley, would you say you developed as a manager?*

61 A great deal (+) . . . not very much (−)

> *As a result of Henley would you say you developed as a person?*

62 A great deal (+) . . . not very much (−)

> *Looking at the Henley experience in relation to the subsequent demands of your job, which one of the following best describes your situation?*

63 It had direct relevance to the specific tasks confronted since leaving Henley (+) . . . It had little or no direct relevance to subsequent work (−)

> *Can you say what changes you think should in future be made in the Henley course?*

64 Items suggesting an increase in technical input (+)
Items suggesting an increase in human relations (−)

> *How many changes of job have you had since leaving Henley?*

65 Few (+) . . . Many (−)

> *How many promotions have you had since leaving Henley?*

66 Few (+) . . . Many (−)

> *How many changes of employer have you had since leaving Henley?*

67 Few (+) . . . Many (−)

Variable:

What was your annual salary pre-Henley?

68 Low (+) – under £2,000 . . . High (−) £7,000–£8,000

What is your salary now?

69 Low (+) – under £2,000 . . . High (−) £7,000–£8,000

How would you characterize the work of your organization as a whole?

70 Each job, task, or project is unique and requires individually tailored solutions

71 Most of the jobs, tasks, or projects fall into patterns which are recognizable and to which the organization of effort can be geared

72 Most of the work is in a fixed pattern with problems arising primarily from human factors

73 Most of the work is in a fixed pattern with problems arising primarily due to technical and economic factors

How would you characterize the part of the organization in which you are now involved?

74 Each job, task, or project is unique and requires individually tailored solutions

75 Most of the jobs, tasks, or projects fall into patterns which are recognizable and to which the organization of effort can be geared

76 Most of the work is in a fixed pattern with problems arising primarily from human factors

77 Most of the work is in a fixed pattern with problems arising primarily due to technical and economic factors

Comparing what you do in your present job with the one you had just prior to going to Henley, have any of the following things changed:

78 Number of decisions taken without referring to higher authority – Increased (+) . . . Decreased (−)

79 Magnitude of decisions taken without referring to higher authority – Increased (+) . . . Decreased (−)

80 Amount of involvement with others of different specialities – Increased (+) . . . Decreased (−)

Variable:

81 Amount of dealings with people outside the firm – Increased (+) . . . Decreased (−)
82 Amount of your work that can be done by machine aids – Increased (+) . . . Decreased (−)
83 Amount of your work that you can delegate to other people – Increased (+) . . . Decreased (−)
84 Participation in long-term planning – Increased (+) . . . Decreased (−)
85 Constraints on your own freedom of action – increased (−) . . . Decreased (+)

In your own work which of the following presents problems most frequently?

86 Technical
87 Intellectual
88 Economic/financial
89 Human relational
90 Political

In your own work which of the following problems is most irksome to you?

91 Technical
92 Intellectual
93 Economic/financial
94 Human relational
95 Political

How are most of the problems dealt with?

96 By technical experts
97 By strong action from the man on top
98 By complex negotiation among diverse groups

How would you characterize the overall picture in your present work environment?

99 Secure (+) . . . Insecure (−)
100 Exciting (+) . . . Boring (−)
101 Warm (+) . . . Cool (−)
102 Permissive (+) . . . Strict (−)
103 Conventional (+) . . . Unconventional (−)
104 United (+) . . . Divided (−)

Variable:

> *Comparing your pre-Henley work pattern with your present job, indicate your overall feeling of satisfaction in your previous job:*

105 Very satisfied (+) . . . very dissatisfied (−)

> *Comparing your pre-Henley work pattern with your present job, indicate your overall feeling of satisfaction in your present job:*

106 Very satisfied (+) . . . very dissatisfied (−)

> *What was the place of birth of yourself and your parents?*

107 Respondent born in Scotland
108 Respondent born in Wales
109 Respondent born in North of England
110 Respondent born in South of England
111 Mother born in Scotland
112 Mother born in North of England
113 Mother born in South of England
114 Father born in Scotland
115 Father born in North of England
116 Father born in South of England

> *Which of the following categories best describes your father's occupation during your childhood?*

117 Semi-skilled worker
118 Clerical or sales
119 Manager or proprietor
120 Professional

> *Did your father work:*

121 On his own account
122 For the Civil Service
123 For a local authority
124 For a college, university, or school
125 For a large industrial firm (i.e. employing over 500)
126 For a small industrial firm (i.e. employing under 500)

Variable:

> *How would you describe the feelings of your father about his work during the period of your childhood?*

127 Satisfied with occupation (+) . . . dissatisfied about occupation (−)
128 Don't know

> *How would you describe the feelings of your mother about her work during the period of your childhood (if mother had no paid employment, answer in terms of her feelings about being a housewife)*

129 Satisfied with occupation (+) . . . dissatisfied about occupation (−)
130 Don't know

> *Were either of your parents particularly influential in your choice of career?*

131 Yes, father a positive influence
132 Yes, mother a positive influence
133 No, neither

> *How many brothers and sisters do you have? Include stepbrothers and sisters or deceased brothers and sisters if you grew up with them.*

134 No or few brothers (+) . . . Many brothers (5+) (−)
135 No or few sisters (+) . . . Many sisters (5+) (−)

> *How many times during your childhood (up until age 15) did your family change the locality of their residence?*

136 No change (+) . . . More than five changes (−)

> *How would you describe the general family atmosphere in your family as a child?*

137 Secure (+) . . . Insecure (−)
138 Exciting (+) . . . Boring (−)
139 Warm (+) . . . Cool (−)
140 Permissive (+) . . . Strict (−)
141 Conventional (+) . . . Unconventional (−)
142 United (+) . . . Divided (−)

> *What type of secondary school did you attend?*

143 Grammar (+); Independent (i.e. Public or Private) (−)

Variable:

Did you go to boarding school?

144 Yes (+) ... No (—)

What was your age on leaving school?

145 Under 14 (+) ... 18 or over (—)

Did you have any higher education?

146 No formal training
147 Full-time or part-time university course, graduated with degree
148 Full-time or part-time university course, did not complete degree
149 Full-time or part-time technical college course (including sandwich courses)
150 Other training leading to a recognized professional qualification

What were your main areas of academic interest at school?

151 Humanities (history, English, etc.), arts (painting and applied arts), economics, social science
152 Natural sciences (biology, etc.)
153 Physical sciences (mathematics, physics, etc.)
154 Engineering and applied sciences
155 No specific academic interest

What were your main areas of academic interest at university or other institution of higher education?

156 Humanities and arts
157 Physical sciences (mathematics, physics, etc.)
158 Engineering and applied sciences
159 Economics, social science, administration

At the time you completed your school education, did you have:

160 A very clear or fairly clear idea of your future career interests and intentions (+) ... No idea at all of your future career interests and intentions (—)

At the time you completed your higher education, did you have:

161 A very clear or fairly clear idea of your future career interests and intentions (+) ... No idea at all of your future career interests and intentions (—)

Variable:

> *For those who had a very clear or fairly clear idea of their future career interests, indicate whether, in relation to the ideas at leaving school, these ideas correspond to the work you are now doing:*

162 Yes, are related (+) . . . No, are not related (−)

> *For those who had a very clear idea or fairly clear idea of their future career interests, indicate whether, in relation to your ideas at leaving university, these ideas correspond to the work you are now doing:*

163 Yes, are related (+) . . . No, are not related (−)

> *Managers vary considerably in their general opinions and attitudes about the principles of management. All of the following attitudes are found among contemporary managers; indicate what your general opinion is:*

(N.B. for the range of variables 164–181, the scale runs from 'Strongly Agree' (+) to Strongly Disagree' (−).

164 'Too much of most senior managers' energy goes into work, to the detriment of other aspects of living.'

165 'The most important skill for the manager/administrator in future will be planning and controlling change.'

166 'The man who gets ahead is the man who knows the right people.'

167 'The same personal qualities are really required of the man at the top whether he is running an industrial organization, a bank, or a Ministry.'

168 'Most managerial jobs require a person to compromise with his moral standards.'

169 'The quality of individual decisions is generally higher than the quality of group decisions.'

170 'The burdens of senior posts outbalance the rewards.'

171 'Most workers are capable of accepting more responsibility than they are usually given.'

172 'Most people who rise to the top find that they are less happy than when they were in more junior posts.'

173 'The top manager is willing to make decisions that hurt others.'

174 'The most important objective of an organization is to

Variable:

 facilitate the maximum development of its employees as individuals.'

175 'A clear-cut hierarchy of authority and responsibility is the cornerstone of a well-functioning organization.'

176 'A young man who is aiming for a top post should be careful in selecting a wife to make sure she will fit into his career plans.'

177 'It is more important than ever today that the man at the top be a bold leader more than a skilled administrator.'

178 'The average worker prefers to avoid responsibility, has little ambition, and above all wants security.'

179 'In management decisions, the human factor is at least as important as the economic factor.'

180 'There are many sound principles of management that should not be changed even if economic and technological conditions seem to require that they be modified.'

181 'It is the tough, driving, impersonal man who gets to the top.'

If ever married, how many children do you have?

182 None or few (+) . . . Many (4) (−)

If currently married, does your wife:

183 Work only as a home-maker (+) . . . have a part-time or full-time job other than home-making (−)

Has your wife undertaken any of the following:

184 Full-time or part-time university course
185 Full-time or part-time technical college course
186 Professional course in teaching or nursing, etc.

From the favourable and unfavourable adjectives listed below choose the ones that best describe you:

187 Adaptable
188 Ambitious
189 Aggressive
190 Calm
191 Cautious
192 Competitive
193 Conventional

Variable:

194 Cooperative
195 Creative
196 Cultured
197 Dominant
198 Efficient
199 Emotional
200 Energetic
201 Fun-loving
202 Happy
203 Hard-driving
204 Idealistic
205 Impetuous
206 Intellectual
207 Intuitive
208 Lazy
209 Loyal to an organization
210 Methodical
211 Middle-brow
212 Moody
213 Physically strong
214 Quiet
215 Rational
216 Rebellious
217 Reserved
218 Self-sufficient
219 Shy
220 Talkative
221 Tense
222 Unconventional
223 Witty

Has your life changed in relation to the following activities since you have been to Henley? (The scale on variables 224–229 runs from Increased (+) . . . Decreased (−))

224 Amount of time spent on leisure activities individually
225 Amount of time spent on leisure activities with family
226 Amount of time spent on leisure activities with others
227 Amount of time spent at home with your family
228 Amount of time spent at work

Variable:

229 Amount of time spent in organized community or public service activities

> *People at mid-career sometimes experience new, often surprising feelings about themselves as persons, their work situations, and their family situations – which they must face and deal with at this period of their lives. Indicate what characterizes your own feelings in the past six months:*

230 How often do you have a feeling of rage and despair in the work situation? Frequently (+) . . . Rarely (−)

231 How often do you have feelings of pride and fulfilment in the work situation? Frequently (+) . . . Rarely (−)

232 What is your usual feeling in work situation: despair (−) . . . joy and fulfilment (+)

233 How often do you have a feeling of rage and despair in your family situation? Frequently (+) . . . Rarely (−)

234 How often do you have feelings of pride and fulfilment in your family situation? Frequently (+) . . . Rarely (−)

235 What is your usual feeling in your family situation? Despair (−) . . . Joy and fulfilment (+)

236 How often do you have a feeling of rage and despair about yourself and your life generally? Frequently (+) . . . Rarely (−)

237 How often do you have feelings of pride and fulfilment about yourself and your life generally? Frequently (+) . . . Rarely (−)

238 What is your usual feeling about yourself and your life generally? Despair (−) . . . Joy and fulfilment (+)

> *A number of ex-members as well as recent surveys have indicated that sheer health is an important factor in career development. Please indicate for each of the following items whether it applies to you: (Yes = +, No = −).*

239 Do you feel that you are bothered by all sorts of pains and ailments in different parts of your body?

240 For the most part do you feel vigorous enough to carry out the extra things you would like to do?

241 Are you sometimes bothered by shortness of breath when you are not exercising or working hard?

242 Have you suffered from ulcers?

Variable:

243   Are you sometimes bothered by your heart beating hard?
244   Do you sometimes have trouble getting to sleep or staying asleep?
245   Would you call your general physical health good?
246   Are there times when you are bothered by feelings of nervousness and tenseness?
247   Are you sometimes troubled by your hands sweating so that you feel damp and clammy?
248   Are you troubled by backache?
249   Would you call your general mental–emotional health good?

Please indicate the relative importance to you personally of the following eight factors which may have contributed to your personal ideals for a career pre-Henley:

250   An opportunity to work with people rather than exclusively with things or ideas
252   A chance to work at an interesting job with a minimum of disturbance
254   A chance to use intellectual problem-solving abilities
256   An opportunity to be helpful to other people
258   An opportunity to show what I can accomplish
260   A reasonable, stable, and secure future
262   Relative freedom from supervision by others
264   An opportunity to be creative

Please indicate the relative importance to you personally of the following eight factors which may have contributed to your personal ideals for a career now:

251   An opportunity to work with people rather than exclusively with things or ideas
253   A chance to work at an interesting job with a minimum of disturbance
255   A chance to use intellectual problem-solving abilities
257   An opportunity to be helpful to other people
259   An opportunity to show what I can accomplish
261   A reasonable, stable, and secure future
263   Relative freedom from supervision by others
265   An opportunity to be creative

Variable:

Present pattern of work:

266   Strength (i.e. like) managerial skills (+) . . . weakness (i.e. dislike) managerial skills (−)
267   Strength/weakness – technical knowledge, knowledge of organization
268   Dislikes routine work
269   Strength/weakness – human relations
270   Strength/weakness – self-expression, creativity
271   New problems and challenges either technical or human relational
272   Functional to general job change (following Henley)

Type of organization employed in:

273   Private Sector
274   Bank
275   Nationalized Industry
276   Civil Service

Main job pre-Henley

277   Production
278   Research
279   Marketing, sales, etc.
280   Accounting
281   General management

Miscellaneous:

282–286   Staff assessments of members' performance
287   Age at time of attending Henley
(+) = 30 . . .
(−) = 40 +

Appendix II · A Note on the McQuitty Hierarchical Linkage Analysis

The questionnaire forms were punched on to IBM punch cards from which all subsequent analyses were made.

Descriptive analyses were made on the basis of marginal counts and selected cross-tabulations. Additionally:

(a) A total matrix of coefficients of correlations between each variable and all other variables in the questionnaire was constructed. The list of variables is given in Appendix I. The Pearson product-moment correlations were used for the linear-linear scales, Guttman's coefficient of predictability for nominal-nominal correlations, and the Goodman-Kruskal for ordinal-ordinal correlations.

(b) A McQuitty Hierarchical Linkage analysis was performed on the total matrix, and nearly 50 clusters were discerned, averaging seven variables per cluster. A cut-off point of ·1 was used in defining clusters. Thirteen clusters were selected because they contained variables which were highly correlated (i.e. had a coefficient of correlation of at least ·25) with either variable 61 – development as a manager – or 62 – development as a person – or both.

The study of these thirteen clusters and their relationship to development and to education, age, organization, and occupation, all at the time of attending Henley, was presented in Chapter 8.

For a description of the procedure for the McQuitty Linkage analysis, see McQuitty (1960) and modifications by Emery, Irving, and Hilgendorf (1968).

(c) The clusters isolated in the McQuitty Hierarchical Linkage Analysis link together variables which define dimensions on which people can be described. To use the clusters as scales for rating individuals, a convention was required which would take into account the method by which the clusters were constructed.

Accordingly, a scoring system was developed whereby scores could be assigned, each of which was a power of 2, reflecting the position of the variable in the cluster – i.e. how much weight it carried as a separate variable in making up the total score for the cluster. This was done on the basis of setting a number which could be halved the necessary number of times, proportionately to the branches of the largest cluster in the series; this number was 512. Thus, if a cluster were made up of two variables only, each would receive a weight of 256. If it were made up of two branches, one of which had a pair of variables and the other a single variable, each branch would initially receive a weight of 256, and then the two variables on the branch which had the sub-cluster of two would each receive a weighting score of 128, while the single variable on the other branch would receive the full weight of 256.

A score was thus developed for each individual for each cluster. From these sources a distribution table and correlation matrix were constructed. The correlation matrix was based on the product-moment correlation.

Individuals were allocated to quintile groups within each cluster and the relationships between position in the quintile scale and a number of variables (development as a manager, age, education, organization, and occupational specialism) were examined.

Of the thirteen clusters, ratings for individuals on the scales based on five of them, clusters 1, 3, 6, 8, and 13, were found to be significantly correlated with the sense of having developed as a manager, though the level of intercorrelation was found to be low (see Chapter 8). While the cluster analysis reduced substantially the overall variance, an examination of the intercorrelation matrix for the clusters suggested that further reduction in the variance might be accomplished by the factor analysis of the intercorrelational matrix of cluster scores.

(d) The scores were factor-analysed for principal components. Four factors were discerned. Factor scores were calculated according to the loadings computed through the principal components analysis, and three of the four were found to be correlated with variable 61 (sense of development as a manager as a consequence of Henley) – again using the product-moment coefficient (see Chapters 8 and 9).

Appendix III · List of Variables in Thirteen Key Clusters, and Weights assigned them

The clusters, which were arrived at through the use of McQuitty's Hierarchical Linkage procedure as described in Appendix II, were used to establish scales for scoring individuals by allocating weights to items according to their cluster positions. As described in Appendix II, a number was arrived at that could be subdivided the necessary number of times to accommodate the items in the largest cluster found. This number was 512. Then each branch of the cluster was assigned half the weights successively until all of the items in the cluster were accommodated. Thus, if a cluster had only two branches with one item, the items would each be given a weight of 256. Individuals having both attributes would then be scored 512 for that cluster scale; individuals with one or the other attribute only would be scored 256; and individuals with neither attribute would be scored 0.

The method of weighting is illustrated on cluster 1, the Ambitious/Creative cluster, which was presented on p. 154. All the other weightings are listed in tabular form by cluster.

Cluster 1 *Weights for items in Ambitious/Creative cluster (weightings in parenthesis)*

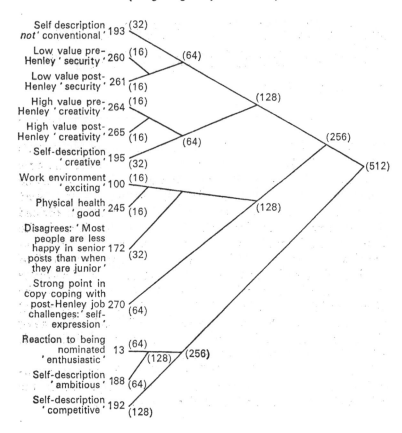

Cluster 2   *Restless/Hard-driving*

Item No.	Item	Weight
67	Changes of employer: *many*	4
148	Went to university, did not complete degree	4
178	Agrees: 'Workers prefer to avoid responsibility'	8
228	Time spent at work since Henley *increased*	2
227	Time spent at home with family *decreased*	2
225	Time spent with family for leisure *decreased*	4
224	Time spent on own leisure *decreased*	8
226	Leisure time with others *decreased*	32

Item No.	Item	Weight
278	Job pre-Henley *not* research	64
212	'Moody'	32
181	Agrees: 'Tough driving manager to the top'	32
173	Agrees: 'Top managers take decisions that hurt'	32
189	'Aggressive'	32
220	'Talkative'	256

Cluster 3 *Environment-oriented*

Item No.	Item	Weight
17	Initially wanted to get from Henley: 'better understanding of own organization in relation to the wider environment'	128
26	Actually got from Henley: as Item No. 17	128
63	Henley experience *directly* relevant to subsequent job	64
216	Self-description 'rebellious'	64
72	The pattern of work in the organization is *not* a fixed one with many human relations problems	128

Cluster 4 *Accommodating*

Item No.	Item	Weight
3	Main reason for being nominated: 'to assess potential'	64
102	Work environment 'strict'	64
32	Recommends *more* syndicate method	32
33	Recommends *fewer* outside visitors	32
247	Suffers from 'sweaty hands'	64
134	Has brothers in family	128
155	No special academic interest in school	128

Cluster 5 *Uncritical*

Item No.	Item	Weight
6	Main reason: 'earmarked'	128
9	Second reason: 'assess potential'	64
167	Agrees: 'Some personal qualities required for man at the top regardless of type of organization'	64
49	Staff most valuable contribution 'direct teaching'	64
59	Not disturbed by residential character of course	32

Cluster 5 (continued)

60	Wife not disturbed by residential character of the course	32
35	Does not want more contact with the staff	64
56	Staff contribution could have been more valuable in 'none' of the suggested ways	64

Cluster 6 *Dogged*

Item No.	*Item*	*Weight*
57	At Henley, worked 'hard'	64
7	Secondary reason for being nominated *not* as a sabbatical experience	64
208	*Not* 'lazy'	128
46	Staff contribution could have been more valuable 'private advice'	64
140	Family environment as a child 'strict'	64
18	Agrees: 'There are many sound principles of management that should not be changed'	64
201	*Not* 'fun-loving'	64

Cluster 7 *Humanistic*

Item No.	*Item*	*Weight*
89	Most frequent problems at work 'human relational'	128
171	Agrees: 'Most workers are capable of accepting more responsibility'	128
165	Agrees: 'Most important skill for manager in future will be planning change'	64
185	Wife attended technical college	64
158	Academic interest at university *not* engineering or applied sciences	128

Cluster 8 *Conflicted*

Item No.	*Item*	*Weight*
133	Career decisions influenced by neither parent	64
160	After school no clear idea of career plans	32
161	After university no clear idea of career plans	32
141	Family atmosphere 'unconventional'	64
242	Suffers from ulcers	64
191	Self-description *not* 'cautious'	256

Cluster 9 *Venturesome*

Item No.	*Item*	*Weight*
99	Work environment 'insecure'	32
273	Private Sector employer	32
281	Main job pre-Henley *not* in general management	64
276	*Not* Public Sector	64
287	*Younger* age-group	64
105	Feeling about pre-Henley job *not* dissatisfied	64
286	Henley staff rating *not* 'average'	64
123	Father did *not* work for a local authority	64
69	Present salary *not* low	32
68	Pre-Henley salary *not* low	32

Cluster 10 *Manipulative*

Item No.	*Item*	*Weight*
90	Most frequent problem at work 'political'	64
168	Agrees: 'Most managerial jobs require a person to compromise with his moral standards'	64
154	Main academic interest at school engineering and applied science	64
176	Agrees: 'A young man aiming at the top should be careful to choose a wife that fits'	64
149	Attended a technical college	256

Cluster 11 *Fulfilled*

Item No.	*Item*	*Weight*
235	Joy and fulfilment in family	4
234	Pride in family: often	4
233	Rage and despair in family: rarely	16
202	'Happy'	8
240	'Vigorous'	16
238	Self: 'Pride and fulfilment' usually	8
237	Self: Frequent feelings of pride and fulfilment	8
249	Mental health 'good'	32
236	Rage about self: rarely	16
230	Rage in work situation: rarely	16
137	Early family 'secure'	8
142	Early family 'united'	8
139	Early family 'warm'	16

Cluster 11 (continued)

138	Early family 'exciting'	16
222	Self-conception *not* 'unconventional'	16
152	Academic interest in school natural science	32
129	Mother 'satisfied'	32
199	*Not* 'emotional'	256

Cluster 12   *Alienated*

Item No.	Item	Weight
2	Main reason for being nominated 'pure chance'	64
101	Work environment 'cool'	64
231	No feelings of pride at work	64
104	Work environment 'divided'	32
232	Usual feelings on job 'rage and despair'	8
106	Job attitude: dissatisfied	8
54	Staff could have been more helpful: 'career advice'	16
268	Most disliked aspect of the work environment 'routine'	256

Cluster 13   *Climbing*

Item No.	Item	Weight
78	Since Henley, *more* decisions without reference to higher authority	32
79	Since Henley, *greater magnitude* of decisions taken	32
85	Since Henley, *fewer* constraints on freedom of action	64
81	Since Henley, *more* dealing with people outside firm	128
84	Since Henley, *more* participation in long-term planning	128
80	Since Henley, *more* involvement with others of different specialities	128

References

ABERCROMBIE, M. L. JOHNSON (1960). *The anatomy of judgement.* London: Hutchinson.

ACKOFF, RUSSELL (1968). Toward an idealized university. (Mimeo.)

ADMINISTRATIVE STAFF COLLEGE, Henley-on-Thames (n.d.). A guide for prospective members.

ALDERFER, CLAYTON P. (1969). An empirical test of a new theory of human needs. *Organizational Behaviour and Human Performances,* 4, 97–111.

ANDREWS, K. (1957). Is management training effective? *Harvard Business Review,* January/February.

ARGYRIS, C. (1962). *Interpersonal competence and organizational effectiveness.* Homewood, Ill.: Irwin Dorsey; London: Tavistock Publications, 1963.

ASHBY, ERIC & ANDERSON, MARY (1966). *Universities: British, Indian, African.* London: Weidenfeld & Nicolson.

AZRAEL, JEREMY R. (1966). *Managerial power and Soviet politics.* Cambridge, Mass.: Harvard University Press.

BAKKE, E. WRIGHT (1959). *A Norwegian contribution to management development.* Labor and Management Center, Yale University.

BARNA, TIBOR (1962). *Investment and growth policies in British industrial firms.* London: Cambridge University Press.

BARRON, FRANK (1968). *Creativity and personal freedom.* Princeton, N.J.: Van Nostrand.

BARRON, FRANK & EGAN, DERMOT (1968). Leaders and innovators in Irish management. *Journal of Management Studies,* 5 (1), 41–60.

BAUMAN, ZYGMUNT (1964). Economic growth, social structure, elite formation: the case of Poland. *International Social Science Journal,* 16 (2), 203–16.

BELBIN, E. & DOWNS, S. M. (1964). Activity learning and the older worker. *Ergonomics,* 7, 429–37.

BELBIN, R. M. (1969). *The discovery method: an international experiment in retraining.* Paris: OECD.

BELL, D. J. (1967). Notes on the post-industrial society (I and II). *The Public Interest* (6 and 7).

BENNIS, W. G. & SLATER, P. E. (1968). *The temporary society.* New York: Harper & Row.

BLAU, PETER M. & STOTT, W. RICHARD (1962). *Formal organizations – a comparative approach.* San Francisco: Chandler.

BONDY, M. (1966). Identification of overlapping capital letters by subjects of different ages. *Ceskoslovenská Psychologie,* **10,** 221–32.

BOTTOMORE, T. B. (1964). *Elites and society.* London: Watts.

BRADFORD, L. P. *et al.* (eds.) (1964). *T-group theory and laboratory method.* New York: Wiley.

BRODIE, M. B. (1965). Trades unions for executives. *The Manager,* **3** (3), 65–67.

BRODIE, M. B. (1967). *Fayol on administration.* London: Lyon, Grant & Green.

BRODIE, M. B. & LIFE, E. A. (1969). Higher executive roles and university attainment. Paper presented to working party on the relation between university attainment and employment requirements of administrative and executive posts, International Social Science Council.

BURNHAM, JAMES (1962). *The managerial revolution.* Harmondsworth: Penguin Books.

BURNS, T. & STALKER, G. M. (1961). *The management of innovation.* London: Tavistock Publications.

CAPLAN, GERALD (1964). *Principles of preventive psychiatry.* New York: Basic Books; London: Tavistock Publications.

CARR-SAUNDERS, A. M. & WILSON, P. A. (1964). *The professions.* London: Cass.

CHILD, JOHN (1968). Organizations and their environments. (Mimeo.)

CHOWDHRY, KAMLA (1964). Management development programmes: moratorium for executives. *Human Organization,* **23,** 254–9.

CLARK, D. G. (1966). *The industrial manager.* London: Business Publications.

COCHRAN, THOMAS C. (1965). Cultural factors in economic growth. In Hugh G. J. Aitken (ed.), *Explorations in enterprise.* Cambridge, Mass.: Harvard University Press.

COGSWELL, BETTY E. (1969). Some structural properties influencing socialization. *Administrative Science Quarterly,* **13,** 417–40.

COLE, ARTHUR H. (1965). An approach to the study of entrepreneurship. In Hugh G. J. Aitken (ed.), *Explorations in enterprise.* Cambridge, Mass.: Harvard University Press.

COLES, R. B. & BRIDGER, H. (1969). The consultant and his roles. *Brit. J. med. Psychol.,* **42,** 241.

COPELAND, MELVIN T. (1958). *And mark an era: the story of the Harvard Business School.* Boston, Mass.: Little, Brown.

CROZIER, MICHEL (1964). *The bureaucratic phenomenon.* London: Tavistock Publications.

CURLE, ADAM (1967). Educational implications of technological change. (Mimeo.)

DAVIES, JOHN (1968). Management with a motive. *The Times*, 17 December. London.

DAVIS, F. (1963). *Passage through crisis*. Indianapolis: Bobbs-Merrill.

DAVIS, F. (1967). Why all of us may be hippies someday. *Trans-action*, 5(2), 10–18. December. St Louis.

DORNBUSCH, SANFORD (1955). The military academy as an assimilating institution. *Social Forces*, 33, 316–21.

EDUCATION, MINISTRY OF (1947). *Education for management*. Report of a Special Committee (Chairman: Lt. Col. L. Urwick). London: HMSO.

EDUCATION, MINISTRY OF (1963). Report of the Committee on Higher Education, 1961–3 (Chairman: Lord Robbins) (Cmnd. 2154). London: HMSO.

EDUCATION & SCIENCE, DEPARTMENT OF (1964). University Grants Committee. Report of the Committee on University Teaching Methods (Chairman: Sir Edward Hale). London: HMSO.

EMERY, F. E. (ed.) (1969). *Systems thinking*. Harmondsworth: Penguin Books.

EMERY, F. E., IRVING, B. & HILGENDORF, L. (1968). Psychological dynamics of smoking. London: Tobacco Research Council (Reg. Paper No. 10).

EMERY, F. E. & THORSRUD, E. (1966). Industrial conflict and 'industrial democracy'. Chapter 32 in J. R. Lawrence (ed.), *Operational research and the social sciences*. London: Tavistock Publications.

EMERY, F. E. & TRIST, E. L. (1960). Socio-technical systems. Pp. 83–97 in C. W. Churchman & M. Verhulst (eds.), *Management sciences, models and techniques*, Vol. 2. Oxford: Pergamon.

EMERY, F. E. & TRIST, E. L. (1965). The causal texture of organizational environments. *Human Relations*, 18, 21–32.

EMMET, DOROTHY (1966). *Rules, roles and relations*. New York: St Martins; London: Macmillan.

ENNIS, R. W. (ed.) (1966). *Accountability in government departments, public corporations and public companies*. London: Lyon, Grant & Green.

ERIKSON, ERIK H. (1968). *Identity: youth and crisis*. London: Faber & Faber.

ETZIONI, AMITAI (1961). *A comparative analysis of complex organizations*. New York: Free Press of Glencoe.

EVAN, WILLIAM M. (1961). Organization man and the due process of law. *American Sociological Review*, 26, 540–7.

FEDERATION OF BRITISH INDUSTRIES (1954). *Education and training for management*. London: FBI.

FEDERATION OF BRITISH INDUSTRIES (1961). Management education at university level. Paper by J. W. Platt in *Stocktaking on management education*. London: FBI.

FLEISHMAN, E. A., HARRIS, E. F. & BURTT, H. E. (1955). *Leadership and supervision in industry: an evaluation of a supervisory training program.* Columbus, Ohio: Ohio State University Bureau of Educational Research Monograph 33.

FOGARTY, M., RAPOPORT, RHONA & RAPOPORT, ROBERT (1968). *Women and top jobs: an interim report.* PEP Broadsheet. London: Political and Economic Planning.

FULTON REPORT, *see under* TREASURY (1968).

GALBRAITH, J. K. (1958). *The affluent society.* Boston, Mass.: Houghton Mifflin; London: Hamilton.

GIBBONS, JOHN (1844). *Practical remarks on the use of the cinder pig in the puddling furnace; and on the management of the forge and the mill.* (Quoted in Pollard, 1965.)

GOFFMAN, ERVING (1958). The characteristics of total institutions. In Walter Reed Army Institute of Research, *Symposium on preventive and social psychiatry* (1957). Washington: US Government Printing Office.

GOLD, BELA (1965). Reorganizing management education. *Journal of Management Studies,* **2** (1), 1–13.

GORDON, ROBERT A. & HOWELL, JAMES E. (1959). *Higher education for business.* New York: Columbia University Press.

GRUENFELD, L. W. (1966). Personality needs and expected benefits from a management development programme. *Occupational Psychology,* **40,** 75–81.

GUTTSMAN, W. L. (1963). *The British political elite.* London: MacGibbon & Kee.

HABAKKUK, H. J. (1962). *American and British technology in the nineteenth century.* London: Cambridge University Press.

HACON, R. J. (ed.) (1969). *Organizational necessities and individual needs.* ATM Occasional Paper 5. Oxford: Blackwell.

HAIRE, M., GHISELLI, E. E. & PORTER, L. W. (1966). *Management thinking: an international study.* New York: Wiley.

HALE REPORT, *see under* EDUCATION & SCIENCE, DEPARTMENT OF (1964).

HALL, NOEL (1964). Education and management. *Journal of Management Studies,* **1** (2), 105–15.

HALL, RICHARD H. (1962–3). Intraorganizational structural variation: application of the bureaucratic model. *Administrative Science Quarterly,* **7,** 295–308.

HANIKA, F. DE P. (1965). *New thinking in management.* London: Hutchinson.

HELLER, FRANK (1969a). Group feedback analysis: a method of field research. *Psychological Bulletin,* **72,** 108–12.

HELLER, FRANK (1969b). Group feedback analysis applied to training.

(Mimeo.) document, HRC 265, Tavistock Institute of Human Relations; *Journal of Management Studies* (forthcoming).

HELSBY, LORD (1968). The Fulton report. *The Listener*, 18 July. London: BBC.

HERBST, P. G. (1962). *Autonomous group functioning*. London: Tavistock Publications.

HERBST, P. G. (1963). Organisational commitment: a decision process model. Reprinted from *Acta Sociologica*, **7**, 34–46.

HESSELING, P. (1966). *Strategy of evaluation research in the field of supervisory and management training*. Assen: Van Gorcum.

HOBSBAWM, ERIC (1968). The Fulton report: a further view. *The Listener*, 18 July. London: BBC.

HORNE, J. H. & LUPTON, T. (1965). The work activities of 'middle' managers. *Journal of Management Studies*, **2**, 14–33.

HOUSE, R. J. (1967). *Management development: design, evaluation and implementation*. Ann Arbor, Bureau of Industrial Relations, Graduate School of Business Administration, University of Michigan.

HUDSON, LIAM (1966). *Contrary imaginations*. London: Methuen.

IBM (1969). (International Business Machines.) Education and industry. Occasional Paper. London: Bow-Towning.

IMEDE (1965). (Institut pour l'Étude des Méthodes de Direction de l'Entreprise.) Handbook.

INKELES, A. (1965). A note on social structure and the socialization of competence. SSRC Conference of the Committee on Socialization, Puerto Rico. (Mimeo.)

INKELES, A. (1968). Society, social structure and child socialization. In J. A. Clausen (ed.), *Socialization and society*. Boston, Mass.: Little, Brown.

JANIS, IRVING (1958). *Psychological stress*. New York: Wiley.

JAQUES, ELLIOTT (1951). *The changing culture of a factory*. London: Tavistock/Routledge.

JAQUES, ELLIOTT (1965). Death and the midlife crisis. *International Journal of Psycho-Analysis*, **46** (4), 502–14.

JEFFERYS, J. B. (1954). *The story of the engineers*. London: Lawrence & Wishart.

JENNINGS, E. E. (1954). The dynamics of forced leadership training. *Journal of Personnel Administration and Industrial Relations*, **1**, 110–18.

JERKEDAL, A. (1967). *Top management education: an evaluation study*. Stockholm: Swedish Council for Personnel Administration.

KAHN, H. & WIENER, A. J. (1967). *The year 2000*. N.Y.: Macmillan.

KAHN, R. L. et. al. (1964). *Organizational stress: studies in role conflict and ambiguity*. New York: Wiley.

LEACH, E. (1968). *A runaway world?* Reith Lectures. London: BBC.

LIFE, E. A. (1968). Behaviour in the working environment. Occasional Paper. Henley-on-Thames: Administrative Staff College.

LIFTON, ROBERT (1961). *Thought reform and the psychology of totalism: a study of 'brainwashing' in China*. New York: Norton; London: Gollancz.

LINDEMANN, ERICH (1944). Symptomatology and management of acute grief. *American Journal of Psychiatry*, **101**, 141–8.

LUPTON, T. (1970). *Management and the social sciences*. London: Lyon, Grant, and Green.

MCGREGOR, DOUGLAS (1960). *The human side of enterprise*. New York: McGraw-Hill.

MCQUITTY, L. L. (1960). Hierarchical linkage and analysis for the isolation of types. *Educational and Psychological Measurement*, **20**, 55–67.

MARCH, J. G. (ed.) (1965). *Handbook of organizations*. Chicago: Rand McNally.

MARCUSE, HERBERT (1964). *One-dimensional man*. London: Routledge.

MARRIS, ROBIN (1966). *The economic theory of 'managerial capitalism'*. London: Macmillan.

MASLOW, A. H. (1962). *Toward a psychology of being*. Princeton, N.J.: Van Nostrand.

MICHAEL, DONALD N. (1968). *The unprepared society*. New York: Basic Books.

MILES, M. B. (1964). On temporary systems. In M. B. Miles (ed.), *Innovation in education*. New York: Columbia University Press.

MILLER, E. J. & RICE, A. K. (1967). *Systems of organization*. London: Tavistock Publications.

MIT (1949). Report of the Committee on Educational Survey to the Faculty of the Massachusetts Institute of Technology. Cambridge, Mass.: MIT Press.

MOMENT, DAVID (1966). Pathways of career development revisited. *Harvard Business School Bulletin*, November–December, 27–9.

MOMENT, DAVID & ZALEZNIK, A. (1963). *Role development and interpersonal competence*. Cambridge, Mass.: Harvard University Press.

MORRIS, J. F. (1968). Mid-career education for management. In Supplement to *Education for management*. Doc. no. 279999. London: HMSO.

NATIONAL ECONOMIC DEVELOPMENT COUNCIL (1963). *Conditions favourable to faster growth*, para. 220. London: HMSO.

NEUGARTEN, BERNICE L. et al. (1964). *Personality in middle and late life*. New York: Atherton.

PAHL, J. & PAHL, R. (1970). *Office and home*. Harmondsworth: Penguin (forthcoming).

PLATT, J. W. (1961). Management education at university level. In

Stocktaking on management education. London: Federation of British Industries.

POLLARD, SIDNEY (1965). *The genesis of modern management.* London: E. Arnold; Cambridge, Mass.: Harvard University Press. Harmondsworth: Penguin Books, 1968.

POSTAN, M. M. (1967). *An economic history of Western Europe, 1945–1964.* London: Methuen.

PUGH, DEREK S., HICKSON, D. J., HININGS, C. R., MACDONALD, K. M., TURNER, C. & LUPTON, T. (1963). A conceptual scheme for organizational analysis. *Administrative Science Quarterly,* **8** (3), 289–315.

RAPOPORT, RHONA V. (1963). Normal crisis, family structure and mental health. *Family Process,* **2.**

RAPOPORT, ROBERT N. (1960). *Community as doctor.* London: Tavistock Publications.

RAPOPORT, ROBERT N. & RAPOPORT, RHONA V. (1969). The dual career family. *Human Relations,* **22,** 3–30.

REDDIN, W. J. (1967). The importance of managerial style and flexibility. *Works Management,* May.

RIDLEY, F. F. (1968). *Specialists and generalists.* London: Allen & Unwin.

ROBBINS REPORT, *see under* EDUCATION, MINISTRY OF (1963).

ROKEACH, MILTON (1960). *The open and closed mind.* New York: Basic Books.

ROSE, T. G. (1954). *A history of the Institute of Industrial Administration, 1919–1951.* London: Pitman (for IIA).

ROTH, JULIUS (1963). *Timetables.* Indianapolis: Bobbs-Merrill.

SCHECHTER, ALAN H. (1968). Businessmen as government policymakers. *Columbia Journal of World Business,* **3** (3), 67–72.

SCHEIN, EDGAR H. (1961). *Coercive persuasion: a socio-psychological analysis of the brainwashing of American civilian prisoners by the Chinese communists.* New York: Norton.

SCHEIN, EDGAR H. (1965). Career orientations and perceptions of rewarded activity in a research organization. *Administrative Science Quarterly,* **9,** 333–49.

SCHEIN, EDGAR H. (1967). Attitude change during management education. *Administrative Science Quarterly,* **11,** 601–28.

SCHEIN, EDGAR H. & BENNIS, WARREN G. (1965). *Personal and organizational change through group methods: the laboratory approach.* New York: Wiley.

SCHULTZ, T. W. (1961). Investment in human capital. *American Economic Review,* **51,** 1–17.

SCOTT MYERS, M. (1964). Who are your motivated workers? *Harvard Business Review,* January–February, **42** (1), 73–88.

SCOTT MYERS, M. (1966). Conditions for manager motivation. *Harvard Business Review*, January–February, **44** (1), 58–71.

SELF, PETER (1965). Bureaucracy of management. LSE Inaugural Lecture. London: Bell.

SHONFIELD, ANDREW (1966). *Modern capitalism: the changing balance of public and private power.* London: Oxford University Press.

SHONFIELD, ANDREW (1969). Thinking about the future. *Encounter*, **32** (2).

SIMON, HERBERT A. (1960). *The new science of management decision.* New York: Harper & Row.

SISSON, C. H. (1959). *The spirit of British administration.* London: Faber & Faber.

SODDY, K. (1967). *Men in middle life.* London: Tavistock Publications; Philadelphia: Lippincott.

STEWART, ROSEMARY (1967). *Managers and their jobs: a study of the similarities and differences in the way managers spend their time.* London: Macmillan.

TAGIURI, RENATO (1965). Value orientations of managers and scientists. In Orth, C. D. *et al.*, *Administering research and development.* Homewood, Ill.: Richard D. Irwin; London: Tavistock Publications.

TALLAND, G. (1966). Visual signal selection as a function of age, in-put rate, and signal frequency. *Journal of Psychology*, **63**, 105–15.

THOMAS, HUGH (1961). *The story of Sandhurst*, p. 20. London: Hutchinson.

TREASURY (1958). *University development, 1952–1957.* University Grants Committee Report (Cmnd. 534). London: HMSO.

TREASURY (1968). *The Civil Service*, Vol. 1. Report of the Committee, 1966–8 (Chairman: Lord Fulton) (Cmnd. 3638). Paras. 15, 42. London: HMSO.

TRIST, E. L. (1968). The relation of welfare and development in the transition to post-industrialism. Working Paper 1. Socio-technical Systems Division, Western Management Science Institute, University of California, Los Angeles.

TRIST, E. L., HIGGIN, G. W., MURRAY, H. & POLLOCK, A. B. (1963). *Organizational choice.* London: Tavistock Publications.

TROLLOPE, ANTHONY (1870). *The Vicar of Bullhampton.*

TYHURST, JAMES S. (1958). *The role of transition states including disasters in mental illness.* Washington: US Government Printing Office.

UNIVERSITY GRANTS COMMITTEE, *see under* TREASURY (1958) and EDUCATION & SCIENCE, DEPARTMENT OF (1964).

URWICK REPORT, *see under* EDUCATION, MINISTRY OF (1947).

VICKERS, GEOFFREY (1968). *Value systems and social process.* London: Tavistock Publications; New York: Basic Books.

WALLE, ARNE (1969). When competence precedes education: a problem on management development training programs. In Pepinsky, H. B. (ed.), *People and information*. New York: Pergamon.

WARNER, W. LLOYD (1960). The corporation man. In Edward S. Mason (ed.), *The corporation in modern society*. Cambridge, Mass.: Harvard University Press.

WARNER, W. LLOYD & MARTIN, NORMAN H. (1959). *Industrial man: businessmen and business organizations*. New York: Harper.

WATSON, W. (1964). Social mobility and social class in industrial communities. In Gluckman, M. (ed.), *Closed systems and open minds*. Edinburgh: Oliver & Boyd.

WELFORD, A. T. (1958). *Ageing and human skill*. London: Oxford University Press.

WHITE, ROBERT W. (1966). *Lives in progress*. (2nd edition.) New York: Holt.

WHYTE, WILLIAM H. (1956). *The organization man*. New York: Simon & Schuster; London: Cape, 1957.

WILLINGS, DAVID R. (1968). *The human element in management*. London: Batsford.

WILSON, A. T. M. (1966). Some sociological aspects of systematic management development. *Journal of Management Studies*, 3, 1–18.

WILSON, A. T. M. (1967). Organizational development and the integrative need of the executive. A paper prepared for the McGregor Memorial Conference, MIT.

WOLSTENHOLME, G. E. W. (ed.) (1963). *Man and his future*. London: Churchill.

WOODWARD, JOAN (1965). *Industrial organization*. London: Oxford University Press.

WRIGHT MILLS, C. (1956). *The power elite*. London: Oxford University Press.

YOUNG, MICHAEL (ed.) (1968). *Forecasting and the social sciences*. London: Heinemann.

Name Index

Subject Index

For Product Safety Concerns and Information please contact our EU
representative GPSR@taylorandfrancis.com Taylor & Francis Verlag GmbH,
Kaufingerstraße 24, 80331 München, Germany

Printed and bound by CPI Group (UK) Ltd, Croydon, CR0 4YY
08/05/2025
01864426-0001